Microsoft IIS 10.0 Cookbook

Task-oriented recipes to manage your web server with ease

Ashraf Khan

BIRMINGHAM - MUMBAI

Microsoft IIS 10.0 Cookbook

First published: June 2017

Production reference: 1220617

Published by Packt Publishing Ltd.
Livery Place
35 Livery Street
Birmingham
B3 2PB, UK.

ISBN 978-1-78712-667-1

www.packtpub.com

Credits

Author
Ashraf Khan

Reviewer
Anwarul Haque

Acquisition Editor
Heramb Bhavsar

Content Development Editor
Sharon Raj

Technical Editor
Mohit Hassija

Copy Editor
Madhusudan Uchil

Project Coordinator
Virginia Dias

Proofreader
Safis Editing

Indexer
Aishwarya Gangawane

Graphics
Kirk D'Penha

Production Coordinator
Aparna Bhagat

About the Author

Ashraf Khan works as the Head Of Network Operating System Unit, with a diverse background in production systems, Network Administration, and Solutions Architecture. He has the MCSE-Server, MCSE-Messaging, MCSE-Cloud, CCNA, ITIL & Prince2 certifications. He has more than 13 years of experience in sectors such as IT infrastructure and private and government sectors located in India and the UAE and remote support for USA and worldwide for physical and virtual server environment IT management, implementation, planning, disaster recovery, testing, and technical support.

I would like to express my gratitude to the many people who saw me through this book and to all those who provided support, talked things over, read, wrote, offered comments, allowed me to quote their remarks, and assisted in the editing, proofreading, and design.

I would like to thank my editors Heramb Bhavsar and Sharon Raj and reviewer, Anwarul Haque, for enabling me to publish this book. Above all, I want to thank my wife, Shama, and the rest of my family, who supported and encouraged me in spite of all the times it took me away from them. It was a long and difficult journey for them.

I would like to thank Sharon Raj for helping me in the process of selection and editing. Thanks to Packt who encouraged me.

Last but not least, I beg forgiveness of all those who have been with me over the years and whose names I have failed to mention.

About the Reviewer

Anwarul Haque has been creating applications professionally since 2004. Haque has worked as a consultant for over 12 years in the enterprise and consumer domains. He is a Microsoft SharePoint 2007 Application Development certified since 2007, Microsoft Dynamics NAV 2013 C/Side Development certified since 2014, and Microsoft Certified Professional Developer since 2014. He also worked on SharePoint 2010 and 2013 offline premises, online SharePoint Office 365, and IIS Server management with hosting management skills at the administration level. He managed web servers at various platforms and technology applications hosted on Windows IIS Server, Azure Server, and Unix Server. Apart from IIS Server, he also managed and hosted websites on Apache Tomcat Server.

In the development area, he has worked on various IDEs, tools, and technologies, such as Microsoft Office Designer applications for SharePoint development, Microsoft CRM Portal, ASP.Net, VB.Net, ADO.Net, WCF, SSRS, ASP 3.0, Entity Framework, SQL Server 2005, 2008, 2012, 2015, Oracle, Visual Basic 6.0 & VBA macro, VB Script, JavaScript, Ajax, jQuery, dynamic Excel reports and charts, and add-on developers for Microsoft Office products. He has also used subversion control tools such as Microsoft Visual SourceSafe, SVN, and the IBM Rational ClearCase tool.

As a professional, he has worked with small and large enterprises in Matrix InfoSoft, MetaOption LLC, and currently works as a software analyst in GCE Solutions, which is based in New Delhi.

You can follow him on LinkedIn at `https://www.linkedin.com/in/anwarul-haque-b 4824b21/`.

I would like to thank my lovely wife, Zeenat Haque, for her patience, support, and understanding!

www.PacktPub.com

For support files and downloads related to your book, please visit www.PacktPub.com.

Did you know that Packt offers eBook versions of every book published, with PDF and ePub files available? You can upgrade to the eBook version at www.PacktPub.com and as a print book customer, you are entitled to a discount on the eBook copy. Get in touch with us at service@packtpub.com for more details.

At www.PacktPub.com, you can also read a collection of free technical articles, sign up for a range of free newsletters and receive exclusive discounts and offers on Packt books and eBooks.

https://www.packtpub.com/mapt

Get the most in-demand software skills with Mapt. Mapt gives you full access to all Packt books and video courses, as well as industry-leading tools to help you plan your personal development and advance your career.

Why subscribe?

- Fully searchable across every book published by Packt
- Copy and paste, print, and bookmark content
- On demand and accessible via a web browser

Customer Feedback

Thanks for purchasing this Packt book. At Packt, quality is at the heart of our editorial process. To help us improve, please leave us an honest review on this book's Amazon page at https://www.amazon.com/dp/1787126676.

If you'd like to join our team of regular reviewers, you can e-mail us at customerreviews@packtpub.com. We award our regular reviewers with free eBooks and videos in exchange for their valuable feedback. Help us be relentless in improving our products!

Table of Contents

Preface   1

Chapter 1: Integrating IIS 10.0 with Windows Server 2016   7

Introduction   7

  Understanding IIS 10.0   8

  Basic requirements of IIS 10.0   9

    OS requirements   9

    Hardware requirements   10

      Windows Server 2016   10

      Windows 10   10

    Operating system media   10

IIS 10.0 architecture   10

  Getting ready   11

  How to do it...   11

  How it works...   13

    Introducing the IIS 10.0 architecture's components and modules   14

      Overview of an HTTP request   14

      Details of an HTTP request inside the worker process   16

Installing IIS 10.0 on Windows Server 2016   17

  Getting ready   17

  How to do it…   17

  How it works...   24

IIS Manager   25

  Getting ready   26

  How to do it...   26

    How to manage remote IIS?   28

  How it works...   33

Basic configuration of IIS 10.0   34

  Getting ready   34

  How to do it...   34

  How it works...   38

Hosting static web page   39

  Getting ready   39

  How to do it...   39

  How it works...   43

Testing a static-page website   43

  Getting ready   44

How to do it...	44
How it works...	44

Chapter 2: Creating an Application Pool in IIS 10.0 — 45

Introduction	45
Understanding application pools in IIS 10.0	46
Getting ready	46
How to do it...	47
How it works...	49
Installation of lower framework version	49
Getting ready	49
How to do it...	50
How it works...	57
Creating different application pools in IIS 10.0	57
Getting ready	57
How to do it...	57
How it works...	60
Configuration of application pool on IIS 10.0	61
Getting ready	61
How to do it...	62
How it works...	67
Hosting .NET web page	68
Getting ready	68
How to do it...	68
How it works...	72
Hosting different versions of a .NET website	73
Getting ready	73
How to do it...	73
How it works...	75
Testing different versions of a website	75
Getting ready	76
How to do it...	76
How it works...	77

Chapter 3: Hosting Multiple Websites on IIS 10.0 — 79

Introduction	79
Hosting multiple websites	80
Getting ready	80
How to do it...	80
How it works...	87

Creating a website folder   87
    Getting ready   87
    How to do it...   87
    How it works...   90
Configuring websites   90
    Getting ready   91
    How to do it...   91
    How it works..   94
Configuring ports   94
    Getting ready   94
    How to do it...   94
    How it works..   98
Configuring the website IP   99
    Getting ready   99
    How to do it...   99
    How it works...   104
Deploying websites   104
    Getting ready   104
    How to do it...   104
    How it works...   107
Testing websites   107
    Getting ready   108
    How to do it...   108
    How it works...   110
Chapter 4: Constructing Virtual Directories in IIS 10.0   111
    Introduction   111
    Constructing a virtual directory in IIS 10.0   112
       Getting ready   112
       How to do it...   112
       How it works...   115
    Understanding IIS 10.0 virtual directories   115
       Getting ready   116
       How to do it...   116
       How it works...   117
    Configuring virtual directories in IIS 10.0   117
       Getting ready   117
       How to do it...   117
       How it works...   122
    Configuring virtual directories with different application pools   122

Getting ready	123
How to do it...	123
How it works...	126
Uploading a .NET web page	**127**
Getting ready	127
How to do it...	127
How it works...	130
Testing the uploaded web page	**130**
Getting ready	130
How to do it...	130
How it works...	132
Chapter 5: Installing HTTP/2 on IIS 10.0	**133**
Introduction	**133**
Understanding HTTP/2	**134**
Getting ready	134
How to do it...	134
How it works...	136
Installing HTTP/2 on IIS 10.0	**136**
Getting ready	137
How to do it...	137
How it works...	142
Configuring HTTP/2 on IIS 10.0	**143**
Getting ready	143
How to do it...	143
How it works...	148
Uploading .NET web pages	**149**
Getting ready	149
How it do it...	149
How it works...	152
Testing uploaded web pages	**152**
Getting ready	152
How to do it...	152
How it works...	155
Chapter 6: Getting Your Wildcard Host Up and Running	**157**
Introduction	**157**
Understanding wildcard hosts	**158**
Getting ready	158
How to do it...	158

How it works...	161
Creating a wildcard host	161
Getting ready	161
How to do it...	162
How it works...	167
Configuring a wildcard host	167
Getting ready	167
How to do it...	167
How it works...	171
Uploading .NET web pages to a wildcard host	172
Getting ready	172
How to do it...	172
How it works...	175
Testing uploaded website pages	175
Getting ready	175
How to do it...	176
How it works...	180

Chapter 7: Deploying IIS 10.0 on Nano Server — 181

Introduction	181
Understanding IIS 10.0 on Nano Server	182
Getting ready	182
How to do it...	182
How it works...	185
Installing IIS 10.0 on Nano Server	185
Getting ready	186
How to do it...	186
How it works...	195
Managing IIS 10.0 on Nano Server	195
Getting ready	195
How to do it...	195
How it works...	199
Creating an IIS 10.0 website on Nano Server	199
Getting ready	199
How to do it...	199
How it works...	203
Configuring an IIS 10.0 website on Nano Server	203
Getting ready	203
How to do it...	203
How it works...	208

Uploading website pages	209
Getting ready	209
How to do it...	209
How it works...	211
Testing uploaded web pages	211
Getting ready	212
How to do it...	212
How it works...	214

Chapter 8: Configuring IIS Administration with PowerShell Cmdlets	215
Introduction	215
IIS administration with PowerShell cmdlets	216
Getting ready	216
How to do it...	217
How it works...	223
Creating an advanced IIS 10.0 website on Nano Server	223
Getting ready	223
How to do it...	223
How to do it...	230
Configuring IIS 10.0 websites on Nano Server	231
Getting ready	231
How to do it...	231
How it works...	236
Uploading IIS 10.0 websites to Nano Server	236
Getting ready	236
How to do it...	236
How it works....	240
Testing uploaded web pages	241
Getting ready	241
How to do it...	241
How it works...	246

Chapter 9: Enabling ASP.NET Core with IIS on Nano Server	247
Introduction	247
Understanding ASP.NET Core with IIS on Nano Server	248
Getting ready	248
How to do it...	248
How it works...	251
Configuring ASP.NET Core with IIS on Nano Server	251
Getting ready	252

How to do it...	252
How it works...	259
Creating an IIS 10.0 virtual directory on Nano Server	259
Getting ready	259
How to do it...	259
How it works...	263
Configuring a virtual directory in IIS 10.0	263
Getting ready	263
How to do it...	263
How it works...	267
Uploading and testing web pages in a virtual directory	268
Getting ready	268
How do to it...	268
How it works...	272

Chapter 10: Installing and Configuring SSL Websites	273
Introduction	273
Understanding SSL websites in IIS 10.0	274
Getting ready	274
How to do it...	274
How it works...	276
Installing SSL	276
Getting ready	276
How to do it...	276
How it works...	283
Creating an SSL certificate	283
Getting ready	284
How to do it...	284
How it works...	286
Configuring websites with an SSL port and certificate	286
Getting ready	287
How to do it...	287
How it works...	289
Using PowerShell commands to create SSL certificates	290
Getting ready	290
How to do it...	290
How it works...	292
Testing SSL websites	293
Getting ready	293
How to do it...	293

How it works...   296

Chapter 11: Extending IIS 10.0 to FTP   297

Introduction   297
Understanding FTP   298
  Getting ready   298
  How to do it...   298
  How it works...   301
Installing FTP on IIS 10.0   302
  Getting ready   302
  How to do it...   302
  How it works...   305
Creating, securing, and configuring an FTP site   306
  Getting ready   306
  How to do it...   306
  How it works...   314
Creating an FTP user and managing user permissions   314
  Getting ready   314
  How to do it...   314
  How it works...   320
Testing our FTP server   320
  Getting ready   321
  How to do it...   321
  How it works...   324

Chapter 12: Securing Your Websites on IIS 10.0   325

Introduction   325
Understanding available security on IIS 10.0   326
  Getting ready   326
  How to do it...   326
  How it works...   333
Configuring security on IIS 10.0   334
  Getting ready   334
  How to do it...   334
  How it works...   340
URL authorization and authentication   340
  Getting ready   341
  How to do it...   341
  How it works...   346
IP address and domain restrictions   347

Getting ready	347
How to do it...	347
How it works...	351
Testing security on IIS 10.0	351
Getting ready	351
How to do it...	351
How it works...	355
Chapter 13: Managing and Troubleshooting IIS 10.0	357
Introduction	357
Managing IIS 10.0	358
Getting ready	358
How to do it...	359
How it works...	361
Installing Health, Diagnostics, and Performance features	361
Getting ready	361
How to do it...	361
How it works...	367
Configuring Health and Diagnostics	367
Getting ready	367
How to do it...	367
How it works...	375
Configuring Failed Request Tracing Rules	375
Getting ready	375
How to do it...	375
How it works...	383
Configuring static content compression	383
Getting ready	383
How to do it...	383
How it works...	388
Index	389

Preface

IIS 10.0 is the latest version of Internet Information Services (IIS), which is an extensible web server developed by Microsoft. IIS 10.0 was introduced with Windows Server 2016 and the Windows 10 operating system. New features of IIS 10.0 are HTTP/2, IIS on Nano Server, wildcard host headers, and PowerShell 5 Cmdlets. IIS 10.0 supports all previous features: HTTP, HTTPS, SMTP, and SNMP, FTP and FTPS.

What this book covers

Chapter 1, *Integrating IIS 10.0 with Windows Server 2016*, starts with some basic information about IIS 10.0. After that, we are going to integrate IIS 10.0 with Windows Server 2016 and configure and test our first sample webpage.

Chapter 2, *Creating an Application Pool in IIS 10.0*, explains application pools, installation of different versions of application pool, creation of application pools, and configuration of application pools. We'll upload and test .NET 3.5 and .NET 4.0 web applications.

Chapter 3, *Hosting Multiple Websites on IIS 10.0*, starts with multiple web hosting on the same IIS 10.0 instance, and we will access these websites by their hostname (domain name). We will configure a dedicated IP address for the website.

Chapter 4, *Constructing Virtual Directories in IIS 10.0*, starts with the creation of a virtual directory and its use in an existing website. If you have a different web application that needs an application pool in the website, you can create a virtual directory and add the required application pools.

Chapter 5, *Installing HTTP/2 on IIS 10.0*, explains HTTP/2 and installation, configuration, and testing of HTTP/2.

Chapter 6, *Getting Your Wildcard Host Up and Running*, shows how to create a subdomain demo prefixed with main domain such as demo.v2mysite.com. We can create different names and unlimited wildcard hosts for our parent domain.

Chapter 7, *Deploying IIS 10.0 on Nano Server*, starts with installing IIS 10.0 on Nano Server. We will remote connect Nano Server, import the IISAdministration module in PowerShell, and create and manage the website on Nano Server.

Chapter 8, *Configuring IIS Administration with PowerShell Cmdlets*, uses PowerShell to perform administration work on IIS Server.

Chapter 9, *Enabling ASP.NET Core with IIS on Nano Server*, teaches how to enable ASP.NET and create virtual directories in IIS on Nano Server.

Chapter 10, *Installing and Configuring SSL Websites*, starts with installation of third-party SSL certificates; we will create a local self-signed certificate and test it.

Chapter 11, *Extending IIS 10.0 to FTP*, shows how to install the FTP server role on Windows Server 2016. We create and configure an FTP site.

Chapter 12, *Securing Your Websites on IIS 10.0*, explains IIS 10.0 security and available security configurations such as IP, domain, and URL.

Chapter 13, *Managing and Troubleshooting IIS 10.0*, explains configuration and management of health and performance of IIS 10.0.

What you need for this book

In order to work with IIS 10.0, the following hardware and software should be available:

- **Software Required (with version)**: IIS 10.0, FileZilla FTP client software, Visual Studio 2015 or later, HTML files, PowerShell 5 cmdlets
- **Hardware specifications**: 4 GB RAM, 300 GB HDD, 2vProcessor.
- **OS required**: Windows Server 2016, Nano Server 2016 and Windows 10

Who this book is for

This book is for those who have been working as IIS administrators, system administrators, website administrators, and web developers, such as site builders, backend developers, and frontend developers, and those who are eager to see what awaits when they start using IIS 10.0.

Sections

In this book, you will find several headings that appear frequently (Getting ready, How to do it..., How it works..., There's more..., and See also).

To give clear instructions on how to complete a recipe, we use these sections as follows:

Getting ready

This section tells you what to expect in the recipe, and describes how to set up any software or any preliminary settings required for the recipe.

How to do it...

This section contains the steps required to follow the recipe.

How it works...

This section usually consists of a detailed explanation of what happened in the previous section.

There's more...

This section consists of additional information about the recipe in order to make the reader more knowledgeable about the recipe.

See also

This section provides helpful links to other useful information for the recipe.

Conventions

In this book, you will find a number of text styles that distinguish between different kinds of information. Here are some examples of these styles and an explanation of their meaning.

Code words in text, database table names, folder names, filenames, file extensions, pathnames, dummy URLs, user input, and Twitter handles are shown as follows: "Create a new user for JIRA in the database and grant the user access to the `jiradb` database we just created using the following command."

A block of code is set as follows:

```
<Contextpath="/jira"docBase="${catalina.home}
/atlassian- jira" reloadable="false" useHttpOnly="true">
```

Any command-line input or output is written as follows:

```
mysql -u root -p
```

New terms and important words are shown in bold. Words that you see on the screen, for example, in menus or dialog boxes, appear in the text like this: "Select **System info** from the **Administration** panel."

Warnings or important notes appear in a box like this.

Tips and tricks appear like this.

Reader feedback

Feedback from our readers is always welcome. Let us know what you think about this book-what you liked or disliked. Reader feedback is important for us as it helps us develop titles that you will really get the most out of.

To send us general feedback, simply e-mail feedback@packtpub.com, and mention the book's title in the subject of your message.

If there is a topic that you have expertise in and you are interested in either writing or contributing to a book, see our author guide at www.packtpub.com/authors.

Customer support

Now that you are the proud owner of a Packt book, we have a number of things to help you to get the most from your purchase.

Downloading the example code

You can download the example code files for this book from your account at http://www.packtpub.com. If you purchased this book elsewhere, you can visit http://www.packtpub.com/support and register to have the files e-mailed directly to you.

You can download the code files by following these steps:

1. Log in or register to our website using your e-mail address and password.
2. Hover the mouse pointer on the **SUPPORT** tab at the top.
3. Click on **Code Downloads & Errata**.
4. Enter the name of the book in the **Search** box.
5. Select the book for which you're looking to download the code files.
6. Choose from the drop-down menu where you purchased this book from.
7. Click on **Code Download**.

You can also download the code files by clicking on the **Code Files** button on the book's webpage at the Packt Publishing website. This page can be accessed by entering the book's name in the **Search** box. Please note that you need to be logged in to your Packt account.

Once the file is downloaded, please make sure that you unzip or extract the folder using the latest version of:

- WinRAR / 7-Zip for Windows
- Zipeg / iZip / UnRarX for Mac
- 7-Zip / PeaZip for Linux

The code bundle for the book is also hosted on GitHub at `https://github.com/PacktPublishing/Microsoft-IIS-10Dot0-Cookbook`. We also have other code bundles from our rich catalog of books and videos available at `https://github.com/PacktPublishing/`. Check them out!

Downloading the color images of this book

We also provide you with a PDF file that has color images of the screenshots/diagrams used in this book. The color images will help you better understand the changes in the output. You can download this file from `https://www.packtpub.com/sites/default/files/downloads/MicrosoftIIS10Dot0Cookbook_ColorImages.pdf`.

Errata

Although we have taken every care to ensure the accuracy of our content, mistakes do happen. If you find a mistake in one of our books-maybe a mistake in the text or the code-we would be grateful if you could report this to us. By doing so, you can save other readers from frustration and help us improve subsequent versions of this book. If you find any errata, please report them by visiting http://www.packtpub.com/submit-errata, selecting your book, clicking on the **Errata Submission Form** link, and entering the details of your errata. Once your errata are verified, your submission will be accepted and the errata will be uploaded to our website or added to any list of existing errata under the Errata section of that title.

To view the previously submitted errata, go to https://www.packtpub.com/books/content/support and enter the name of the book in the search field. The required information will appear under the **Errata** section.

Piracy

Piracy of copyrighted material on the Internet is an ongoing problem across all media. At Packt, we take the protection of our copyright and licenses very seriously. If you come across any illegal copies of our works in any form on the Internet, please provide us with the location address or website name immediately so that we can pursue a remedy.

Please contact us at copyright@packtpub.com with a link to the suspected pirated material.

We appreciate your help in protecting our authors and our ability to bring you valuable content.

Questions

If you have a problem with any aspect of this book, you can contact us at questions@packtpub.com, and we will do our best to address the problem.

1
Integrating IIS 10.0 with Windows Server 2016

In this chapter, we will cover the following recipes:

- IIS 10.0 architecture
- Installing IIS 10.0 on Windows Server 2016
- IIS Manager
- Basic configuration of IIS 10.0
- Hosting a static page
- Testing a static-page website

Introduction

IIS 10.0 is the latest version of Internet Information Services (IIS), which is an extensible web server developed by Microsoft. IIS 10.0 was introduced with Windows Server 2016 and Windows 10. The new features of IIS 10.0 are HTTP/2, IIS on Nano Server, Wildcard Host Headers, and PowerShell 5 cmdlets, and so on. In addition, it supports all the previously supported features: HTTP, HTTPS, SMTP, SNMP, FTP, and FTPS.

The recipes in this chapter will primarily focus on the integration of IIS 10.0 with Windows Server 2016.

We will start with some basic information about IIS 10.0. After that, we will integrate IIS 10.0 with Windows Server 2016 and configure and test our first sample web page.

Understanding IIS 10.0

In this recipe, we will understand how to work with IIS 10.0's new features. We will have an overview of the following new features added to IIS 10.0:

- **HTTP/2**

  HTTP/2 requests are now faster than ever. This feature is active by default with IIS 10.0 on Windows Server 2016 and Windows 10.

- **IIS 10.0 on Nano Server**

  IIS 10.0 is easy and quick to install on Nano Server. You can manage IIS 10.0 remotely with PowerShell or the IIS Manager console. Nano Server is much faster, and consumes less memory and disk space that the full-fledged Windows Server. Rebooting is also faster so that you can manage time effectively.

- **Wildcard Host Headers**

  IIS 10.0 support the subdomain feature for your parent domain name. This will really help you manage more subdomains with the same primary domain name.

- **PowerShell 5 cmdlets**

  IIS 10.0 adds a new, simplified PowerShell module for quick and easy management. You can use PowerShell to access server-management features remotely. It also supports existing `WebAdministration` cmdlets.

- **FTP**

  FTP is a simple protocol for transferring files. This system can transfer files inside your company LAN and WAN using the default port, 21. IIS 10.0 includes an FTP server that is easy to configure and manage.

- **FTPS**

  FTPS is the same as FTP, with the only difference that it is secure. FTPS transfers data with SSL. We are going to use HTTPS port 443. For this, we need to create and install an SSL certificate that encrypts and decrypts data securely. SSL ensures that all data passed between web server and browser remains private and consistent during upload and download over private or public networks.

- **Multi-web hosting**

  IIS 10.0 allows you to create multiple websites and multiple applications on the same server. You can easily manage and create a new virtual directory located in the default location or a custom location.

- **Virtual directories**

  IIS 10.0 makes it easy to manage and create the virtual directories you require.

Basic requirements of IIS 10.0

Before we run our web server either in operations or staging mode, we have to plan it. What type of website and application are we going to publish? For example, our website needs a server that supports .NET framework 4.5 on IIS 10.0. We need to know the supported operating system and hardware requirements.

Let's take a look at the requirements in detail.

OS requirements

The following subsections detail the estimated system requirements for Windows Server 2016. If your computer has less than the minimum requirements, you will not be able to install this product correctly. Actual requirements will vary based on your system configuration and the applications and features you install. Unless otherwise specified, these minimum system requirements apply to all installation options (Windows 2016 Server Core, Windows Server 2016, Nano Server, and Windows 10) and both the Standard and DataCenter editions. IIS 10.0 Express supports Windows 7 Service Pack 1, Windows 8.1, Windows 8, Windows Server 2008 R2, Windows Server 2012, Windows Server 2012 R2, Windows 10, and Windows Server 2016.

> For the best results, conduct test deployments to determine the appropriate system requirements for your particular deployment scenario.

Hardware requirements

Let's look at the minimum hardware requirements to run Windows Server 2016 and Windows 10:

Windows Server 2016

- Processor: 1.4 GHz 64 bit
- RAM: 2 GB for 64-bit OSes
- Hard disk space: 32 GB

Windows 10

- Processor/SoC: 1 GHz
- RAM: 1 GB for 32-bit or 2 GB for 64-bit OSes
- Hard disk space: 16 GB for 32-bit or 20 GB for 64-bit OSes
- Graphics card: DirectX 9 with the WDDM 1.0 driver

Operating system media

IIS 10.0 installation requires operating system media. While installing IIS 10.0 on Windows Server 2016, sometimes, it asks for the operating system media for required files. We have to insert the media either in CD or USB drive form.

To install IIS 10.0 Express only, we need the IIS 10.0 Express software, which is available on the Microsoft IIS website (`https://www.microsoft.com/en-us/download/details.aspx?id=48264`). You only need the software and an Internet connection.

IIS 10.0 architecture

We need to understand what resources are available to your IIS application; how it handles content files of different types, such as static files, ASP files, or ISAPI files; and how it groups content files into applications. An introduction to the client/server relationship is included for first-time readers unfamiliar with web servers.

IIS 7 and later provide a request-processing architecture. We get the following additional benefits of request processing, since the default configuration monitors each request and validates implemented security rules:

- The Windows Process Activation Service (WAS), which enables sites to use protocols other than HTTP and HTTPS
- A web server engine that can be customized by adding or removing modules
- Integrated request-processing pipelines from IIS and ASP.NET

Getting ready

We require an up-and-running IIS 10.0 instance. Security components should be installed. You should have administrative privileges.

How to do it...

Now, we are going to review the components and modules.

1. Start Server Manager on Windows Server 2016, which already should have IIS 10.0 installed on it.
2. Go to the **Tools** menu at the top.
3. You will be able to see **Internet Information Service Manager (IIS)**.

4. Click on **IIS Server**, which is to the left-hand side of the **IIS Manager** window, as shown here:

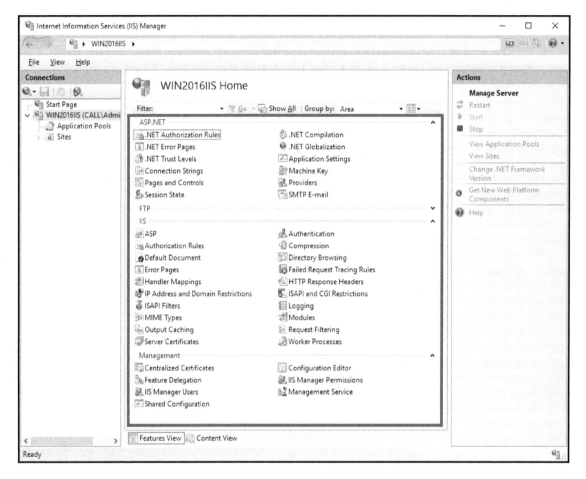

5. In the **Server Manager** panel, you will see the list of default components installed. You can configure them as per your requirements. For example, you can configure security and management options.
6. Let's understand where the modules are. In the previous figure, you will see the icon called **Modules**, which will open the default configuration at this stage.

7. Double-click on **Modules**, and you will get the list of modules available in IIS 10.0:

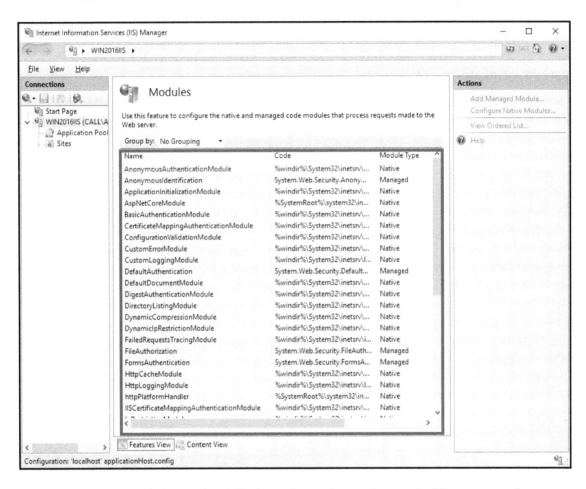

8. All the modules are by default configured to native mode. We can reconfigure them as per our application requirements.

How it works...

The combination of components and modules helps us implement application request processes and security settings quickly.

Introducing the IIS 10.0 architecture's components and modules

Let's discuss the components and modules available in IIS 10.0 Server in detail.

Overview of an HTTP request

Let's observe HTTP requests of IIS 10.0 IIS 7 and later versions have an HTTP request-processing flow similar to that of IIS 6.0 and below.

1. When a client browser initiates an HTTP request for a resource on the web server, **HTTP.sys** intercepts the request.
2. **HTTP.sys** contacts **Windows Activation Service (WAS)** to obtain information from the configuration store.
3. WAS requests configuration information from the configuration store, **applicationHost.config**.
4. The **World Wide Web Publishing Service (WWW Service)** receives configuration information, such as application pool and site configuration.
5. The **WWW Service** uses the configuration information to configure **HTTP.sys**.
6. WAS starts a worker process for the application pool to which the request was made.
7. The **Worker Process** processes the request and returns a response to **HTTP.sys**.
8. The client receives a response.

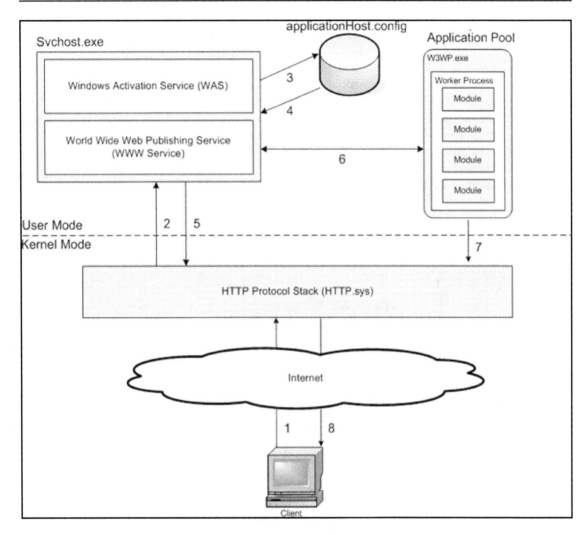

https://media-www-iis.azureedge.net/media/7188132/introduction-to-iis-architecture-101-overviewofhttprequest.png

Details of an HTTP request inside the worker process

In a worker process, an HTTP request passes through several ordered steps, called events, in the **Web Server Core**. At each event, a native module processes part of the request, such as authenticating the user or adding information to the event log. If a request requires a managed module, the native **Managed Engine** module creates an **AppDomain**, where the managed module can perform the necessary processing, such as authenticating a user with **Forms Authentication**. When the request passes through all of the events in the **Web Server Core**, the response is returned to HTTP.sys. The following figure shows an HTTP request entering the **Worker Process**:

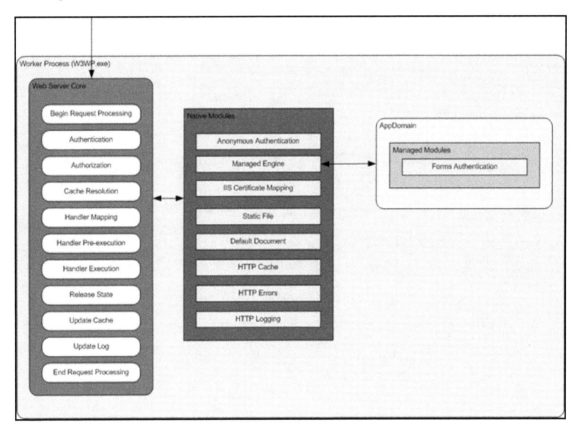

https://media-www-iis.azureedge.net/media/7188126/introduction-to-iis-architecture-101-httprequestworkerproc.png

Installing IIS 10.0 on Windows Server 2016

From the previous recipes, we've understood the basics of IIS 10.0. Now we will go install IIS 10.0 on Windows Server 2016. We are already aware of the requirements. We will use GUI-mode installation, which will show you how to install and which options you need to select.

Getting ready

To step through this recipe, you will need a running Windows Server 2016 instance and installation media. You should have administrative privileges.

How to do it...

1. Log in to Windows Server 2016 with an account with administrative privileges.
2. Open Server Manager from the Start menu or use the search window to find it.

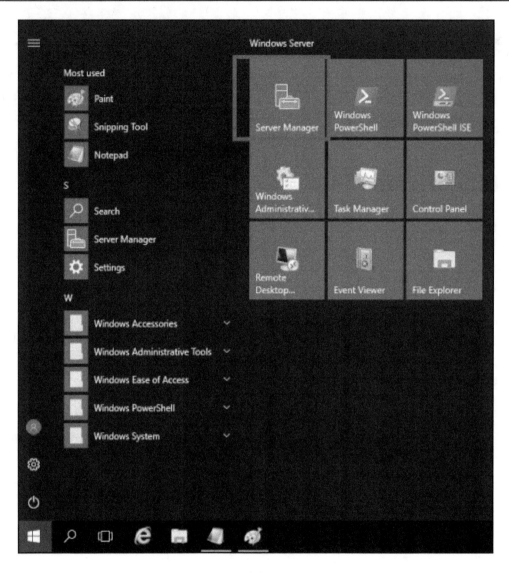

3. You have to click on **Add roles and features**, or you can find the same option in top **Manage** menu.

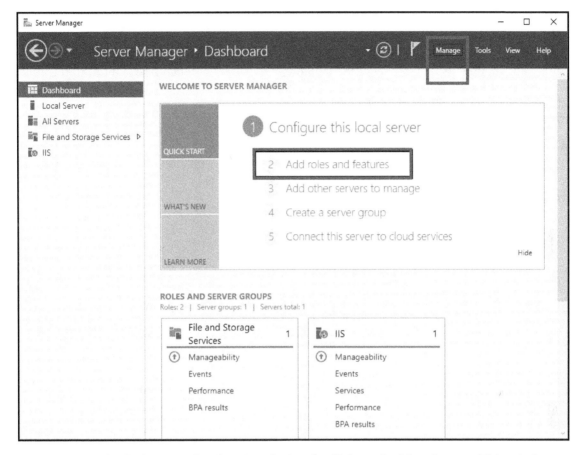

4. On the **Before you begin** wizard, simply click on the **Next** button. This window is just for information about installation prerequisites.

5. On the **Select installation type** wizard, leave the default option **Role-based or feature-based installation** selected and click on **Next**.

6. Now we have to select which server we have to install IIS 10.0 on. We are installing to our local machine, so leave **Select a server from the server pool** with the current machine selected and click on **Next**. Alternatively, you can select another server that you are managing from here. You can figure it out in the following diagram:

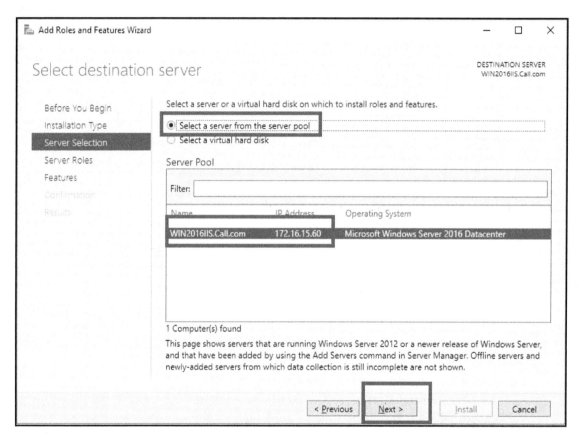

7. Now we have to select the role from the **Select server roles** wizard. Check the box next to **Web Server (IIS)**. Doing this may open up a new pop-up window advising that additional features are required; simply click on the **Add Features** button to install them as well. Click on **Next** on the **Select server roles** menu once this is complete.

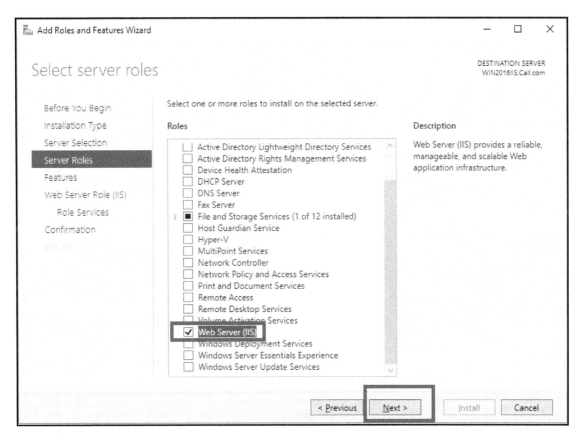

8. Once we have selected **Web Server (IIS)**, we will get a list of additional features, which we can select from. At this stage, we are not going to select any features, so simply click on **Next** in the **Select features** wizard.

9. Click **Next** on the **Web Server Role (IIS)** wizard after reading the information provided.

10. The next window in the **Select role services** wizard allows you to install additional services for IIS, if required. You can always come back and add more later, so just click on **Next** for now to install the defaults.

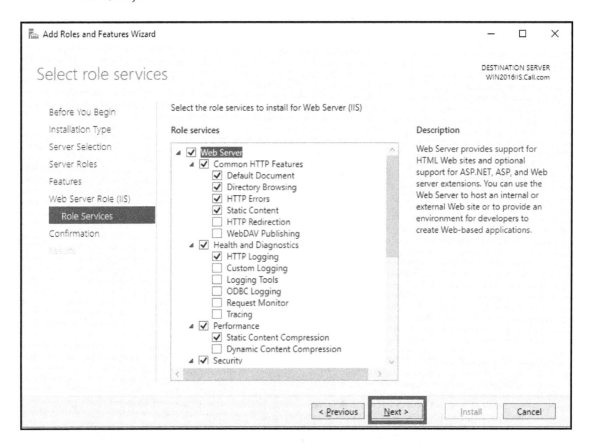

11. Now we are on the **Confirm installation selections** wizard, so review the items that are to be installed and click on **Install** to proceed with installing the IIS 10.0 web server on Windows Server 2016.

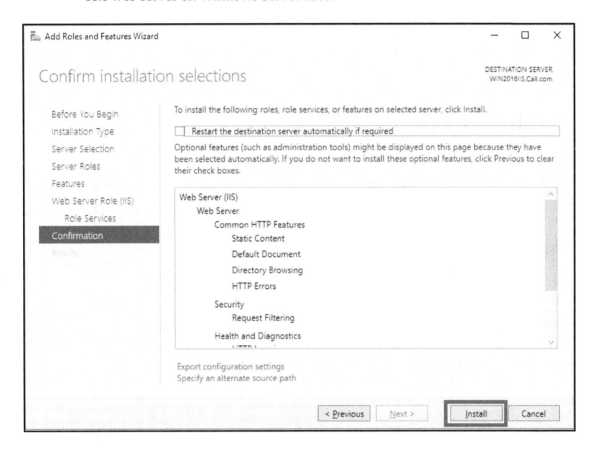

12. Here, you can see the restart checkbox. No need to mark it for a normal IIS 10.0 installation--only when you uninstall something from the server or install an additional component that requires restarting the server do you need to reboot the system.

13. Once the installation has succeeded, you can click on the close button. IIS 10.0 by default runs on port 80. It will auto-enable the **World Wide Web Services (HTTP Traffic-In)** firewall rule in Windows Firewall.

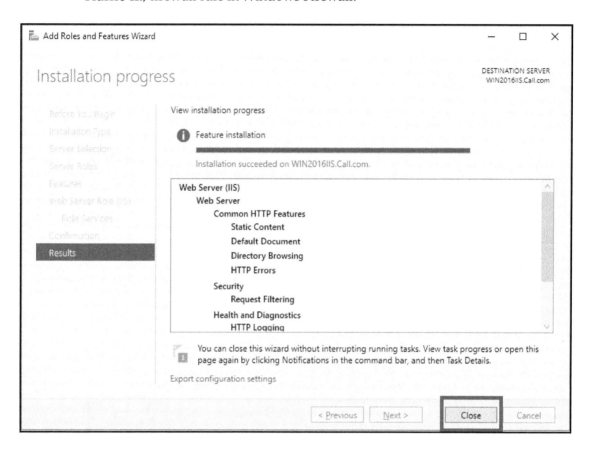

How it works...

When your are running your web server, it will process the request through the default `http` port, which has a numeric value of 80. The firewall rule was already enabled in the installation process. Now we need to know whether it's working fine.

We will perform a simple test by opening a web browser such as Internet Explorer and type the server IP address, `http://127.0.0.1/`, or `http://localhost/` in the browser address bar and hit *Enter* to run the application. You will see the default IIS welcome page.

Look at this screenshot, which shows IIS 10.0 running on Server 2016.

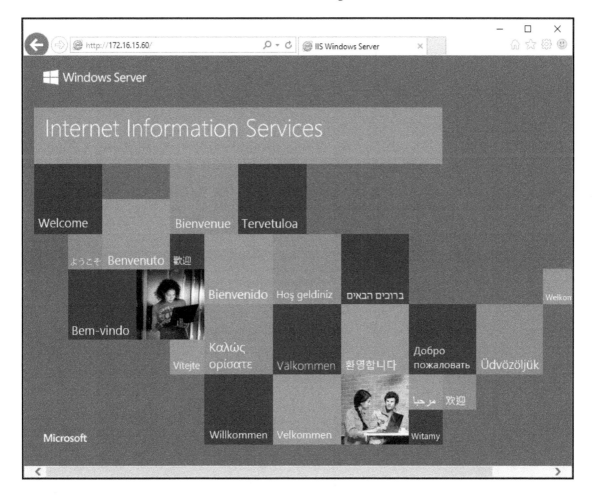

IIS Manager

Now that we know how to install IIS 10.0, let's take a look at IIS Manager, which comes as a part of the IIS 10.0 Management tools provided by Microsoft. IIS 10.0 can be managed in either GUI mode or with PowerShell commands. The IIS Manager GUI interface comes with Windows Server 2016 by default.

We will also learn how we can connect a remote IIS server with IIS Manager.

Getting ready

To step through this recipe, you will need a running IIS 10.0 instance on Windows Server 2016. For remote IIS management, you need to Install IIS management tools.

How to do it...

1. Start Server Manager on Windows Server 2016, which already has IIS 10.0 Installed on it.
2. Click on the **Tools** menu.
3. At the top, you will be able to see **Internet Information Service Manager (IIS)**. This figure will show you how to get there:

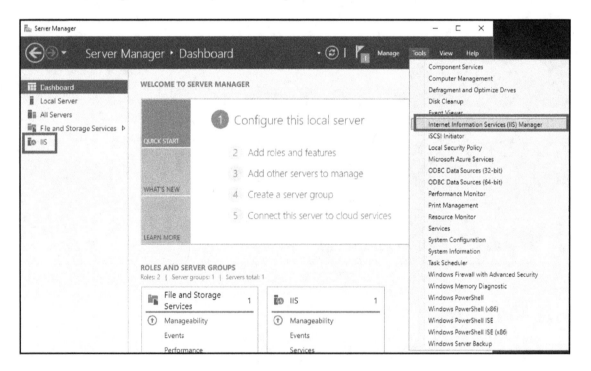

4. You will now see the IIS Manager home screen.

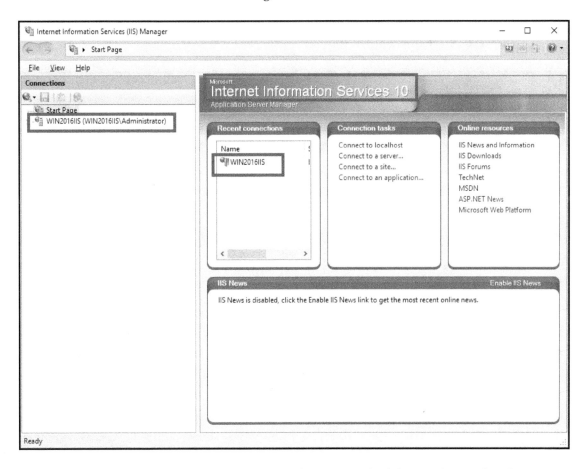

5. IIS Manager shows you its connected servers, which have IIS 10.0 already installed on it.

6. Then, we select **WIN2016IIS (WIN2016IISAdministrator),** which is at the left-hand side.

7. The IIS Manager home screen will display the default features of IIS 10.0.

8. As you can see in the following figure, there is an **Application pool** on the left-hand side along with your **Default Web Site**. Then, there are feature configuration options available in the middle section and then **Manage Server**, **Restart**, **Start**, and **Stop** at the right. You can browse the website from here.

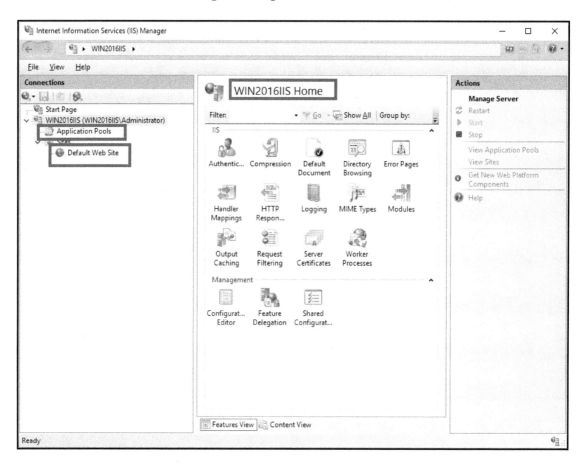

How to manage remote IIS?

1. You have more than one IIS Server instance available to manage even only website or web application want to manage from IIS Manager.
2. We are going to connect a remote IIS Server instance with IIS Manager on Windows Server 2016. This you can do with any operating system that supports IIS 10.0.

3. First, you have to install the **Management Service** role on the remote IIS server.
4. Follow these path indicated by the next screenshot. You only have to select the **Management Service** feature.

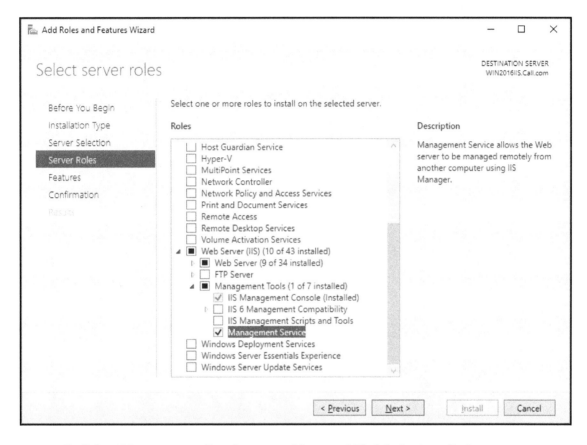

5. Select **Management Service**, press **Next**, and **Finish** the installation.

6. Now open IIS Manager on remote server `172.16.15.212`--this is the IP address in my case, but in your case, it will be your local machine's IP address. The default local machine IP address is `127.0.0.1`. We have to enable remote connections, so select the IP of the server and set the **Default port** to `80`. Allow access, **Apply**, and then **Start**. You can refer to this screenshot:

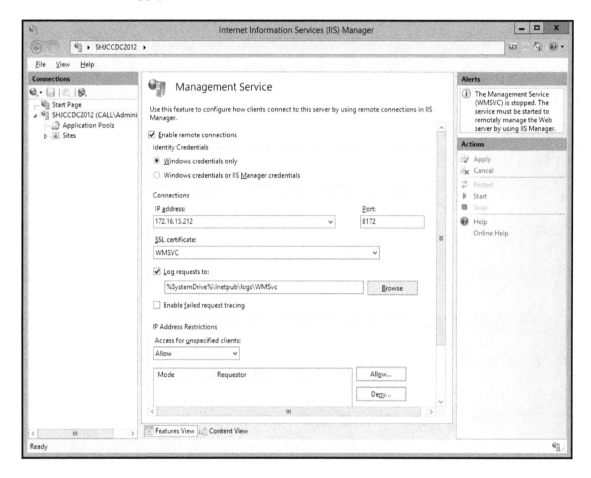

7. Now we have to come to Windows Server 2016, which has IIS 10.0 Installed.

8. Right-click on the **Start Page** icon or click on the globe below **Connections**. You will see the option to connect to an IIS Server, a website, or application.

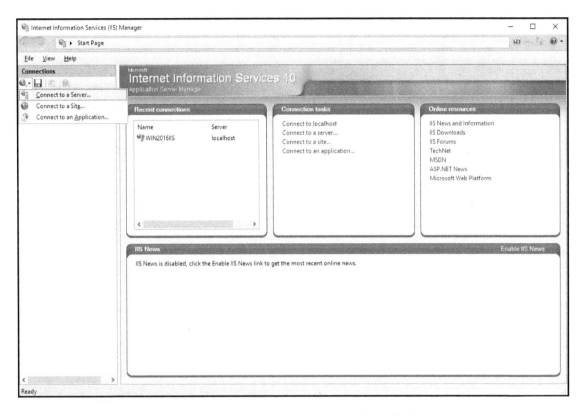

9. We will work on the server connection option first. Click on **Connect to Server**, which is listed in the previous screenshot. On the next screen, it will ask you whether you want to select a remote server IP or **Computer Name**.

10. Enter the server IP address, which is `172.16.15.212`. You will see the next screen. Click on the **Next** button to finish the current step.

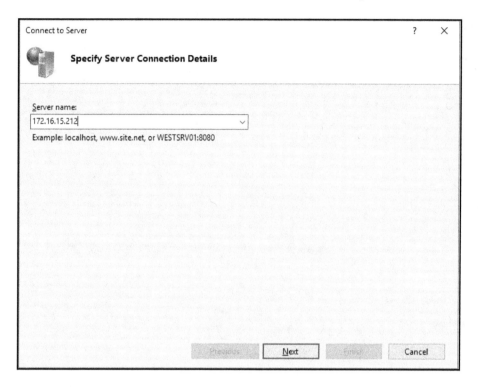

11. Now you have to enter your username and password, after which a server certificate confirmation alert pop-up message comes up on a successfully authenticated username and password. Click on the **Connect** button.

12. Then, provide the server name. We are using `remote IIS` as the server name. Click on **Finish**. That's it; you're done. In the next screenshot, you can see the remote IIS server connected in the left-hand panel of connections for remote IIS management.

How it works...

Remote management for IIS Server is an easy way to manage several IIS servers at the same time from a single window. You can manage websites and application pools remotely as well.

Basic configuration of IIS 10.0

In this recipe, we will learn about the basic configuration of IIS 10.0. We are going to review the `Inetpub` folder, `wwwroot` folder, and `logs` folder.

We will also be covering binding options and limits.

Getting ready

We require an up-and-running IIS 10.0 instance. You should have administrative privileges for IIS management.

How to do it...

1. When we installed IIS 10.0 on Server 2016, the default installation folder location was `C:\inetpub`.

2. Log in to Windows Server 2016, go to the `C:\` drive, and find the default IIS folder called `inetpub`. You can see this in the following figure:

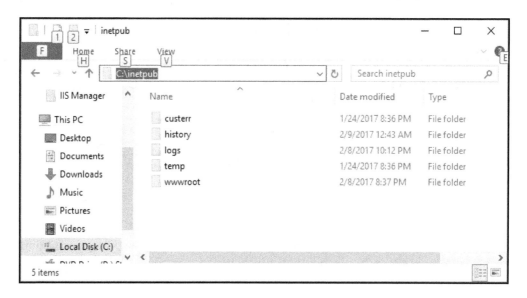

3. By default, all the website files will be stored in the `wwwroot` folder. The path is `C:\inetput\wwwroot`. The following screenshot shows the default IIS 10.0 website files:

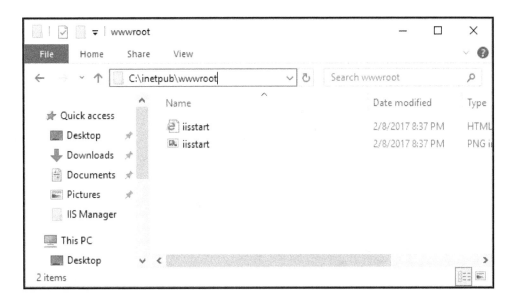

4. Now, we are going to see the `logs` folder. It is located at `C:\inetpub\logs`:

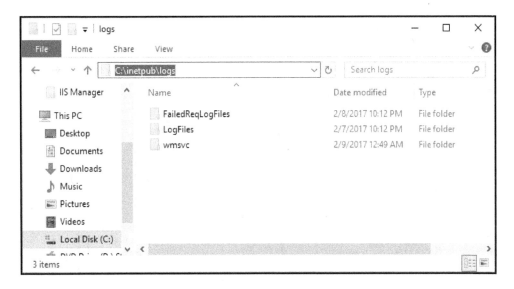

5. Start IIS Manager and select the **Default Web Site**. You will get the **Actions** window on the right-hand side. Inside the **Actions** list, we have the **Edit Site** option.

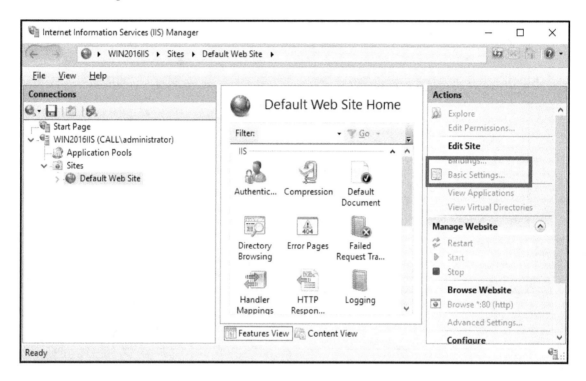

6. Click on the **Basic Setting...** text button. You will get the following window for basic settings:

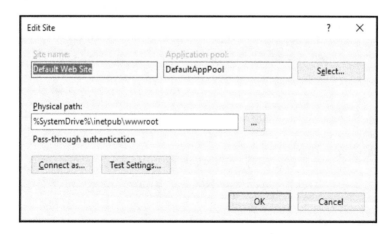

7. We selected the **Default Web Site**; now you can see the **Site name**, **Application pool**, **Physical path**, and **Connect as...** authentication option.

8. In the **Edit Site** window, you can change the **Application pool** and define your website folder path or default type of authentication. Finally, you can test the default settings.

9. Let's look at some binding options. In the **Actions** list, you will see that there is a **Bindings...** option. Bindings are used for defining your website parameters: **Type** http, **Host Name** www.xyz.com, **Port** 80, and **IP Address** * for example, as shown here:

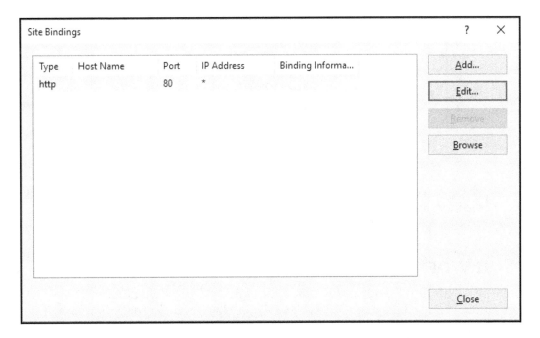

10. Now, set the **Limits** for website access. In the **Actions** list, which is available on the right-hand side of IIS Manager, go to the **Default Web Site** properties.

11. On the configuration screen, click on **Limits...**. You will get the following pop-up window:

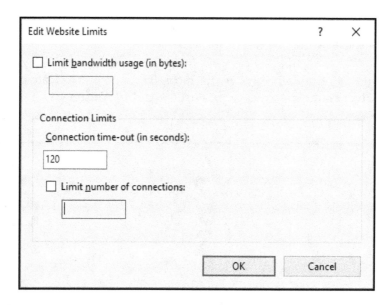

12. Here, we can limit the bandwidth usage in bytes, limit the connection timeout in seconds, and also limit the number of connections.

How it works...

We have installed IIS 10.0 with the default options and IIS 10.0 default website configuration. We also had an overview of wwwroot, logs, and the configuration window. This will help us find out where the wwwroot and logs folders are located. We also reviewed the basic and default configuration of websites, binding options, and limits.

In the next recipe, we will create and configure our own settings.

Hosting static web page

In this recipe, we will host our simple HTML web page.

Getting ready

We need to create an HTML web page and have IIS 10.0 running. You will also require user administrator rights for hosting the site.

How to do it...

1. Open Notepad and type something, like the text shown in the following screenshot. You can write anything you want.
2. Save the Notepad file on your desktop with the name of index.html.

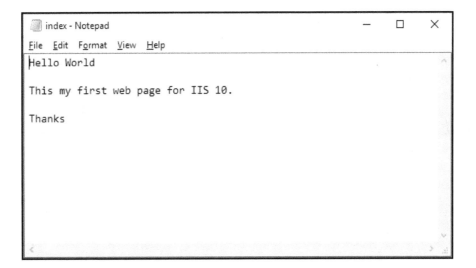

3. Next, you have to open IIS Manager, select the **Default Web Site**, and right-click on it:

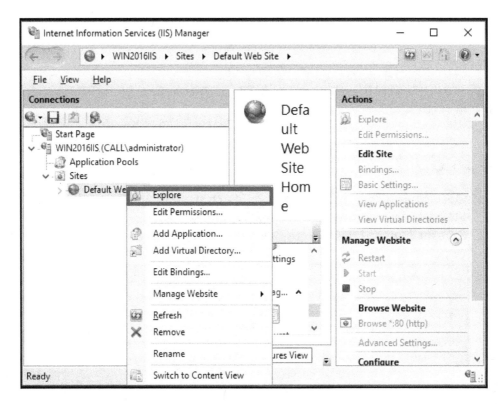

4. Click on the **Explore** option from the pop-up menu.
5. It will open the `Inetpub` folder from the `C:\inetpub\wwwroot` default website folder location, where you will have kept your web application or website files. The `wwwroot` folder is your hosting directory.

6. Copy `index.html` from the desktop and paste it in
   the `C:\inetpub\wwwroot` folder, as shown here:

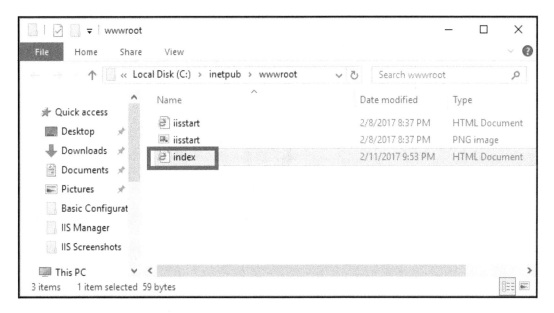

7. Select the **Default Web Site**, which is listed on the left-hand side of IIS Manager.
   You will get the D**efault Document** module.

8. Now you have to open the **Default Document**. There is already a list of filenames
   and extensions available. These names exist by default. If you want your custom
   filenames and extension to get listed there, you can add them to the **Default
   Document** and make sure you move the custom extension to the top of the
   default document settings.

9. Click on **Default Web Site**. You will see the property page come up:

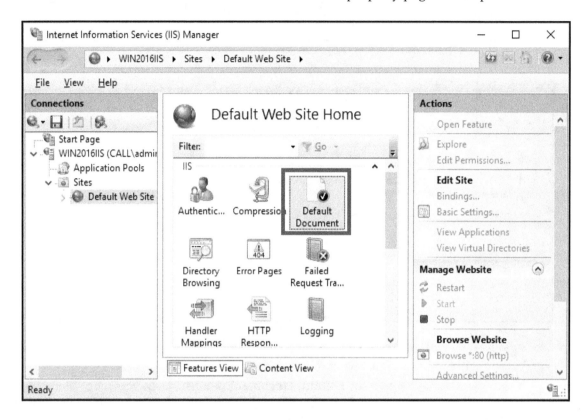

10. Open the **Default Document**. You will find `Default.htm`, `Default.asp`, `Index.html`, and many names listed. Our filename is `Index.html`, and the default document already has the same name.

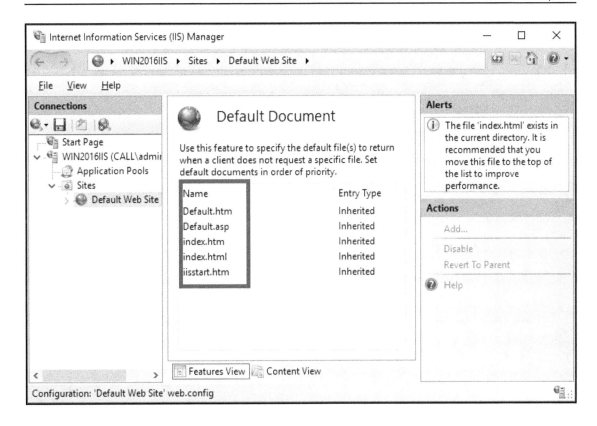

How it works...

Once we check the **Default Document** configuration and find the index.html name already listed, we have to open the web page, and the default home page will open. The **Default Document** setting is very helpful for launching your website as you will select it and you need to tell IIS Server what your home page is.

Testing a static-page website

We've already uploaded the static index.html page to the wwwroot folder, and we've checked the Default Document settings for the default home page. Now let's see how to test the static web page.

Getting ready

We have to test whether the web page is working. You need an up-and-running IIS 10.0 server instance and a static HTML web page.

We have already created the index.html page and uploaded it in the IIS wwwroot directory.

How to do it...

1. Open Internet Explorer.
2. You have to provide the URL of your web page in the address bar. We have IIS 10.0 installed on the localhost (local server).
3. Type the URL http://localhost/ and press **Enter**. Your page will look like this:

How it works...

Once you access your web page through IIS, the page is displayed through HTTP port 80. You can try uploading more pages.

2
Creating an Application Pool in IIS 10.0

In this chapter, we will cover the following recipes:

- Understanding application pools in IIS 10.0
- Installing a lower-version framework
- Creating different application pools in IIS 10.0
- Configuring application pools in IIS 10.0
- Hosting .NET web pages
- Hosting different versions of a .NET website
- Testing different versions of a web application

Introduction

When you finish your IIS 10.0 installation, you will get the default **application pools** and **default web site.** The application pool works on worker process or a set of worker processes for one or more websites.

Application pools are used to separate sets of IIS worker process that share the same configuration and application-level boundaries as your web applications. This is a really great feature of IIS and helps us run our web applications.

The benefit of application pools is that if you have an issue with one of the application pools, it will only effect the associated application pool.

Application pools enable us to isolate our web application for better security, reliability, and availability.

Two types of application pipelines are available. We can select integrated mode (supports IIS 7.5 or later versions) or classic mode (IIS 6.0).

Understanding application pools in IIS 10.0

In this recipe, we will understand application pools. We can simply say that the application pool is the heart of IIS 10.0. Application pools are logical groupings of web applications that will execute in a common process, thereby allowing greater granularity over which programs are clustered together in a single process. For example, if you require every web application to execute in a separate process, you simply go and create an application pool for each application of different framework versions.

Let's say that we have more than one version of a website, one that supports framework 2.0 and another one supporting framework 4.0 or some different application such as PHP or WordPress. All these website process are managed through application pools.

Getting ready

To step through this recipe, you will need a running IIS 10.0 instance. You should also have administrative privilege.

How to do it...

1. Open Server Manager on Windows Server 2016. Click on the **Tools** menu and open IIS Manager.

2. Expand the IIS server (**WIN2016IIS**); this is the localhost server named **WIN2016IIS**. We get the list of application pools and sites.

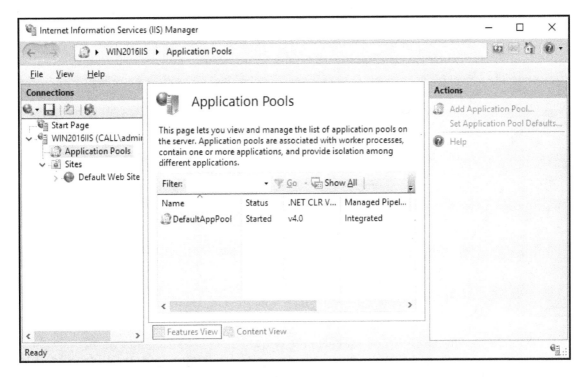

3. In the **Application Pools** section, you get the IIS 10.0 **DefaultAppPool**, as shown in the previous screenshot. You also get the **Actions** panel in the right-hand side of the screen, where you may add application pools.

3. Click on **DefaultAppPool**, and then you will get the **Actions** panel of **DefaultAppPool**. Here, you will get the option **Application Pool Tasks** highlighted in the right-hand side, with which you may **Start**, **Stop**, and **Recycle** the services of IIS 10.0.

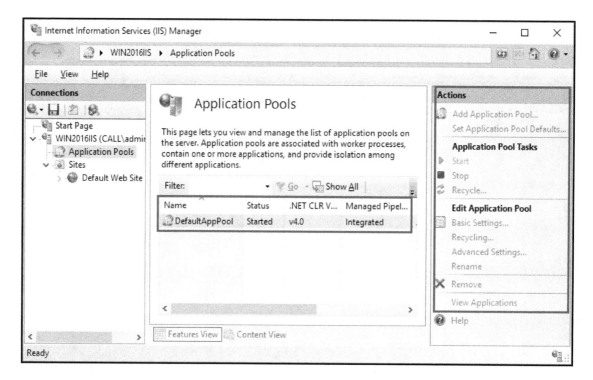

5. In the **Edit Application Pool** section, you can change the settings of the application pool to **Basic Settings...** and **Advanced Settings...**, **Rename** the application pool, and also perform **Recycling....**

How it works...

Let's take a look at what we explored in IIS Manager and application pools. We understood the basics of application pools and the properties in which we can get the changes we want made. The default IIS 10.0 application pool framework is v4.0, which is supported up to v4.6, but we have some more options for installing different versions of the application pool. We can easily customize the application pool, which helps us fulfill our typical web application requirements.

We have several options for application pools in the action pane. We can add a new application pool and we can start, stop, and recycle application pool tasks. We can perform editing and automated recycling as well.

In the next recipe, we will learn more about application pools to install lower framework versions.

Installation of lower framework version

In this recipe, we are going to install framework 3.5 on Windows Server 2016. By default, IIS 10.0 has framework version 4.0. We will install the lower version of the framework, which supports web applications with .NET framework versions 2.0 through 3.5.

For example, if you have a web application you created a few years back and it was developed in the v2.0 .NET framework, you can use this recipe in order to make it run on IIS 10.0. Let's begin.

Getting ready

To step through this recipe, you need to install framework v3.5, which is based on the v2.0 framework. You will need a Windows Server 2016 instance. You should have the Server 2016 OS media for the framework 3.5 files or an Internet connection. You also need admin privileges.

How to do it...

1. Open Server Manager on Windows Server 2016, and click on the highlighted **Add roles and features** option.

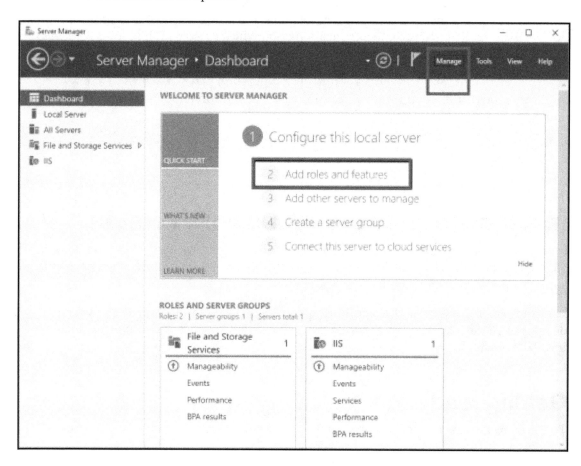

2. Click on **Next** until you get the **Select features** wizard.

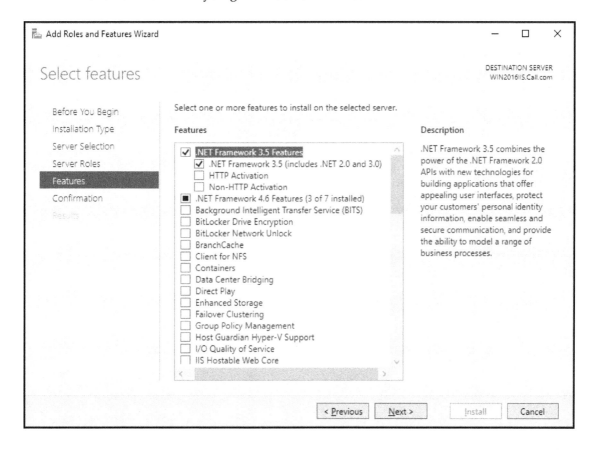

3. Click on the **Features** tab and click on the checkbox for **.NET Framework 3.5 Features**. It will also install the supported 2.0 framework. Move to the next screen:

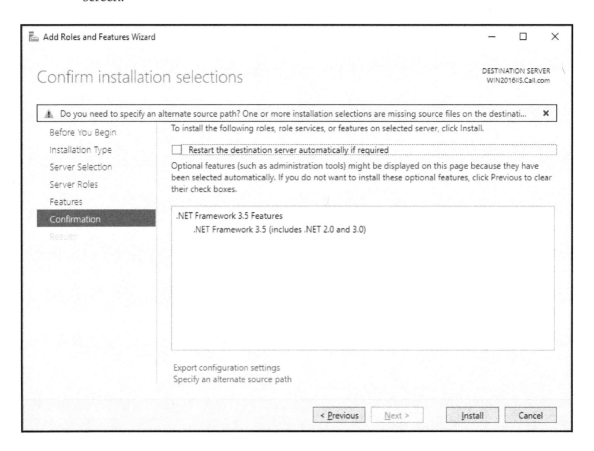

4. There is a warning displayed before installation: **Do you need to specify an alternate source path? One or more installation selection are missing sources files on the destinati...** (it goes on for a bit; hover on it to read the full warning).

5. We have to provide the installation media's `sources\sxs` folder path. Click on **Specify an alternate source path**. You'll get this screen:

Add Roles and Features Wizard   ✕

Specify Alternate Source Path

Some servers might not have all source files available to add all roles, role services, or features. The source files might not have been installed, or might have been removed by users after the operating system was installed.

If the server on which you want to install roles or features does not have all required source files, the server can try to get files by using Windows Update, or from a location that is specified by Group Policy.

You can also specify an alternate path for the source files, if the destination server does not have them. The source path or file share must grant Read permissions either to the Everyone group (not recommended for security reasons), or to the computer (local system) account of the destination server; granting user account access is not sufficient.

The following are examples of a valid source file path where the destination server is the local server, and where the E: drive contains the Windows Server installation media.

Source files for .NET Framework 3.5 Features are not installed as part of a typical installation, but are available in the side-by-side store (SxS) folder:
    E:\Sources\SxS\

Source files for other features are available in the Install.wim file. Add the WIM: prefix to the path, and a suffix to indicate the index of the image from which to get source files. In the following example, the index is 4:
    WIM:E:\Sources\Install.wim:4

Path: D:\sources\sxs

                                                    OK   Cancel

6. Here, I have the Windows Server 2016 media in the **D:** drive. This is the media path in my case, which I have downloaded, but in your case, it can be different or be an actual optical drive. There is a folder called `sources` and a subfolder, `sxs`. Inside this folder, the installation file is available:

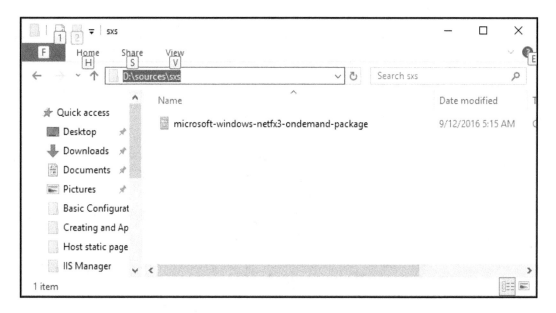

7. Now you know where the source folder is. Go to the confirmation screen and click on **Install**. The next screenshot shows the installation progress on WIN2016IIS:

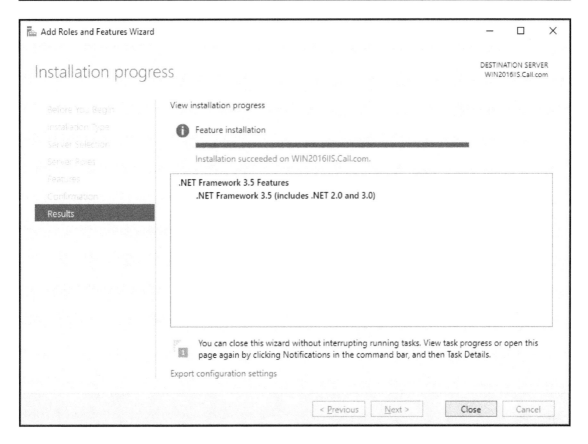

8. Click on **Close** when the installation is complete; you now have framework 3.5 available on your server.
9. Now you have to verify that framework 3.5 has been installed. It should be available in the **Features** wizard.
10. Open Server Manager and click on **Add roles and features**.

11. Keep clicking on **Next** until you get the **Select Features** wizard. You will see the .NET framework 3.5 checkbox checked, and the box will be gray, meaning it's disabled:

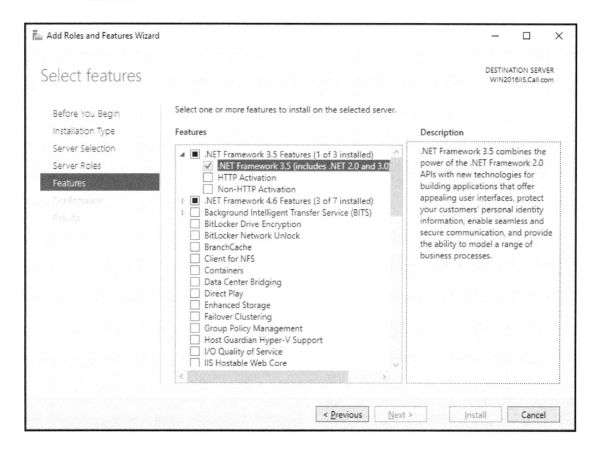

12. We've confirmed that .NET v3.5 has been installed on our server.

This can be installed through PowerShell. We can also install it directly from Windows Update, but you need Internet connectivity and the Windows Update service running on Window Server.

How it works...

In this recipe, the IIS administrator was installed on framework v3.5. The version 3.5 framework on Windows Server 2016 helps us run built-in .NET v2.0 or v3.5 applications. Framework v3.5 processes applications built in framework v3.5 or v2.0.

We also found out where the sources\sxs folder is, and after installation, we verified that .NET framework v3.5 is available.

We will now create an application pool that will support .NET framework v3.5 .

Creating different application pools in IIS 10.0

In this recipe, we are going to create an application pool that supports .NET versions 2.0 to 3.5. We already have the default application pool available for 4.0. This recipe will guide you through creating the different application pools you require.

Getting ready

In this recipe, we need IIS 10.0 and .NET framework 3.5. You should have administrative privileges.

How to do it...

1. Open Server Manager on Windows Server 2016. Click on the **Tools** menu and open IIS Manager.

2. Expand the IIS server (**WIN2016IIS**). You'll get the listed **Application Pools.** Have a look:

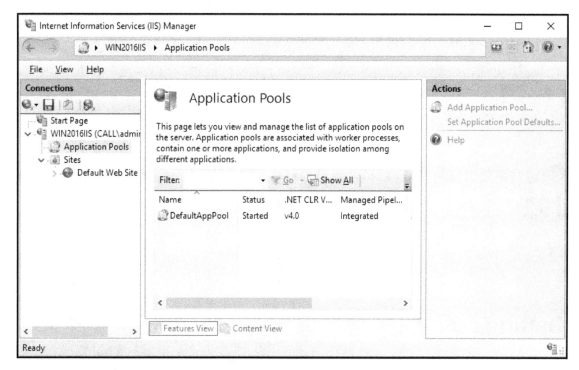

3. This screenshot shows that under the application pools, we have **DefaultAppPool** with the **Status** showing **Started**, version **v4.0**, and **Managed Pipeline** showing **Integrated**.

4. Let's create a new application pool for v2.0 and an integrated pipeline.

5. Click on **Add Application Pool** in the **Actions** window, which is available on the right-hand side. You will get the **Add Application Pool** wizard:

6. Choose an application display name according to your application name to identify it easily. I've named my pool **2and3.5AppPool**. The name shows that it will support both 2.0 and 3.5 .NET framework versions.

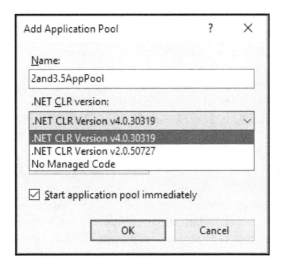

7. Next, we have **.NET CLR version**. Click on the dropdown menu and select **.NET Version V2.0.50727**. This .NET CLR version supports 2.0 and 3.5 framework websites.

8. Next, we have the **Managed pipeline mode** dropdown menu. We can select from **Integrated** or **Classic** mode. We will select the **Integrated** managed pipeline mode in this example.

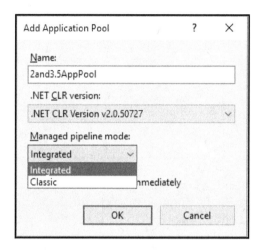

9. You can also select the auto-start option while creating the application pool. Select **Start application immediately** so that once the application pool is created, it starts automatically. If you uncheck the start application checkbox, you can start it later manually from the **Actions** window. Click on the **OK** button. Now you have successfully created your application pool. You can find the newly created application pool in the **Application Pools** list.

How it works...

Application pools process one or more web applications. We created an application pool, for which we have to set the website property to update configurations. You may set the property of the framework to one that your web application supports.

In the previous screenshot, you will see the **Edit Site** property, where you can select your own application pool in the drop-down list. In the next section, we will get into more detail regarding application pool configuration.

Configuration of application pool on IIS 10.0

In this recipe, we will have an overview of application pool properties. We will check out the default configurations under **Basic Settings**, **Recycling**, and **Advanced Settings**. This is very helpful for a developer or system administrator as one can configure different properties of different application pools based on application requirements.

Getting ready

For this recipe, we need IIS 10.0 and any version of the .NET framework installed on IIS 10.0. You must have administrative privileges.

How to do it...

1. Open Server Manager on Windows Server 2016. Click on the **Tools** menu and open IIS Manager.

2. Expand the IIS server (**WIN2016IIS**). You'll get the listed **Application Pools**:

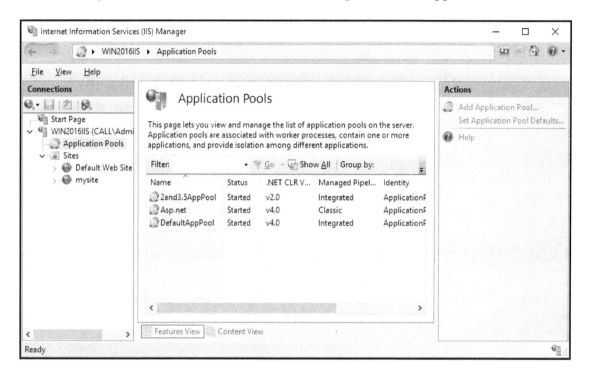

3. We have already created an application pool, which is displayed in the **Application Pools** window. We've created **2and3.5AppPool**, **Asp.net**, and **DefaultAppPool** (the default one).

4. In the **Actions** panel, we can add several application pools, and we can set any one of the created application pools as the default. The default application pool is useful when creating a website: it is the one selected as the application pool unless set otherwise.

5. Select the **2and3.5AppPool**. You will see the **Actions** pane with a list of available properties, in which you can make some changes if needed. The version of the **2and3.5AppPool** is v2.0:

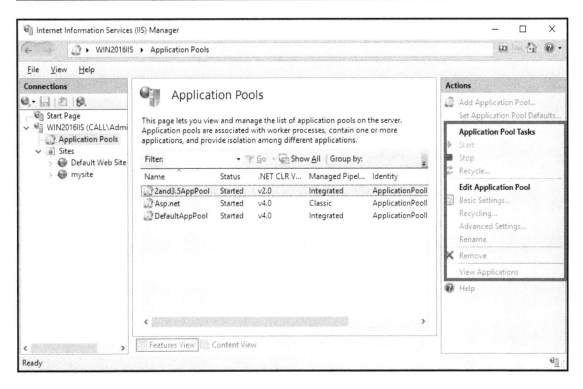

6. Take a look at the **Actions** panel, with the **Application Pool Tasks** and **Edit Application Pool** options. From the **Application Pool Tasks** list, we can **Start**, **Stop** and **Recycle...** the application pool.

7. Now let's come to the basic properties of the application pool. Click on **Basic Settings...** from **Edit Application Pool**, and you'll see this popup:

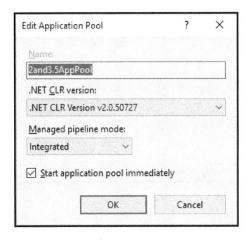

8. **Basic Settings...** has nothing but quick settings to change a limited number of things. We can change the .NET framework version to framework v4.0 or framework v3.5 (version 2.0 is updated to version 3.5).

9. We can change the **Managed pipeline mode** to **Integrated** or **Classic**, and we can check or uncheck the auto-start option.

10. Next is **Advanced Settings...**, which has more options to customize the application pool.

11. Click on **Advanced Settings...**; this screen will open:

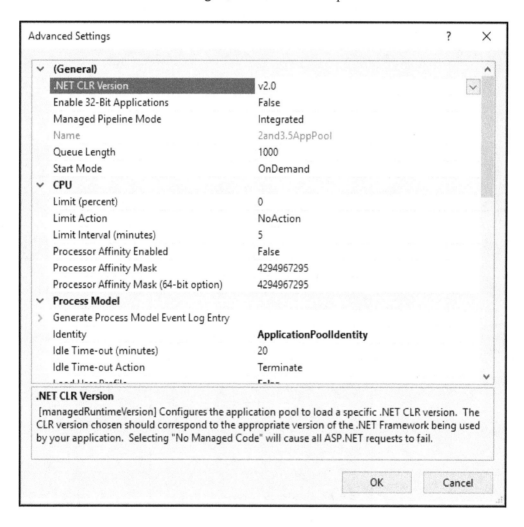

12. We have more options available in the **Advanced Settings...** window. You may change the .NET framework version, or you can turn 32-bit application support on or off. **Queue Length** is **1000** by default. You may reduce or increase it as you need. **Start Mode** should be **OnDemand** or **Always Running**.

13. We can also customize **CPU** utilization, which helps us to manage the load of each application and its performance.

14. The **Process Model** will help you define tasks for application pool availability and accessibility:

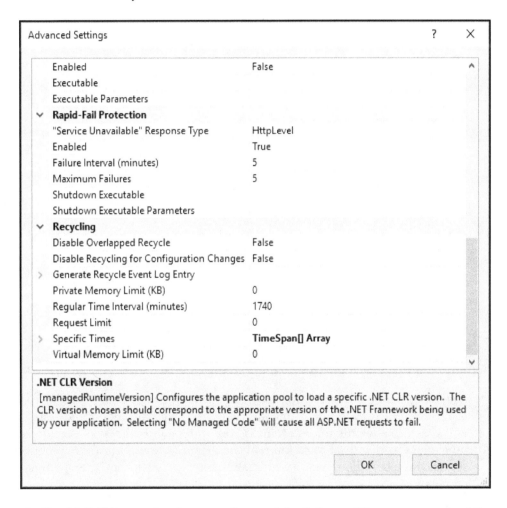

15. **Rapid-Fail Protection** is generally used for failover. We can set up the failover server and its configuration.

16. **Recycling** is to refresh the application pool overlap. We can set a default recycling value.

17. We can add more specific settings through the **Recycling** settings by clicking on **Recycling....** This is what the window looks like:

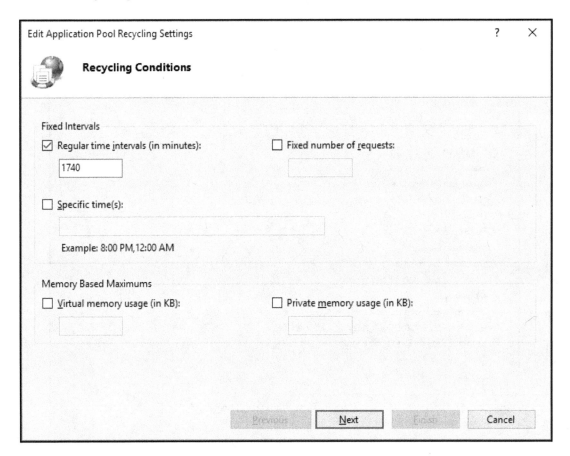

18. Recycling is based on conditions such as virtual memory usage, private memory usage, specific time, regular time intervals, and fixed number of requests. Also, it will generate a log file for you to help you understand what was executed at what time. Here, you will set fixed intervals based on time and number of requests or specific time based on memory utilization and virtual and private memory. Click on **Next**.

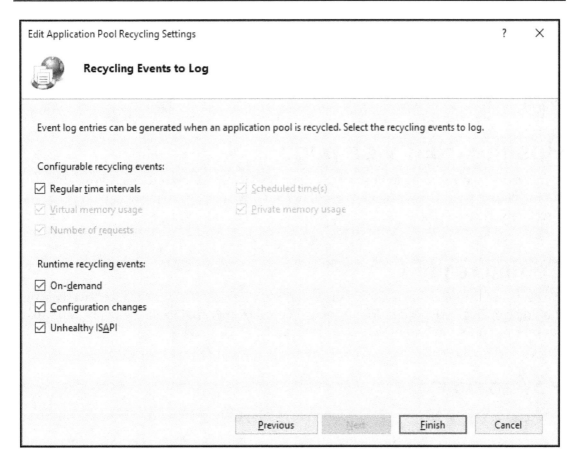

19. In the **Recycling Events to Log** window, we can generate a log of the recycling events.

How it works...

In this recipe, we learned about three types of properties of IIS applications: basic properties, advanced properties, and recycling. We can use these properties for the web applications we will host in IIS Server to process them through the application pool. When hosting a web application, there are always some requirements we need to configure in the application pool settings.

For example, our management may decide that we need to limit the queue of **2and3.5apppool** applications. We can just go to the advanced settings and change it.

In the next section, we will host a v4.0 .NET framework website and make use of the v4.0 application pool.

Hosting .NET web page

In this recipe, we are going to host a .NET default v4.0-supported web page. We will check out the default website properties. We will upload the web page to the default wwwroot directory.

Getting ready

We need a v4.0 application to be installed on IIS 10.0 Server, and our v4.0 .NET web page should be ready. We'll need to install some IIS components not installed already in IIS 10.0. For this, you must have administrative privileges.

How to do it...

First, we have to install some .NET supported components.

1. Open Server Manager on Windows Server 2016 and click on the **Manage** menu. Once in there, click on **Add Roles and features**.
2. Click on **Next** until you get the **Select server roles** wizard. Follow the exact route highlighted in this figure:

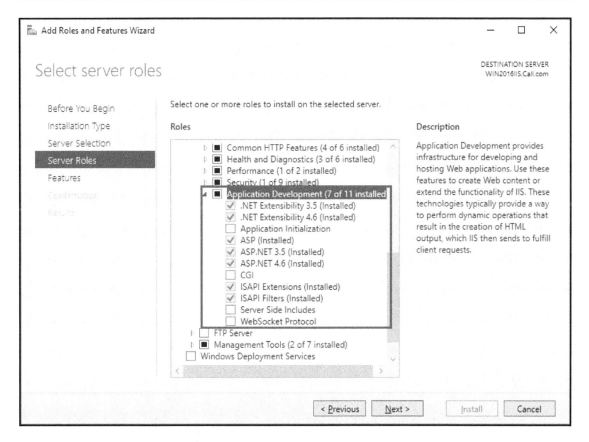

3. Expand **Application Development**. You have to select **.NET Extensibility 3.5**, **.NET Extensibility 4.6**, **ASP**, **ASP.NET 3.5**, **ASP.NET 4.6**, **ISAPI Extensions**, and **ISAPI Filters**.

4. Click on **Next** to finish. Now let's go on and upload the .NET framework web pages we created for demo purposes.

5. Open IIS Manager, click on **Default Web Site**, and you will see this screen:

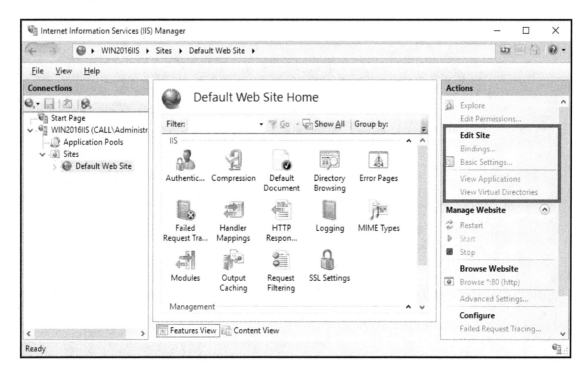

6. In the **Actions** pane, you have to click on **Basic Settings...** and check which version of the application pool is associated with the default web site.

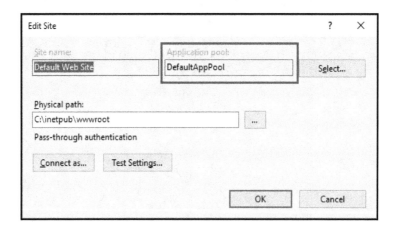

7. We have selected **DefaultAppPool**. Click on the **Select...** button; you'll see the screen shown in the next figure. Select **DefaultAppPool** from the dropdown and click on the **OK** button to finish the pool section.

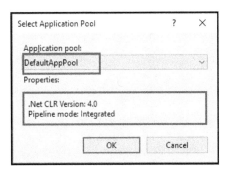

8. Right-click on **Default Web Site**, click on **Explore**, which is in the top-right corner or can be called using the context menu of **Default Web Site** in the left-hand panel, as highlighted in the next figure. You will get the `wwwroot` directory, where you have to upload .NET web files.

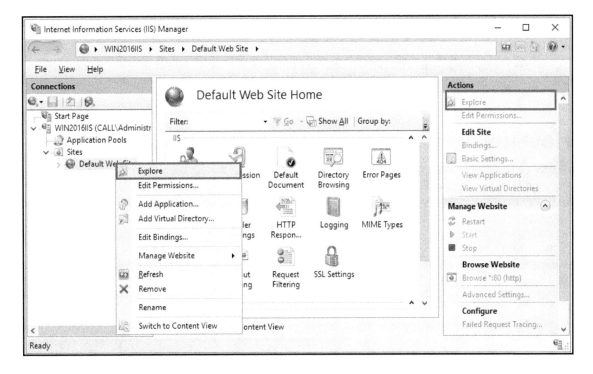

9. We have created ASP.NET v4.0 files, which we need to paste in the `wwwroot` folder, as shown here:

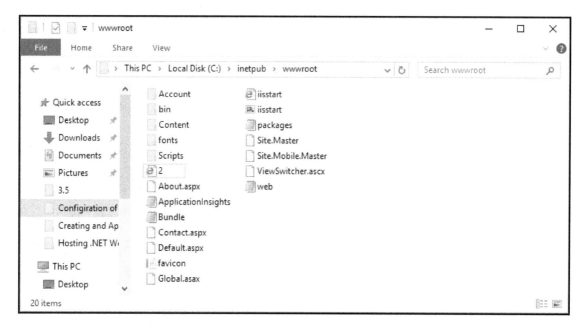

10. Here, we've uploaded the .NET application files we created for testing and demo purposes. We will test the application in the last recipe of this chapter later.

How it works...

In this recipe, we installed the NET Extensibility 3.5 and 4.6 components. We also installed support for asp, asp.NET, and ISAPI, which are not available in a default installation of IIS 10.0. We explored application pool properties and uploaded v4.0 .NET application files we created for demo purposes.

Now, upload your files to the `wwwroot` directory, which is associated with the default website. Once you access the default website URL, your .NET application files will be processed by the application pool.

Hosting different versions of a .NET website

In this recipe, we are going to host a .NET v2.0-supported web page. We will change the property of the **Default Web Site**. We will upload the web page to the default `wwwroot` directory.

Getting ready

We already have the v2.0 and v3.5 framework versions installed on IIS 10.0 Server. The v4.0 .NET web page we created should be ready. You must have administrative privileges.

How to do it...

1. Open IIS Manager and click on **Default Web Site.**
2. In the **Actions** pane, click on **Basic Settings...** and then click on the **Select...** button, highlighted in the next figure:

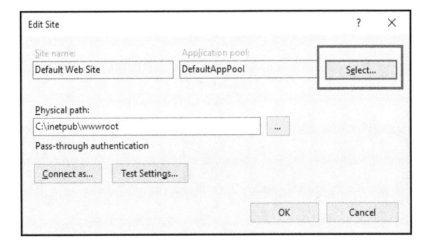

3. The application pool window will pop up. Click on the **Application pool:** drop-down menu, select **2and3.5AppPool** under **Application Pools**, and click on **OK** to finish this step.

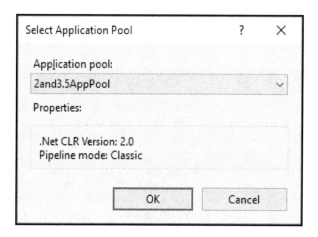

4. Now, in the site properties, you will see the v2.0 application pool associated with the **Default Web Site**:

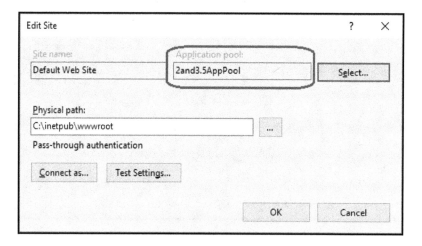

5. Next, right-click on **Default Web Site**, click on **Explore**, and you will get the wwwroot directory, where you have to upload the v3.5 .NET web files:

6. We have thus uploaded the v3.5 files to the wwwroot directory.

How it works...

In this recipe, we changed the application pool property from v4.0 to v2.0 .NET. We had already uploaded our v3.5 .NET files to the wwwroot directory, which is associated with **Default Web Site**.

Once you access the **Default Web Site** URL, your .NET application files will be processed by the selected application pool.

Testing different versions of a website

In this recipe, we are going to test the v3.5 application pool we created. Also, we will test the default v4.0 application pool.

We are going to test the v4.0 and v3.5 frameworks. We have created both the files and already uploaded them to wwwroot folder.

Getting ready

In this recipe, we need the already configured v4.0 and v3.5 frameworks. For the web pages, we've already created the v4.0 and v3.5 framework application files. One by one, we will test the `localhost` URL and see the result. We will also test across versions of frameworks and web application files.

How to do it...

1. We are going to test the v4.0 application, which is **DefaultAppPool**. You already uploaded the web application files to the `wwwroot` folder in the previous recipe.
2. Open Internet Explorer, type `http://localhost/` in the address bar, and press **Enter**. You will see the following screen:

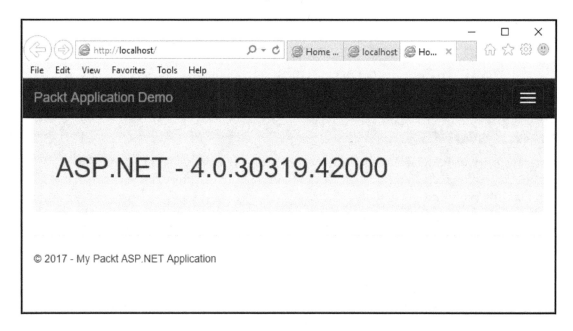

3. Now we are going to test the v3.5 application, which is **2and3.5AppPool**. You already uploaded the web application files to the `wwwroot` folder in the previous recipe.

4. Open Internet Explorer, type `http://localhost/` in the address bar, and press *Enter*. You will see this page:

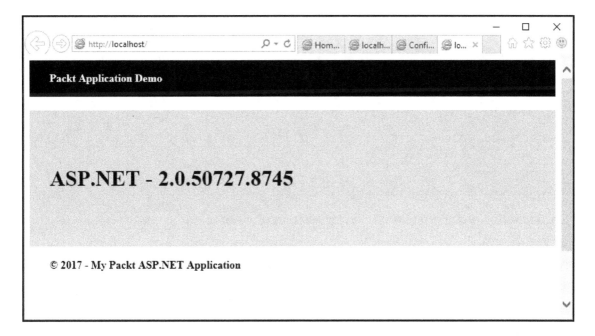

5. We've got the result. We have created both the application files to demonstrate the running application pool version.

How it works...

In this recipe, we tested both application pools framework versions. Each application pool can be used for one or several websites.

We can check what happens if our application pool is v3.5 and we host a web application made for v4.0:

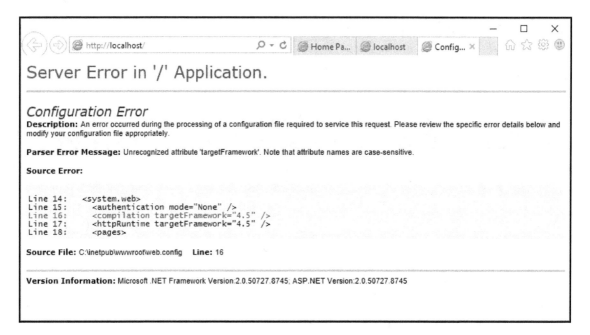

We get an error here. At the bottom of page, you can see the suggestion, which is **Version Information: Microsoft .Net Framework Version 2.0.50727.8745; ASP.NET Version 2.0.50727.8745** and your web application framework is v4.5.

You must make sure to upload the supported .NET web application version and check the application pool associated with the website. Both should be the same framework version in order for the web page to run.

3
Hosting Multiple Websites on IIS 10.0

In this chapter, we will cover the following recipes:

- Hosting multiple websites
- Creating a website folder
- Configuring websites
- Configuring ports
- Configuring the website IP
- Deploying websites
- Testing websites

Introduction

Using multiple web hosts in Microsoft IIS 10 Server, you can host one or more websites on the same IIS 10 server. The website can be hosted using SSL (Secure Socket Layer) over **Hyper Text Transfer Protocol (HTTPS)** using the default port, 80. In general, all websites get access on default port 80 using either HTTP or HTTPS. If you run your website encrypted, the protocol protocol is HTTPS secure port.

A website is needed to access a network, either through LAN, which can be called **intranet**, or **Wide Area Network (WAN)**, which can be called **internet**.

You need a domain name, IP address, and port to run your website or web application.

We have already performed the installation and created application pools. Now let's start multiple web hosts on the same IIS 10 server and access the websites using their host names (domain names).

Hosting multiple websites

In this recipe, we will create three websites in IIS 10.0: mysite.com, v2mysite.com, and v4mysite.com. We will make the hostname entries in the `hosts` file later in this chapter. We will access the website with its hostname.

Let's move on to the next section, where we will be covering this in detail.

Getting ready

To step through this recipe, you will need a running IIS 10 instance and administrator user account. You are going to create and configure the website's properties.

How to do it...

1. Open Server Manager in Windows Server 2016. Click on the **Tools** menu and open IIS Manager.
2. Expand the IIS server from the **Connections** panel. We get the listed **Application Pools** and **Sites** folder.
3. Expand the **Sites** menu in the left-hand side panel under the computer name and click on **Default Web Site**. You can find it using this figure:

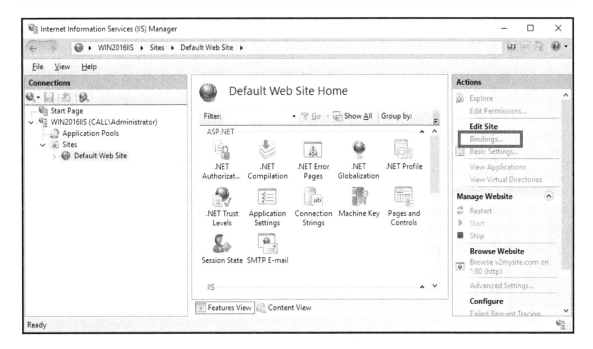

5. Go to the **Actions** panel at the top-right and click on **Bindings** under **Edit Site**. You will get the default **Site Bindings** option:

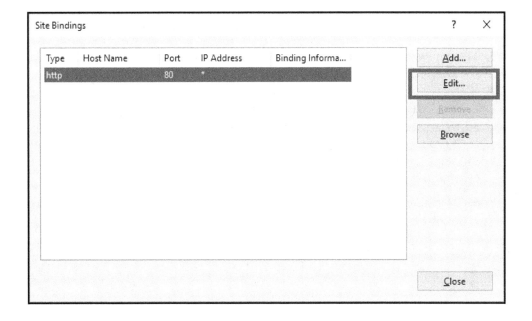

6. Here, you can see the only default information available, which has Type as **http**, **Port** number **80**, and IP address * (asterisk), which means one IP address will be assigned automatically for each site. One server can have multiple IP addresses; for example, one IP is used for shared hosting, and we can also set up a different dedicated IP for individual sites for better bandwidth and performance.

7. Click on the **Edit** button, and you will get the **Edit Site Binding** option, as highlighted in this figure:

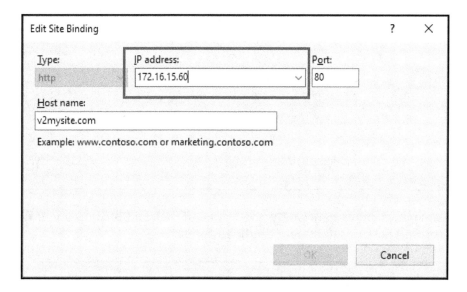

8. You know that we have selected the **Default Web Site** binding property. Hence, we are configuring the **Default Web Site** to be accessed through the hostname or IP.

9. Enter the IP address; we are going to enter IP address 172.16.15.60. This IP address used in our demo case, but in your case it can be different. Before you start typing the IP address, make sure that it is your IP address, but you can keep the same example domain name. Enter the new hostname or domain name. We entered the host name v2mysite.com.

10. Leave the default **Port 80**. Click on **OK**.

11. Go to the **Site** menu of IIS Server Manager, which is available in the left side panel and select the **Default Web Site**. Rename it as v2mysite.com by either right-clicking on the get context pop-up menu to select **Rename** or under the **Actions** pane by clicking on **Basic Settings** to get the same option to rename it. Renaming the website is only for identifying the website.

12. Now we are going to add v4mysite.com. Inside the **Connections** pane, click on the Sites menu, go to the **Actions** panel, and click on **Add Websites....** You will get the **Add Websites...** window:

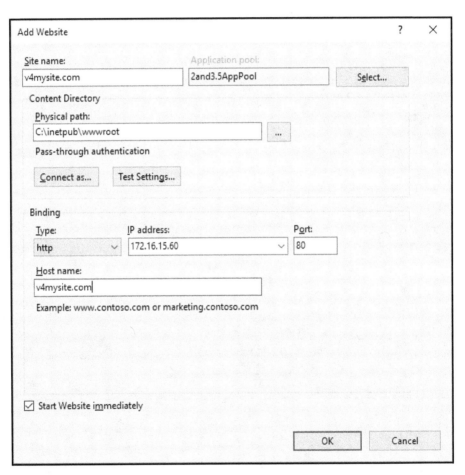

13. We add the **Site name** v4mysite.com and select the **Application pool** 2and3.5AppPool.

14. Leave the default directory as wwwroot. We add the IP address same as the server IP.

15. Leave the port number as the default port number, which is 80. The hostname is v4mysite.com. **Start Website immediately** is the default option, checked. Click on the **OK** button.

16. We will follow the same steps for adding more websites; we will create one more website with the name mysite.com.

17. Now we have three websites created with three different names with the same IP address:

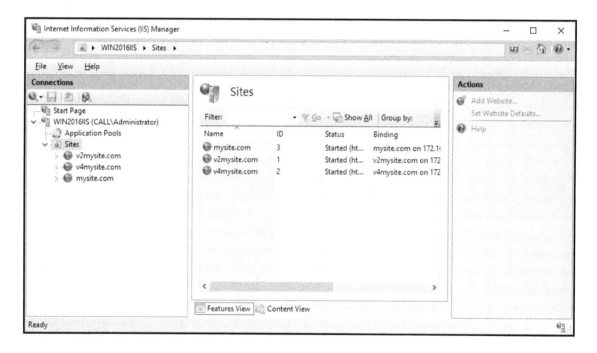

18. Let's move to configure a few more steps to access these websites through the domain name.

19. Go to the `C:\` drive, open the `Windows` folder, and search for `System32`. Inside the `System32` folder, open the `drivers` folder.

20. There is an `etc` folder inside the `drivers` folder:

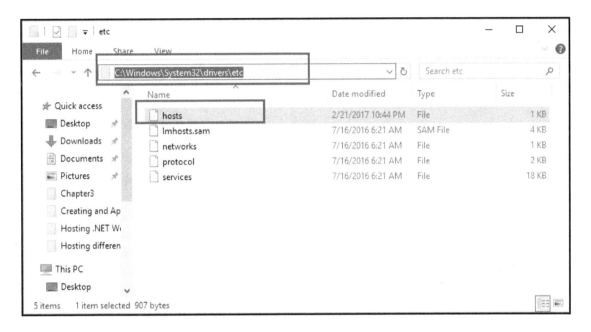

21. Open the `hosts` file in Notepad. Make sure that Notepad opens with administrator privileges by right-clicking on the Notepad icon and clicking on **Run as Administrator**; it will only allow you to save the changes. Now we have to make the web site hostname entry:

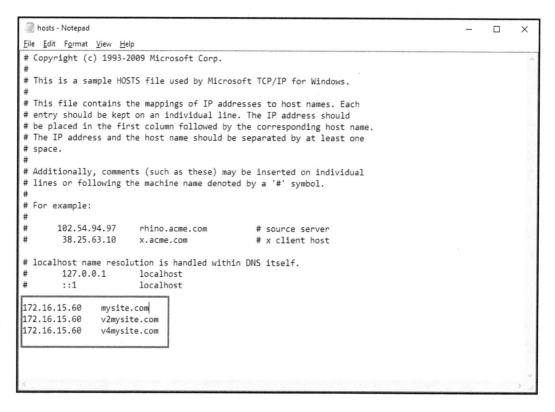

22. As shown in the previous figure, we made three website entries, which are `mysite.com`, `v2mysite.com`, `v4mysite.com`. All the site IPs are the same, `172.16.15.60`. In your case, the IP address should be different.

23. Save the `hosts` file and close it. Now you are done with all the configurations for multiple website hosting.

How it works...

Multiple website hosting on the same IIS 10 server helps us easily manage all the website-related tasks on the same server. We have just created three websites on the same IIS server. You can create many websites as per your requirements.

A hosts file entry is required when you want to get access to the website with the domain name, for example, mysite.com. You can also use the DNS server to access this website through LAN or WAN.

Creating a website folder

In this recipe, we are going to create a separate website directory for each website, for example, `mysite`, `v2mysite`, and `v4mysite`, inside the `c:\inetpub\wwwroot` path, where we can upload the `website` application files later in the chapter. We were using the default `wwwroot` folder to upload the website files, so now we have to publish more than one website. We have to upload all the web files in their own separate directory.

Getting ready

To step through this recipe, you will need a running IIS 10 instance. You must have administrator privileges, which you need to create the website folders.

How to do it...

We are going to create a website folder inside the `wwwroot` folder for each website.

1. Open the file explorer, and click on **This PC**. On the right hand side, you will see your available drives.
2. Open the `C:\` drive, go to the folder name `inetpub`, and you will get the list of IIS 10.0-related folders. You need to find the `wwwroot` folder.

3. Open the `wwwroot` folder. Inside the `wwwroot` folder, you have to create `mysite`, `v2mysite`, and `v4mysite` subfolders:

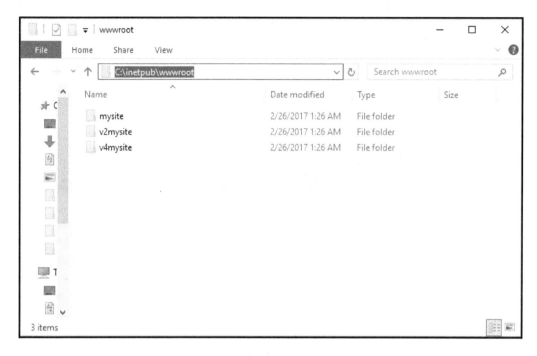

4. Now we have to configure the physical path of the website; we already have three websites: `mysite.com`, `v2mysite.com`, and `v4mysite.com`. Let's configure them one by one.

5. Go to **Server Manager**, click on the **Tools** menu, and open IIS Manager.

6. Expand your IIS server from the **Connections** pane, expand the **Sites** folder, and you have three listed websites. Select **mysite.com**.

7. Go to the **Actions** pane, click on **Basic settings**, and you will get the properties:

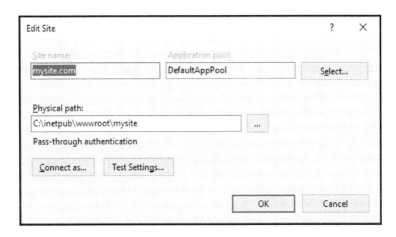

8. We add the **Physical path** `C:\intepub\wwwroot\mysite` of the website directory we want to use for this website, `mysite.com`.

9. Click on the **OK** button to finish.

10. Follow the previous steps to add/update the **Physical path** `C:\intepub\wwwroot\v2mysite` of the website directory we want to use for this website, `v2mysite.com`.

11. Click on the **OK** button.

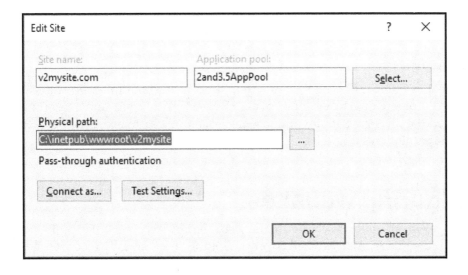

12. We will follow the same steps to add/update the physical path of `v4mysite.com` and `v4mysite.com`:

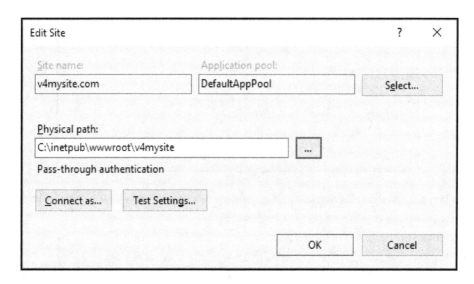

13. Now you can upload the web application files as per the website name and folder. If you need to use different versions of the application pool, you can change the application pool from **Basic Settings**.

How it works...

We first create subfolders inside the wwwroot directory for multiple web applications. We then created separate directories for `mysite.com`, `v2mysite.com`, and `v4mysite.com`. We also changed the physical path for all the websites. Now we can access all the websites with their own separate physical paths.

Configuring websites

In this recipe, we are going to configure the website property. We will explore basic settings and advanced settings. Also, we will cover the settings limit access to the website.

Getting ready

To step through this recipe, you will need a running IIS 10 server and administrator user account to edit the website settings.

How to do it...

1. Open Server Manager on Windows Server 2016. Click on the **Tools** menu and open IIS Manager.
2. Expand the IIS server (**WIN2016IIS**). We get the listed application pools and sites.
3. Click on **mysite.com** from the connections pane, and you will see the properties of **mysite.com** in the **Actions** pane. We get the **Basic Settings...** and **Advanced Settings...**:

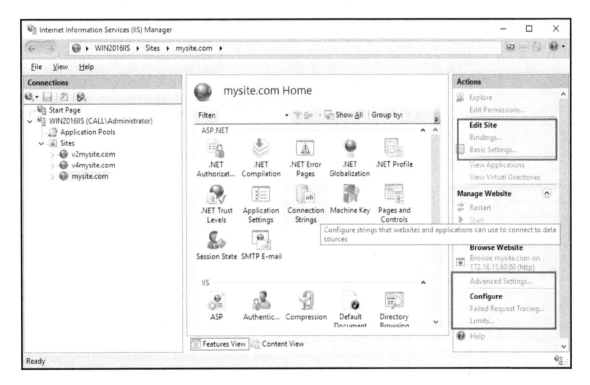

4. Click on **Basic Settings...**, and you will get the **Edit site** property displayed.

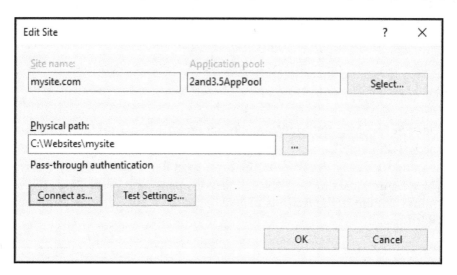

5. The **Edit Site** window shows you the selected website and your assigned application pool.
6. The **Physical path** is the path of the website application files, located in the wwwroot folder. You can customize the **Connect as...** option and test your settings to check whether it is working or not in a browser.
7. Now let's move on to configure the **Advance Settings...** of the selected website.
8. Click on **mysite.com**. In the **Actions** pane, you get the **Advanced Settings...** option. Click on **Advanced Settings...**, and you will get the advanced settings window:

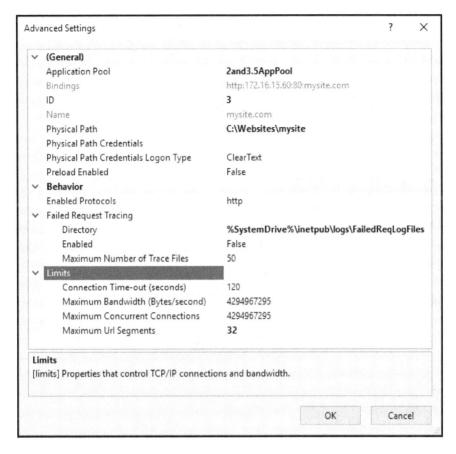

9. **Advanced Settings** has four groups of settings: **General**, **Behavior**, Failed
   Request Tracing, and **Limits**.

10. In **General**, you can change the **Application pool, website ID, website Physical
    Path, Physical Path Credentials Logon Type**, and **Preload Enabled**.

11. In **Behavior,** you change **Enabled** protocols, which are either **http** or **https**.

12. You can configure the settings of **Failed Request Tracing**. **Directory** is where
    you store your tracing information log, tracing service enabled as true or false,
    and maximum number of trace files.

13. You can also set the **Limits** of access to your website on the basis of connection
    timeout, maximum bandwidth per second, maximum concurrent connections,
    and maximum URL segments.

How it works..

In this recipe, we had an overview of the website mysite.com from steps 1 to 3. We went through the Connections pane and expanded the Sites folder to get the properties of mysite.com. From steps 4 to 13, we discussed the basic and advanced settings configuration and customization of the website mysite.com. We understood Failed Request Tracing and how to limit the concurrent connections of mysite.com.

Configuring ports

In this recipe, we are going to configure the website access port; default website access type is HTTP and port number is 80. We will configure some different port to access the website for all individually hosted sites.

Getting ready

To step through this recipe, you will need a running IIS 10 server and administrator user account, which you need to edit the website settings.

How to do it...

1. Open Server Manager on Windows Server 2016. Click on the **Tools** menu and open the IIS Manager.
2. Expand the IIS server (**WIN2016IIS**). We get the listed application pools and sites.
3. We already have the listed websites, which were created earlier. Click on **mysite.com**, you will get the properties of **mysite.com** in the **Actions** pane. We can browse website on IP 172.16.15.60:80; here, 80 is the port number.

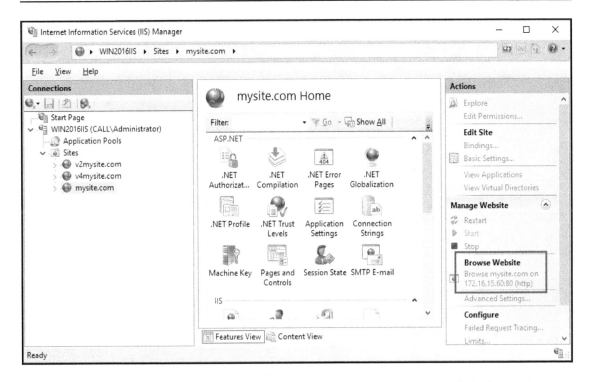

4. Now we have to configure the website port `8080`; the current default port is `80`.

5. Go to the **Actions** pane, click on **Bindings**, and you will get the binding window:

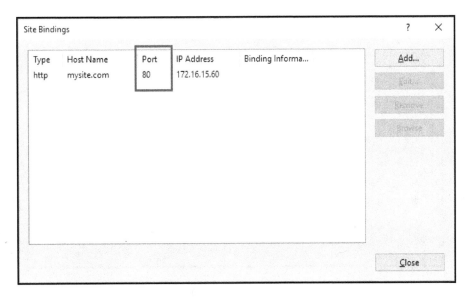

6. Here you will see the **Site Bindings**. The **Type** is http, **Host Name** is **mysite.com**, Port is 80, and IP address 172.16.15.60. Let's move to configure the port number 8080.

7. Select **mysite.com** and the edit button will be active; click on the **Edit** button, and you will get the **Edit Site Binding** window:

8. Change the port to 8080 and then click on the **OK** button. Now, you can see the default port has changed:

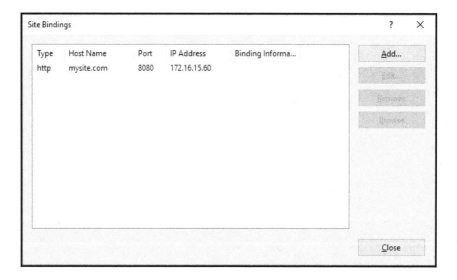

9. Click on the **Close** button, go to IIS Server, select **mysite.com**, and you can see the URL of **mysite.com**, showing `172.16.15.60:8080`:

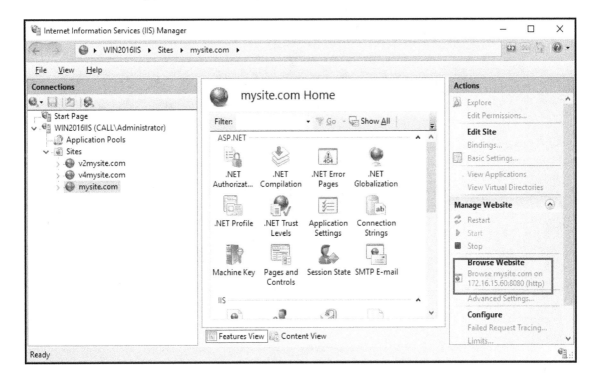

10. Click on **Browse mysite.com on 172.16.15.60:8080**. You will get your website, as shown in this figure:

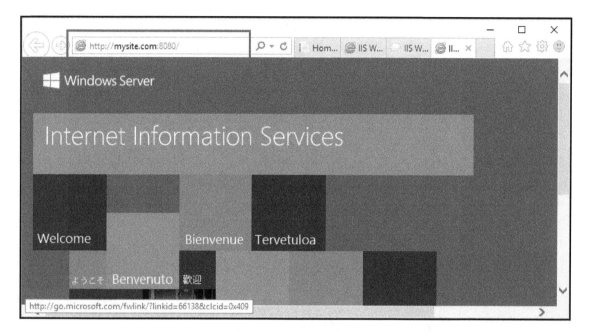

11. You can see the address bar with the URL of `mysite.com: 8080`. It means this website is being accessed through the 8080 port.

How it works..

Throughout this recipe, we configured the port of the website mysite.com, which had the default port of `80`. We had an overview of the default port of mysite.com and added the new port `8080`, after which we accessed the website from the URL mysite.com through the newly added port 8080.

You can also configure a different port as per the availability of servers.

Configuring the website IP

In this recipe, we are going to configure the website IP 172.16.15.61. The default website IP was 172.16.15.60; we will configure a different IP to access the website over this newly configured IP.

Getting ready

To step through this recipe, you will need a running IIS 10 instance, one static IP address, and an administrator user account for editing properties and files.

How to do it...

1. Open Server Manager on Windows Server 2016. Click on the **Tools** menu and open IIS Manager.
2. Expand the IIS server (**WIN2016IIS**). We get the listed application pools and sites.
3. Select the website **v4mysite.com**, click on the **Binding** option, and you will see the **Site Bindings** details of **Host Name**, **Port**, and **IP Address**, as shown in this figure:

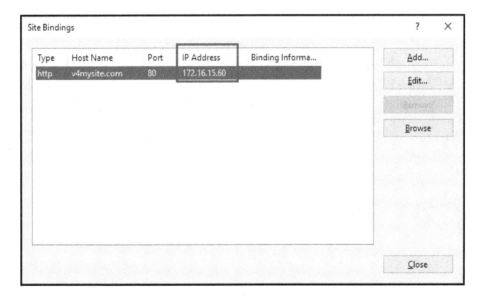

4. **v4mysite.com** has the existing IP 172.16.15.60; it might even be *.

5. Click on the **Edit** button, and you will get the **Edit Site Binding** property window:

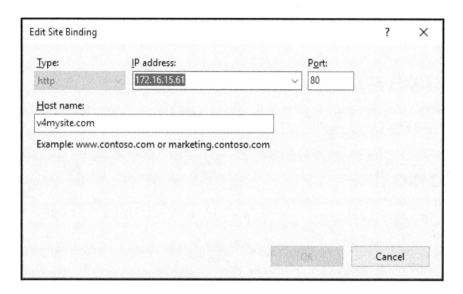

6. You have to add the new IP 172.16.15.61, leave the port as 80, and Host name as it is.

7. Click on the **OK** Button. Now we set the IP for the website bind property. Let's make the required changes in the configuration for the IP 172.16.15.61 so that it will work for the website **v2mysite.com**.

8. Click on Start, go to **Settings**, and click on **Network and Sharing center.**

9. Now, you have to click on **Change adapter settings**:

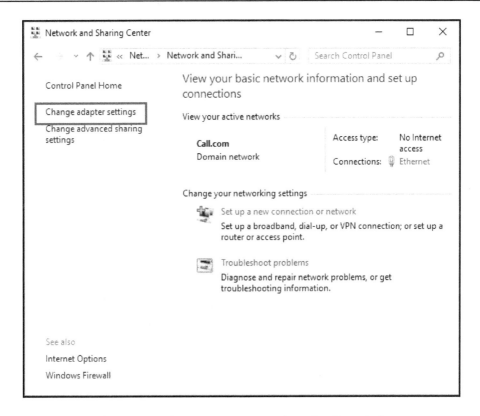

10. You will get the network connections window; In this window, we get the **Ethernet** (server network port) property:

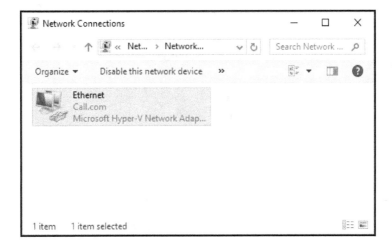

11. Right click on **Ethernet**, and you will get the property context menu of
    Ethernet (Ethernet is the default name; you can rename it), as shown in this
    screenshot:

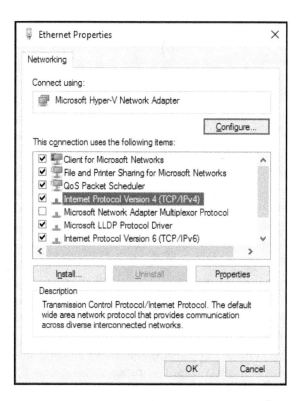

12. In the Ethernet properties, you will get IP version 4 (TCP/IPv4). We are using IP
    version 4, so we will configure only TCP/IP v4. If you have a TCP/IP v6 IP
    address, you can use the TCP/IP v6 protocol.

13. Click on the **Properties** button:

14. You have to add the new IP here.
15. Click on the **Add** button, and enter `172.16.15.61`. It will also ask you to define your **Subnet**. We will add the subnet mask `255.255.255.0` (the given **Subnet mask** is **Default**). Click on the **OK** button. Click on **OK** a few more times till you close the Ethernet properties.
16. Now you've configured the new IP for your website and IIS Server that will recognize additional IP address for IIS server, you have to configure IP address which option is available under Advance TCP/IP Settings property of IP Settings tab, IP settings tab we can add multiple IP on same IIS Server which we can use dedicate to each website.

How it works...

Once we configure the dedicated IP for our website, we have to perform the configuration of TCP/IP protocol settings. We have to add the new IP. The IIS 10 server will check whether the IP is active and configured. Now you can access the website v4mysite.com on IP `172.16.15.61`.

Deploying websites

In this recipe, we will deploy three websites, namely, mysite.com, v2mysite.com, and v4mysite.com. In our case, we already have these sites ready for deployment, but in your case, you have to create your own, or you can use any available older version to upload under the appropriate site folder, which we've learned in our previous examples.

Getting ready

To step through this recipe, you will need a running IIS 10 instance, and websites mysite.com, v2mysite.com, and v4mysite.com configured. You need three sets of website application files as per our demonstration or HTML pages with an administrator user account.

How to do it...

1. Open Server Manager on Windows Server 2016. Click on the **Tools** menu and open IIS Manager.
2. Expand the IIS server (**WIN2016IIS**). We get the listed **Application pools** and **Sites**; inside the **Sites** folder, we have three websites created, namely, `mysite.com`, `v2mysite.com` and `v4mysite.com`.
3. Select **mysite.com**, go to the **Actions** panel, click on **Basic Settings**, and check the physical path of `mysite.com`. You will get the physical path of `mysite.com`.
4. The **mysite.com** physical path is `C:\inetpub\mysite`:

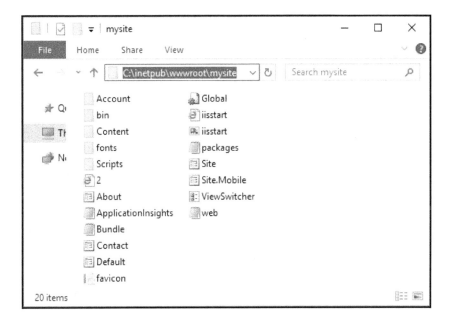

5. Follow the previous steps to copy v2mysite.com to the appropriate folder.

6. Open the IIS Manager, go to the **Connections** panel, right-click on **v2mysite.com** under the **Sites** menu in the left-hand panel, and click on **Explore**. It will open the physical path of v2mysite.com:

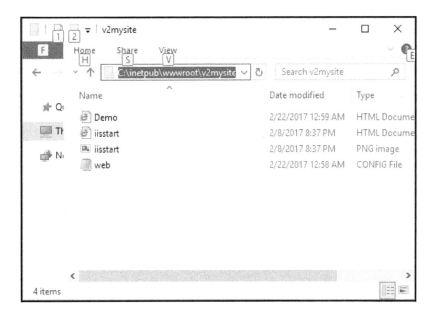

7. We have already created an HTML file called `Demo.html` under the `v2mysite` subfolder of the `wwwroot` directory. Now we have to deploy `v4mysite.com`.

8. Open IIS Manager, select **v4mysite.com**, go to the **Actions** pane, click on **Explore**, and you will get the physical path of `v4mysite.com`:

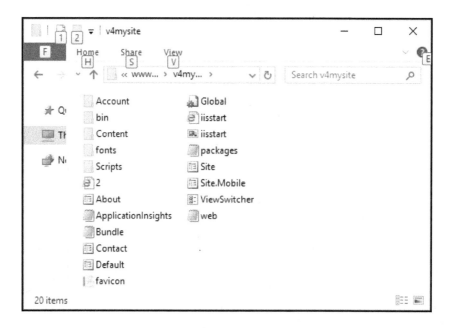

9. We have the uploaded ASP.Net website under the `v4mysite` folder, which is under the `wwwroot` directory, but in your case, you can upload either ASP.Net or HTML files. Its up to your convenience.

10. Now we have to check each website's **Default Documents**, where you can verify the listed Default Home or Index page name, for example, which page comes up first as the home page for someone accessing your website URL. A custom filename can also be used as the default home page through **Default Documents**:

How it works...

In steps 1 to 9, we opened the three different types of physical paths of each website, and we uploaded the website files. In step 10, we know from where to make settings for your home page or default page.

Testing websites

In this recipe, we will test three websites inside IIS 10.0: mysite.com, v2mysite.com, and v4mysite.com. We already created some web files, which we uploaded to the website folders.

Getting ready

You already have a well-configured IIS 10.0 server instance and websites (mysite.com, v2mysite.com, and v4mysite.com). We've also configured and pre-uploaded website application files or HTML pages. You may need an administrator user account, depending on the changes to be made.

How to do it...

1. Open a browser and type in `mysite.com`:

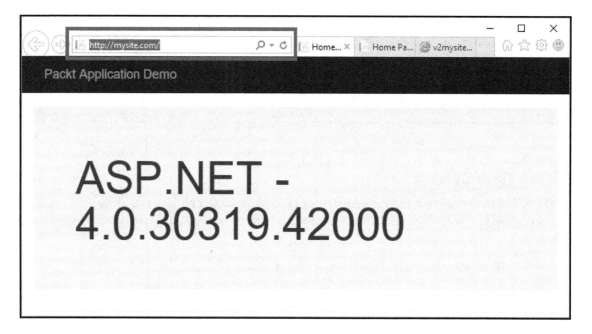

2. Look at the address bar; it by default displays `http://mysite.com`. Let's test `v2mysite.com` in the next step.
3. Type the URL `v2mysite.com` in the address bar:

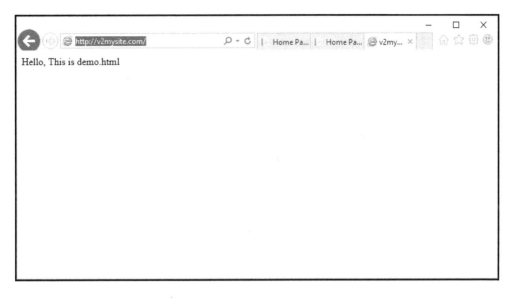

4. Here you can see the `Demo.html` page, which is the default page we configured in the **Default Document** settings.

5. Type the URL `v4mysite.com` in the address bar:

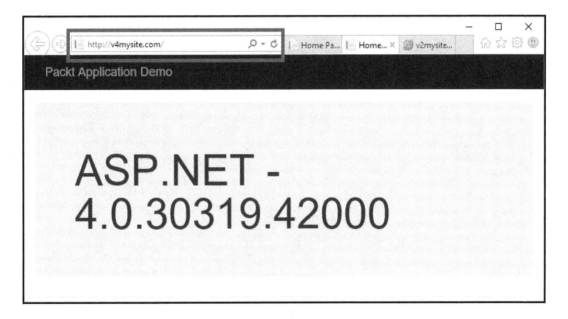

6. We have the IIS 10 server, which has the IP address `172.16.15.60`. We are running two websites, `mysite.com` and `v2mysite.com`, on IP `172.16.15.60`. We added a dedicated IP `172.16.15.61` for the website `v4mysite.com`, and in the same IIS server, you can configure multiple IP address to use specific IPs for individual sites.

How it works...

In this recipe, we tested the website mysite.com with **DefaultAppPool** in steps 1 and 2. In step 3 and 4, we tested website v2mysite.com with the default landing page `Demo.html`, which was configured under the Default Document through IIS Server Manger. In steps 5 and 6, we tested the website v4mysite.com with dedicated IP `172.16.15.61`.

4
Constructing Virtual Directories in IIS 10.0

In this chapter, we will cover the following recipes:

- Constructing a virtual directory in IIS 10.0
- Understanding IIS 10.0 virtual directories
- Configuring virtual directories in IIS 10.0
- Configuring virtual directories with different application pools
- Uploading a .NET web page
- Testing the uploaded web page

Introduction

A **virtual directory** is a friendly name, or alias, for a physical directory on your IIS Server hard drive that does not reside in the home directory. Because an alias is usually shorter than the path of the physical directory, it is more convenient for users to type. A virtual directory appears to client browsers as if it is in the web server's root directory, even though it can physically reside somewhere else.

A virtual directory can be used for different websites' physical folders or different folders of the same website. A virtual directory's physical location can be on the same IIS server or a different server, and we can mount it on an existing website.

For example, you have website pages at different locations in IIS server, such as d:VD. You can create a virtual directory and use it in an existing website. If you have a different web application that needs an application pool in the website, you can create a virtual directory and add the required application pool.

Constructing a virtual directory in IIS 10.0

In this recipe, we are going to create a virtual directory step by step. We will add the alias of the virtual directory (alias is the virtual name of a physical directory). We will also apply the settings of the physical path of virtual directory.

Getting ready

To step through this recipe, you will need a running IIS 10.0 instance. You should also have administrative privileges.

How to do it...

1. Go to the C: drive. We have already created a folder named Websites; under the Websites folder, you have to create a folder called VirtualDirectory, as shown here:

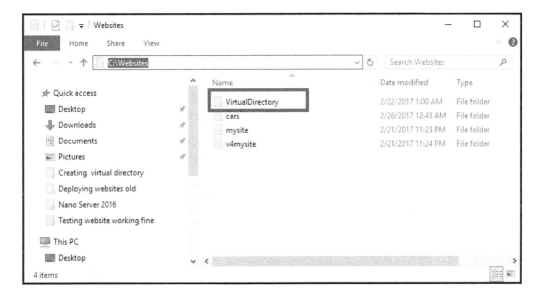

2. Open the `VirtualDirectory` folder, and paste in it some of the HTML files we'd hosted in the previous chapter. We are only using `Demo.html`. You can create your own HTML files:

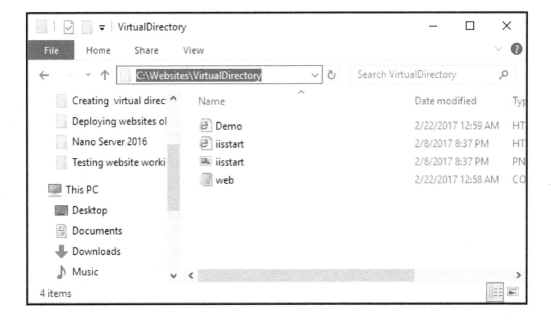

3. Next, you have to open Server Manager on Windows Server 2016. Click on the **Tools** menu and open IIS Manager.

4. Expand the IIS server (**WIN2016IIS**). We get the listed **Application Pools** and **Sites** folders.

5. Expand the **Sites** folder inside the **Connections** pane, right-click on **mysite.com**, and a context window will pop up. You have to select **Add Virtual Directory**, as shown here:

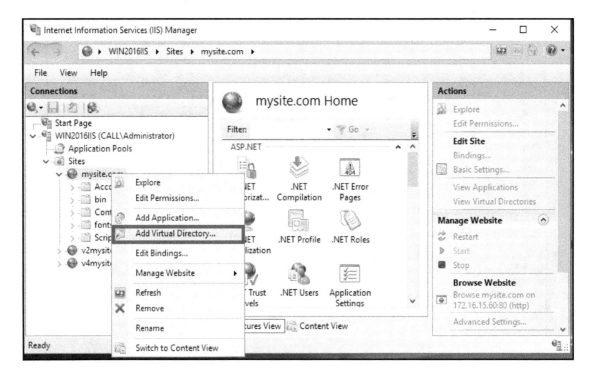

6. In the **Add Virtual Directory** dialog box, type a name in the **Alias** text box. This alias is used to access the content from a URL. You have to provide the physical path of the `Virtual Directory` folder where it is located. In the **Physical path** text box, type the physical path of the content folder, or click on **Browse** to navigate through the filesystem to find the folder. In the `C:\` drive, a `Websites` folder is created to map the physical path of the virtual directory. We added this path:

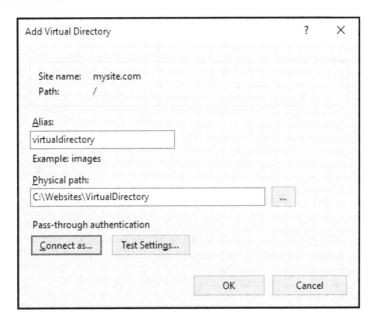

7. Click on on **OK** button. Go to the **Connections** pane, and expand **Sites**.

8. Expand **mysite.com** under the **Sites** folder, and you will see a folder added, called `VirtualDirectory`.

9. Now you have created a virtual directory, and in the next recipe, we will configure it.

How it works...

In steps 1 and 2, we created a physical folder for a virtual directory, and we uploaded site files to this directory. In steps 3 to 7, we created a virtual directory and understood its workings. Step 8 confirmed that the virtual directory has been created.

Understanding IIS 10.0 virtual directories

In this recipe, we are going to understand virtual directories. A virtual directory is an alias of a physical directory; we will get an overview of virtual directories in this recipe.

Getting ready

To step through this recipe, you will need a running IIS 10.0 instance. You should also have administrative privileges.

How to do it...

1. Open Server Manager on Windows Server 2016. Click on the **Tools** menu and open IIS Manager.
2. Expand the IIS server (**WIN2016IIS**). We get the listed **Application Pools** and **Sites**. You will get three listed websites--**mysite.com**, **v2mysite.com**, and **v4mysite.com**--which we've already created. Here, we will use only one.
3. Expand **mysite.com** under the left-hand side **Sites** panel:

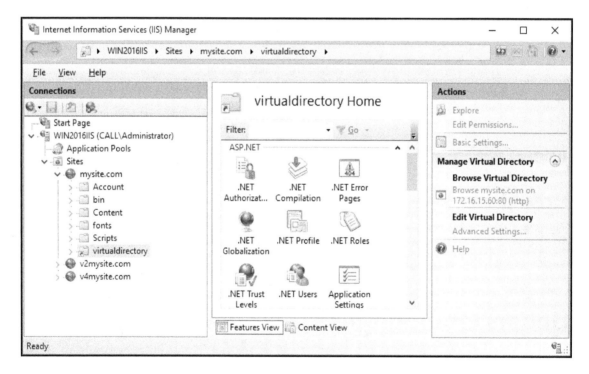

4. We are going to review the virtual directory now. We've already created a virtual directory named `virtualdirectory` inside the website **mysite.com**.

5. Once we select the `virtualdirectory`, we get the properties of `virtualdirectory`--**Edit Permissions...**, **Basic Settings...**, and **Advanced Settings...**--in the right-hand panel under **Actions**. We can also browse the virtual directory.

6. The **virtualdirectory** feature helps us view all the options available in **mysite.com**.

7. In the current example, you can see the sub-website's **virtualdirectory** entry, which is under **mysite.com**.

How it works...

In this recipe, we opened Server Manager and IIS Manager. Inside the **Connections** pane, we selected the **Sites** folder. We expanded **Sites**. We'd already created a virtual directory and named it `virualdirectoy`. Next, we checked the virtual directory and performed a property overview of `virtualdirectory`, where we can managed permissions and basic and advanced settings.

Configuring virtual directories in IIS 10.0

In this recipe, we are going to configure the virtual directory step by step. We will modify the default document settings of the virtual directory and permissions of the physical directory. We'll also set up the basic and advanced settings of the virtual directory.

Getting ready

To step through this recipe, you will need a running IIS 10.0 instance with a virtual directory created. You should also have administrative privilege.

How to do it...

1. Open the Server Manager on Windows Server 2016. Click on the **Tools** menu and open IIS Manager.

2. Expand the IIS server (**WIN2016IIS**). We get the listed **Application pools** and **Sites** folders.

3. Expand the **Sites** folder under the **Connections** panel, click on **mysite.com**, and you will see the **Actions** panel in the top right corner, under which you will see the **Edit Permissions...** option for VirtualDirectory.

4. Click on **Edit Permissions...**, and you will get the properties of **VirtualDirectory**. These are the physical folder properties. Go to the **Security** tab and click on **Edit**.

5. Find the **IUSR** user and **IIS_IUSRS** group and add them to the **Security** tab. Click on the default permission boxes for **Read & execute**, **List folder contents**, and **Read**. These settings are used to access the website through a web user or website application; IIS_IUSRS and IUSR are used for the application pool's internal authentication and communication.

6. IIS_IUSRS is the group for IIS worker process accounts. This means the identity that the application pool itself runs under. IUSR is the anonymous user identity.

7. Click on the **OK** button to finish. Next, you have to click on the **Basic Settings...** of the virtual directory, available in the **Actions** pane:

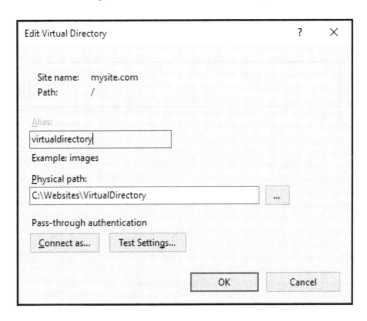

8. In **Basic Settings...**, you have the option to change the physical path of `virtualdiretory`; we can set the **Connect as...** settings as shown in the screenshot, but keep them at the default values.

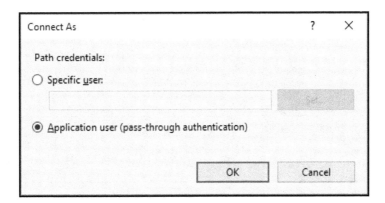

9. We can select a specific user to access this directory or any one of the IIS internal application pool default IUSR users. We have selected the default option, Application user, for the test connection.

10. Click on the **OK** button, go to **Basic Settings...**, and click on the **Test Settings** button, as shown in the screenshot. You will get this option by selecting VirtualDirectory, which was created in the previous recipe. Go to the **Actions** panel on the right-hand side, and click on **Basic Settings...**. A property edit window appears for editing the virtual directory. The last option you will find is Test Setting, which will open the following window. Under **Test Connection**, you will have two Test results, **Authentication** and **Authorization**, which are responsible for validating the application pool and the physical path of the virtual directory.

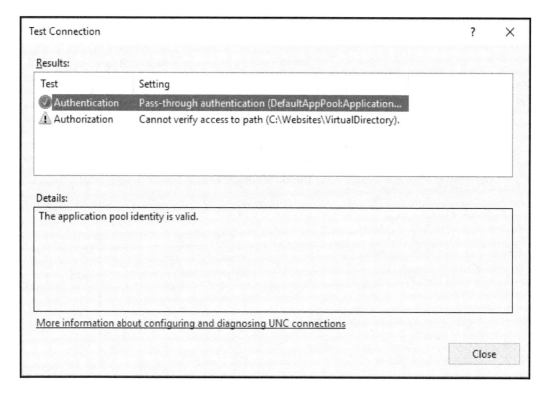

11. The Test Connection window shows that the website's application pool authentication is the pass-through authentication (defaultAppPool) application pool. The application pool authenticates through the default IIS user, IUSR, or the IIS_IUSRS group. We did not set any authorization, so it's showing us **Cannot verify access to path**. Click on the **Close** button, and move to **Advanced Settings....**

12. Click on **Advanced Settings...** in the **Actions** panel, as shown here:

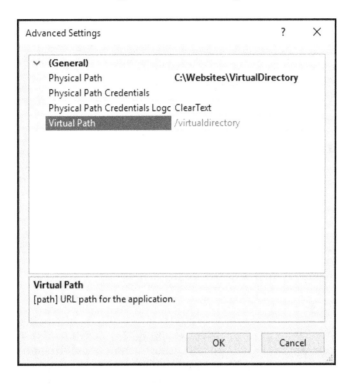

13. Here, **Advanced Settings...** is used to change the **Physical Path, Physical Path Credentials**, and **Physical Path Credentials Logon type** of **virtualdirectory**.

14. Next, we have to apply the settings in **Default Document**, which will help us access the Demo.html page we added in the previous recipe.

15. Expand **mysite.com** from the **Sites** folder and select virtualdirectory. You will see the **Default Document** option in the middle pane.

16. Open the **Default Document** and add the entry `demo.html`; bring this entry to the top of the list:

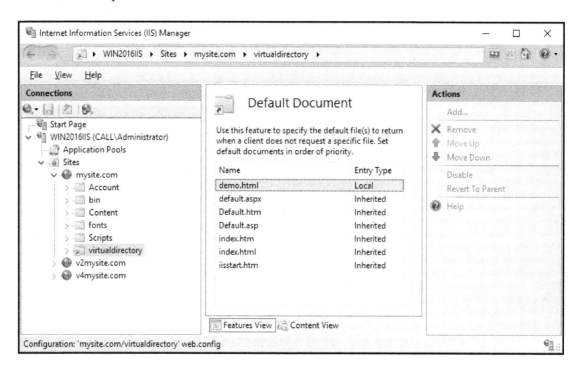

How it works...

In this recipe, we made changes to the physical folder permissions; we searched for the IIS user and IIS user group and assigned permissions to the virtual directory folder in steps 1 to 5. In steps 6 to 10, we reviewed the basic settings of the virtual directory in detail. In steps 11 and 12, we discussed advanced settings, and in steps 13 to 15, we added the default document.

Configuring virtual directories with different application pools

In this recipe, we are going to add a framework version 4 application pool called **DefaultAppPool** and framework version 2.0 application pool called **2and3.5Apppool** to the virtual directory step by step.

Getting ready

To step through this recipe, you will need a running IIS 10.0 instance with a virtual directory created. You should also have administrative privileges.

How to do it...

1. Open Server Manager on Windows Server 2016. Click on the **Tools** menu and open IIS Manager.
2. Expand the IIS server (**WIN2016IIS**). You will get a list of **Application Pools** and **Sites.**
3. Expand **Sites** and select **mysite.com**, and right-click on **mysite.com**. You will see **Add Application**:

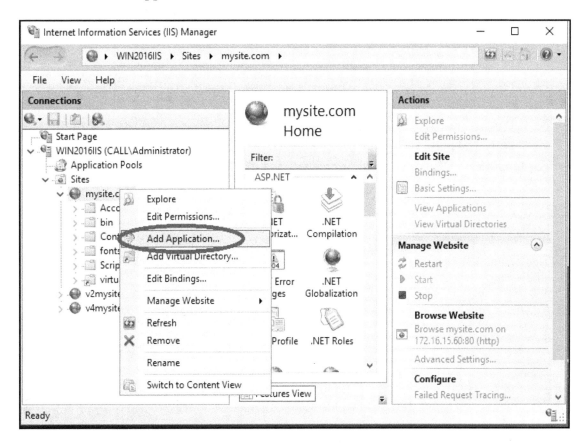

4. Click on **Add Application...**, and you will get the **Add virtual directory with Application Pool** option. Enter the alias name VDApplication; we selected **DefaultAppPool**, which has framework version 4.0.

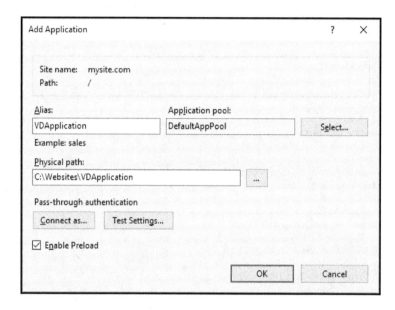

5. We've already created a folder in C:\Websites\VDApplication\. Add the physical path. We've added C:\WebSites\VDApplication\.

6. Click on **OK**. You have now created the virtual directory with an application pool:

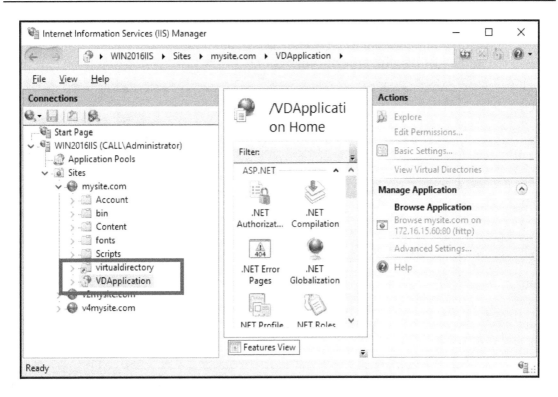

7. In the **Connections** panel, you can see under **mysite.com** that there are two virtual directories: **virtualdirectory**, which does not include the application pool (you can run only normal files such as HTML), and **VDApplication**, which includes the **DefaultAppPool** application pool (you can run your web application here).

8. Let's configure the **virtualdirectory** with framework version 2.0, which has already been created as **2and3.5AppPool.**

9. Right-click on **virtualdirectory** and click on **Convert Application**. Once you have converted it, the virtual directory icon will be changed, and you can see highlighted it in the previous figure:

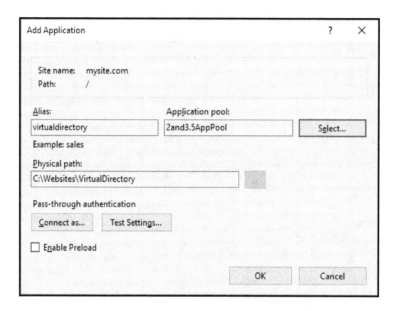

10. Next, you will get an **Add Application** window, as shown in the previous figure. Only the Change Application Pool option is available; you can select the **2and3.5AppPool** application pool. Click on the **OK** button.

11. Now you have two virtual directories created with different application pools: **VDApplication** with **DefaultAppPool** and **Virtual Directory** with **2and3.5AppPool**.

How it works...

In this recipe, we created an application directory and virtual application directory and added an application pool to the virtual directory in steps 1 to 6. In steps 7 to 11, we added custom application pools from an existing virtual directory.

Uploading a .NET web page

In this recipe, we are going to upload website application pages. Website application pages are developed in .NET framework version 4. These website application pages will run from the VDapplicationpool virtual directory.

The website application pages have been developed in .NET framework version 2.0 for the virtualdirectory virtual directory.

Getting ready

To step through this recipe, you will need a running IIS 10.0 instance with a virtual directory created. You should also have administrative privileges.

How to do it...

1. Open Server Manager on Windows Server 2016. Click on the **Tools** menu and open IIS Manager.
2. Expand the IIS server (**WIN2016IIS**). You will get all listed **Application Pools** and **Sites**. You will get three websites listed: **mysite.com**, **v2mysite.com**, and **v4mysite.com**. We have already created them.

3. Expand **mysite.com** under the sites, and you will see there are two virtual directories listed, **VDApplication** and **virtualdirectory**:

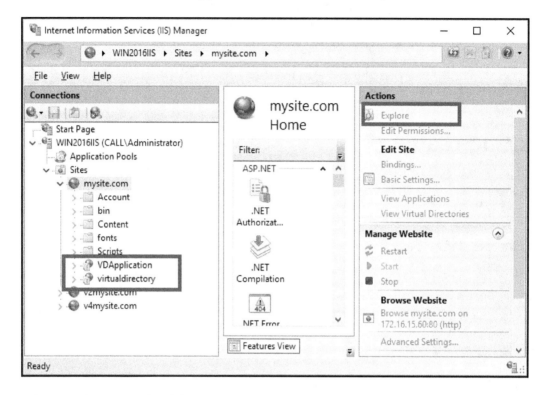

4. We have to upload the version 4.0 website application to the **VDApplication** virtual directory and version 2.0 website application to **virtualdirectory**.
5. We already have the website application pages we created before, but you may create your own to upload.
6. Let's move to uploading the website application pages. Click on the **VDApplication** virtual directory, go to the **Actions** panel, click on **Explore**, and you will get the virtual directory's physical folder, as shown here:

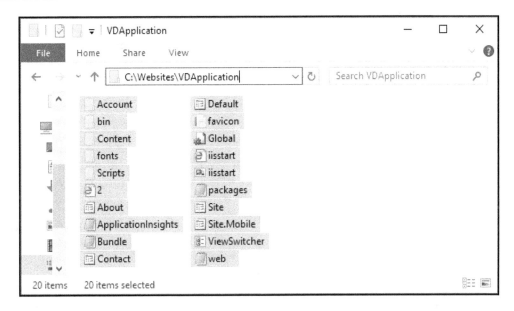

7. Copy your version 4.0 website application pages and paste them in the C:\WebSites\VDApplication\ folder.

8. Now we have to click on **virtualdirectoy** and go to the **Actions** panel. Click on **Explore**, and paste them in the version 2.0 website application pages folder:

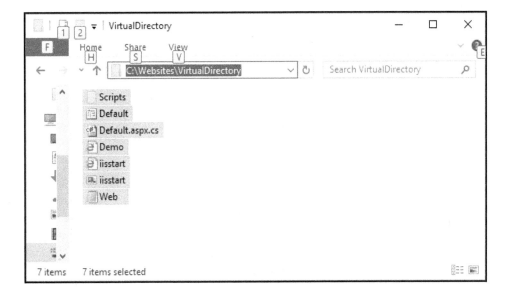

9. Close both the virtual directory and the physical folder.

10. Open IIS Manager, expand **mysite.com**, and click on the **VDapplication** virtual directory. Go to the feature view, open the **Default Document**, and add `default.aspx` to the top. Repeat the same steps for **virtualdirectory.**

How it works...

We have two virtual directories, **VDapplication** and **virtualdirectoy**, already created. We uploaded the version 4.0 website application files to the **VDapplication** virtual directory and the version 2.0 website application files to **virtualdirectory**. We also made the **Default Document** entry for our default landing page.

Testing the uploaded web page

In this recipe, we are going to test web application pages developed in framework version 4 and uploaded into our custom virtual directory VDapplication pool. Web application pages for the lower version, framework 2.0, have been uploaded to the **virtualdirectory** virtual directory.

We will also test a normal HTML page using a custom virtual directory.

Getting ready

To step through this recipe, you will need a running IIS 10.0 instance with a virtual directory created as well as a website application.

How to do it...

1. Open Server Manager on Windows Server 2016. Click on the Tools menu and open IIS Manager.

2. Expand the IIS server (**WIN2016IIS**). You will get a list of **Application Pools** and **Sites** under the **Connections** pane. You will get three websites listed, which we uploaded in previous recipe: **mysite.com**, **v2mysite.com**, and **v4mysite.com**.

3. Go to the **Sites** folder, expand **mysite.com**, and click on **virtualdirectory**. This is a simple virtual directory with the default application pool.

4. Go to the **Actions** panel and click on **Browse**. You will get the `http://mysite.co m/virtualdirectory` URL:

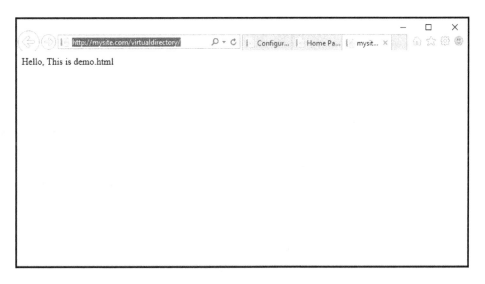

5. Now let's test both custom virtual directory sites we had created in previous steps for **VDapplication** and **virtualdirectory**. You can access both site URLs through any browser, but in my case I used Internet Explorer.

6. Open Internet Explorer and type the URL `http://mysite.com/vdapplication` in the address bar. You will get the website application:

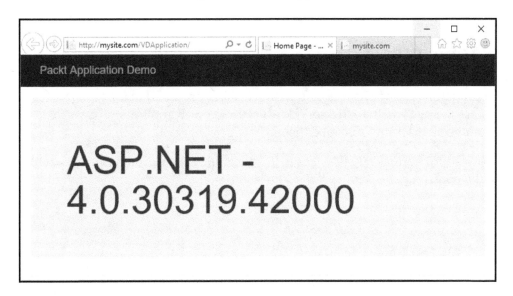

7. In the same way, you can test **mysite.com**, which has a different version of the application pool, **2and3.5AppPool**, which we have already configured in the application pool configuration section.

8. Open Internet Explorer, and type the URL `http://mysite.com/virtualdirecto ry` in the address bar. You will get the website application:

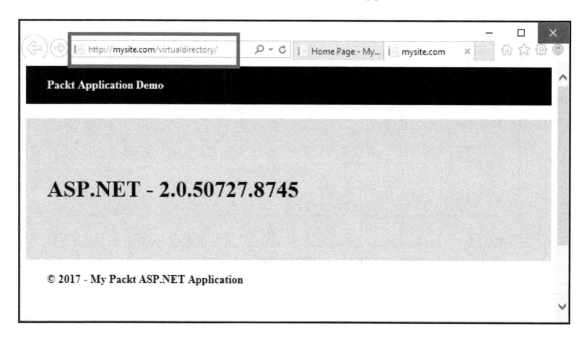

How it works...

We have tested a different .NET CLR version with the appropriate framework version of web application pages, developed in framework 4 and uploaded to the `VDapplicationpool` virtual directory. We also tested web application pages for framework version 2.0 and uploaded them to `virtualdirectory`.

We also tested for normal HTML pages in the **virtualdirectory** virtual directory without an application pool.

5
Installing HTTP/2 on IIS 10.0

In this chapter, we will cover the following recipes:

- Understanding HTTP/2
- Installing HTTP/2 on IIS 10.0
- Configuring HTTP/2 on IIS 10.0
- Uploading .NET web pages
- Testing uploaded web pages

Introduction

HTTP/2 is the newer version of HTTP/1.1, used to reduce the impact of latency and connection load on web servers by semantic flow over TCP connections. The HTTP/2 protocol can work on Windows 10 and Windows Server 2016. Windows 10 and Server 2016 both have the latest version of IIS Server, IIS 10.0. Currently, only IIS 10.0 supports HTTP/2. In HTTP/2, a persistent connection can be used to provide services to multiple simultaneous requests.

We know that every TCP connection requires a round trip to set up a connection between server and client. HTTP/2 sharply reduces the need for a request to wait while a new connection is established or wait for an existing connection to become idle.

HTTP/2 introduces HPACK, a compression scheme for HTTP headers that reduces the redundancy between requests. Compression helps multiplexing, because requests are smaller. This enables clients to make many requests in their first packets on a connection, while TCP flow control windows are still small.

HTTP/2 also introduces the concept of **push**: the server responds to requests the client hasn't made yet, but in a form that the client can cache and reuse on other pages. If **push** is supported by the underlying connection, two things happen:

1. A `PUSH_PROMISE` is sent to the client so that the client can check whether the resource already exists in the cache.
2. A new request is added to the request queue for the pushed resource.

Understanding HTTP/2

In this recipe, we are going to understand HTTP/2. We will visit a few websites and check whether HTTP/2 is supported or not later in this chapter. We are going to see how we can check whether the website is running on HTTP/2 or HTTP/1.1.

Let's cover this in detail.

Getting ready

To step through this recipe, you will need a running HTTP/2 website and internet connection.

How to do it...

1. Open Internet Explorer on your Windows 10 PC or Server 2016; here, we are using a Windows 10 PC.
2. Go to the address bar and type `www.google.ae`:

3. Once you open `www.google.ae`, it will redirect to `https://www.google.ae/`. Now we have to check whether `www.google.com` uses HTTP/2 or HTTP/1.1.

4. Hit *F12*. You can also do the same as the following step:

5. Go to **Settings** and enable F12 Developer Tools; you will get DOM Explorer, Console, Debugger, Network, Performance, and Memory. Now you have to switch to the **Network** tab:

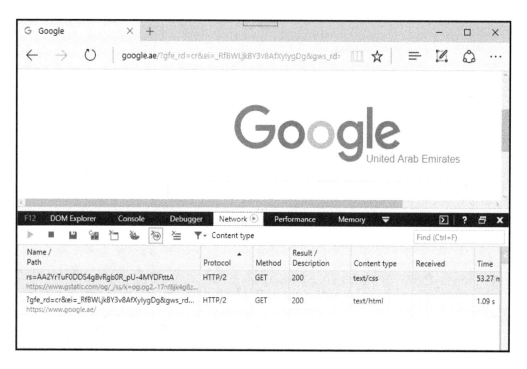

6. Here, you will see that `https://www.google.ae` is using HTTP/2. Next, we will apply HTTP/2 settings on our IIS 10.0 server in order to use the HTTP/2 protocol.

How it works...

In this recipe, we launched the URL `www.google.ae`. The browser was automatically redirected to `https://www.google.ae`. Next, we tested for HTTP/2 through developer tools, which can be run through the *F12* key, or can be enabled from the **Settings** menu.

Installing HTTP/2 on IIS 10.0

In this recipe, we are going to set up HTTP/2 and enable the logging option through IIS 10.0. We will also cover how and where we can perform the necessary changes in the registry.

Let's cover the installation and configuration in detail.

Getting ready

To step through this recipe, you will need a running IIS 10.0 server and an administrator account, which will be used to make changes in IIS 10.0 and Windows Registry.

How to do it...

1. Open Server Manager on Windows Server 2016. Click on the **Tools** menu and open IIS Manager.
2. Click on the IIS server (**WIN2016IIS**); you will get the feature view. Find out the **Logging** setting, as shown in the following figure. You can configure it using Logging on your web server or website to record information about HTTP requests and errors. The information in your log can help you troubleshoot or optimize your website.

3. Double-click on **Logging**. You will see in the next figure that **Site** is selected as the default log file type, and the **Log File** format is **W3C**, with a lot of fields as options.

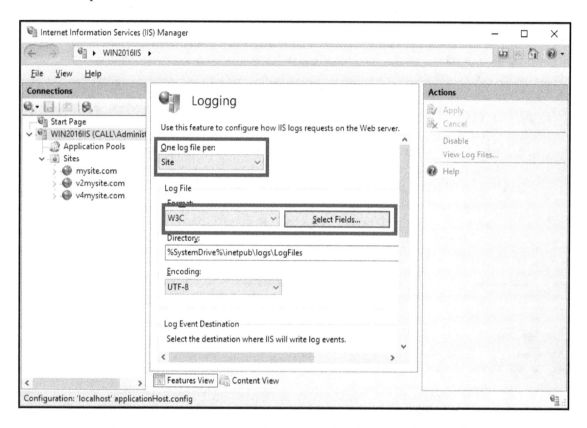

4. Logging configuration steps help us trace log files and check website access through HTTP or HTTP/2.

5. As shown in the figure, **One log file per Site** means each website has its own log file. Hence, it will be easy to use the log file information. We have an option to select the log file for the server, so it will create one log file for your server. This means that if you have hosted many websites per server and you have one log file for that site, it could be very difficult to trace the log information. That's why we have selected site-wise log files--there are a lot of options available in W3C logging fields to identify using Hostname, IP address, and port as well as Client IP address, and so on. We've just verified our recommended selection.

6. Now you have the option to choose a log file Format; the default selected is **W3C**. Now we have to enable one of the protocols.

7. Click on the **Select fields...** option, and you will get the W3C Logging Fields window, as shown here:

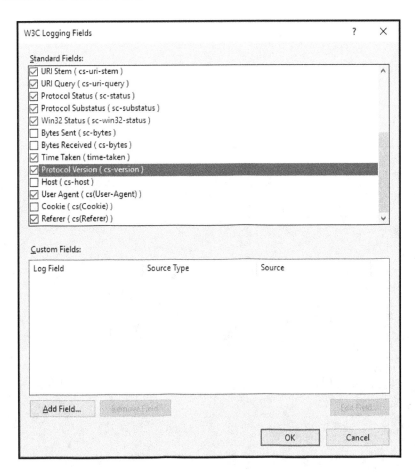

8. You have to mark the checkbox for **Protocol Version**. Protocol Version will generate the log file entry for HTTP/1.1 and HTTP/2. Server Request will generate a site-wise log file for the website and also log the protocol version to the log file as per the client's requested protocol version. You can see the details of this log at `C:\inetpub\logs\LogFiles`.

9. Now we have to make a registry entry for HTTP/2. Internet Explorer is connected to IIS Server over TLS, which negotiates HTTP/2 via TLS extensions, so you do not need to make any changes on the server side. This is because the h2-14 header specifying the use of HTTP/2 Draft 14 is sent by default over TLS .

The protocol version option, which we checked, will generate the log file for website access with either the HTTP or HTTP/2 protocols.

1. Command Prompt, type `regedit` as shown in the screenshot, and press *Enter*. Make sure Command Prompt is running with administrator authentication by right-clicking on its icon and selecting the **Run as Administrator** option.

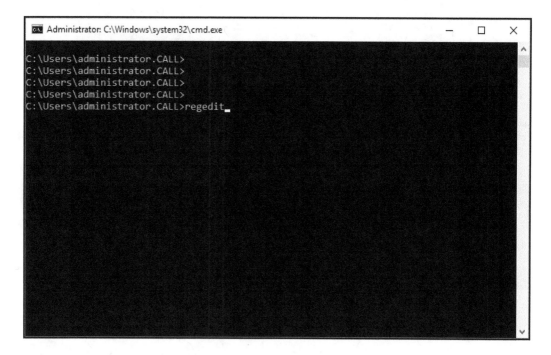

2. It will open the Windows registry editor:

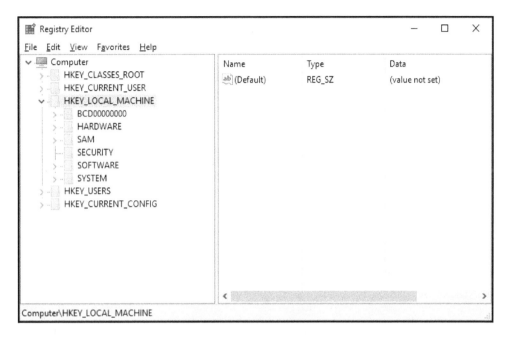

3. Expand the HKEY_LOCAL_MACHINE registry key, the SYSTEM folder, the CurrentControlSet folder, and the Services folder in succession. Expand HTTP and select the Parameters folder.

4. You have to create a new registry entry QWORD value named DuoEnabled inside the Parameters folder. Right-click on the Parameters pane and create a QWORD entry:

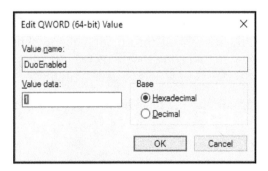

5. You can see a value named `DuoEnabled` with value data 1. Select **Base** as **Hexadecimal**. Click on **OK**.

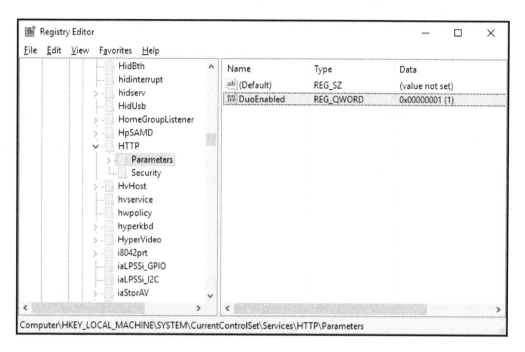

6. Close the **Registry Editor** and reboot.
7. You have successfully completed the setup of HTTP/2.

How it works...

In this recipe, we first opened IIS Manager and set up logging settings to trace the website access log. Logging is nothing but writing information about website activity to a log file. We enabled the protocol version, which will help us get website-access activity information regarding HTTP and HTTP/2.

We then opened Registry Editor and made an entry called **DuoEnabled**, which will work for the HTTP/2 protocol.

Configuring HTTP/2 on IIS 10.0

In this recipe, we are going to configure an HTTP/2 website. The website will get access through the HTTPS port. We will also cover how to add/install a certificate and attach that certificate to a website.

Getting ready

To step through this recipe, you will need a running IIS 10.0 instance. You should also have administrative privileges.

How to do it...

1. Open Server Manager on Windows Server 2016. Click on the **Tools** menu and open IIS Manager.
2. Select the IIS server (**WIN2016IIS**). You will get the **Feature View**, where you will find the `Server Certificates` option:

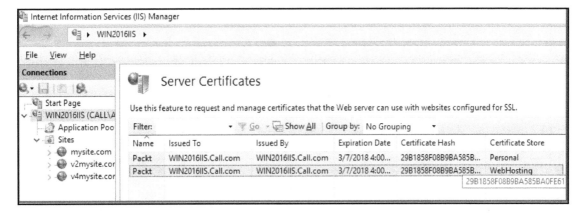

3. We have already created two certificates. These are local certificates for testing. They are not for a live environment. Here, we will use the existing user certificate name, `Packt`; you will see this is issued **Issued To WIN2016IIS.Call.com** and also see its Certificate Hash key. The certificate hash is used for encrypting the website data we access, and it uses a hashing algorithm to encrypt website data and decrypt it. IIS 10.0 uses SHA256 256-bit encryption . Certificate Store has the category of certificate listed; we will use WebHosting.

4. We have had an overview of the Packt certificate and the WebHosting Certificate Store. Let's move on to binding options.

5. Expand the IIS server (**WIN2016IIS**). You will get the listed **Application Pools** and **Sites**. There are three sites listed, which are **mysite.com**, **v2mysite.com**, and **v4mysite.com**.

6. We will use **v4mysite.com**. Click on **v4mysite.com**, go to the **Actions** panel, and click on the **Bindings...** option:

7. Once you click on **Bindings...**, you will get the bind settings property:

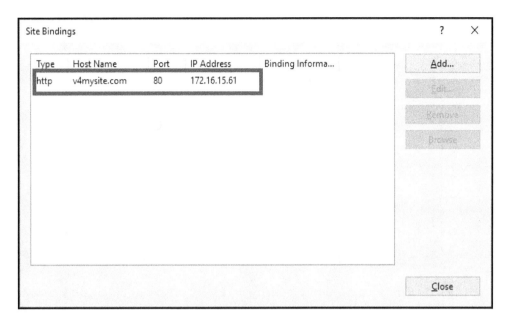

8. In **Site Bindings** we already configured the properties, which are as follows:

Host name: v4mysite.com
Type: http
Port: 80
IP address: 172.16.15.61

Now, we have to add one more site binding for `https`. Click on the **Add** button, and you will get the new window:

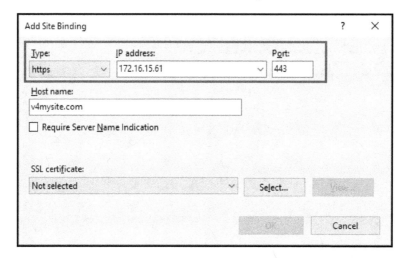

9. Click on the **Type:** drop-down menu and select **https**; it will display the default HTTPS **Port:** 443. You will get the available **IP address:** 172.16.15.61. You also have to add the hostname, which is **v4mysite.com**. Now you have to add the SSL certificate, which has already been installed in the previous recipe. Click on the **SSL certificate:** dropdown and select the certificate you created. Select the **Packt** certificate from the list.

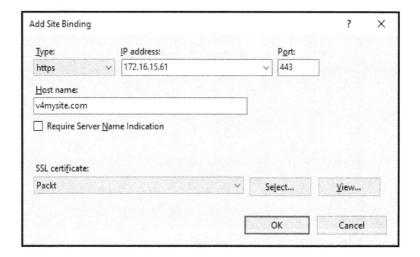

10. You can also check the certificate. Click on the **View** button, and you will get the certificate properties:

11. The certificate properties will show you general information about the certificate, and the `Details` tab will show you full details about the certificate property configuration and type. The certification path has information about whether the certificate is installed on a local or remote server and its status. Now click on **OK**. Click on **OK** again to add the **Site Bindings.** Now you will come to the **Site Bindings** window:

12. In the **Site Bindings** list, both HTTP and HTTPS Binding Type must have the same hostname.

13. Click on **OK** for the **Site Bindings** window. You've now configured the selected website, **v4mysite.com**, to work with HTTP/2.

How it works...

In this recipe, we opened the server certificate settings page and found our created certificate available. A server certificate is used for HTTPS website bindings. We added HTTPS bindings for the website **v4mysite.com**. We also reviewed the certificate properties. Now you have both type bindings, HTTP and HTTPS.

Uploading .NET web pages

In this recipe, we are going to upload website pages made in .NET framework version 4.0 to v4mysite.com. We will have an overview of the associated application pool and also deploy the web pages for the v4mysite.com physical folder path.

Getting ready

We need the version 4.0 application installed on IIS 10.0 Server. You should also have administrative privileges.

How it do it...

1. Open Server Manager on Windows Server 2016. Click on the **Tools** menu and open IIS Manager.
2. Expand the IIS server (**WIN2016IIS**). We get the listed **Application pools** and **Sites**.
3. Expand the **Sites** folder, and you will get three websites: **mysite.com**, **v2mysite.com**, and **v4mysite.com**. Select **v4mysite.com** because we already have the initial settings for HTTP/2 configuration on it. Now you have to upload the .NET framework version 4.0 website pages.

4. Click on **v4mysite.com**. You will see in the **Actions** panel that there are options called **Explore** and **Basic Settings**:

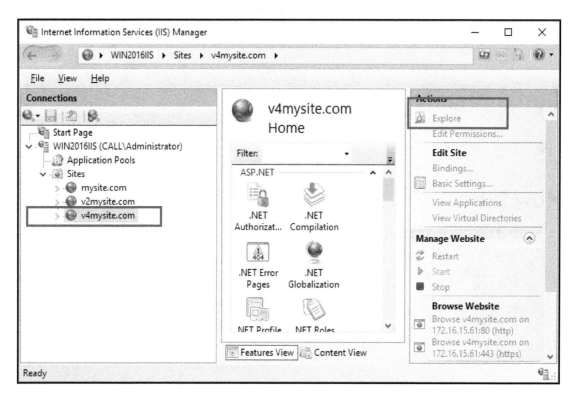

5. You can upload the website **v4mysite.com** in a different way by clicking on **Basic Settings...** and navigating to the physical path of **v4mysite.com**:

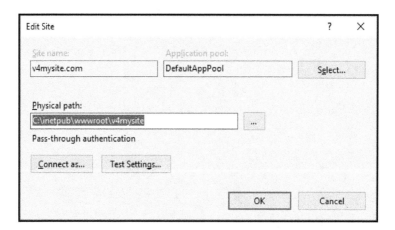

6. The **Edit Site** window gives us details about the physical path
   C:\inetpub\wwwroot\v4mysite of **v4mysite.com**. You can browse the path
   and paste the website pages; also, we can cross-check whether the version 4.0
   application is associated with **v4mysite.com**.

7. Click on the **Select** button in the **Application pool** column. You will get
   the **Application Pool** called **DefaultAppPool**. Once you click on the **Select**
   button, you will get the application pool details window:

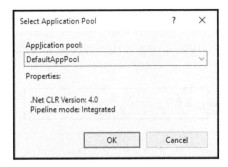

8. You can now see the **DefaultAppPool** property already correctly set up. The
   version of this application pool is 4.0. Close the **Application pool** window and
   Edit site window.

9. Let move to IIS Manager. Expand **Sites** and click on **v4mysite.com**.

10. Go to the **Actions** panel, click on **Explore**, and it will take you to the
    v4mysite.com website's physical path:

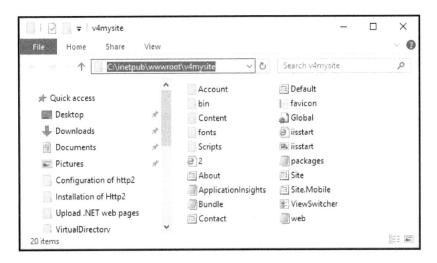

11. Now, you have to paste the .NET web application pages. We have already done this, as you can see in the previous screenshot. We have now uploaded website pages and checked the application pool.

How it works...

In this recipe, we first opened IIS Manager. We then reviewed two different types of websites and learned how to upload website pages. We found out the physical path of **v4mysite.com**. We also checked the Application Pool property and version and uploaded the .NET website pages through the **Explore** option from **Actions**.

Testing uploaded web pages

In this recipe, we are going to test the website v4mysite.com. We have already created and configured HTTP/2 on v4mysite.com and uploaded the .NET web application pages.

Getting ready

To step through this recipe, you will need a running IIS 10.0 instance. You should also have a configured HTTPS website and an administrative account.

How to do it...

1. Open Server Manager on Windows Server 2016. Click on the **Tools** menu and open IIS Manager.
2. Expand the IIS Server (**WIN2016IIS**). We get the listed **Application Pools** and **Sites**.
3. Expand the **Sites** folder; you have three websites listed here: **mysite.com, v2mysite.com**, and **v4mysite.com**. We are going to test **v4mysite.com**.

4. Click on **v4mysite.com** and go to the **Actions** panel. You will see the **Browse v4mysite.com** option, in which there are two URLs available: `http://v4mysite.com:80` and `https://v4mysite.com:443`.

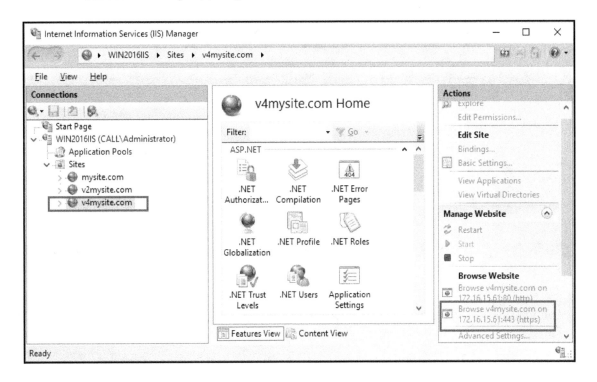

5. Go to the **Actions** panel, click on **Browse v4mysite.com on 172.16.15.61:443**, and you will get a page as shown in this figure:

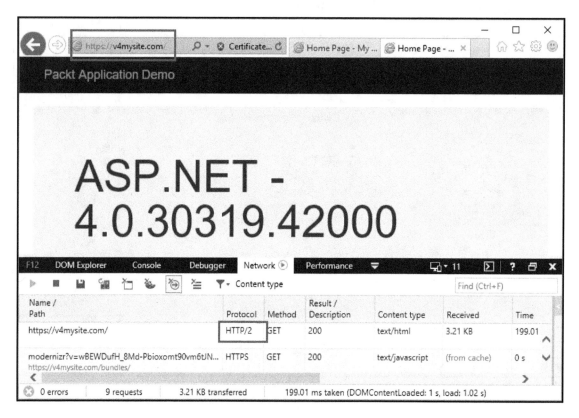

6. In Internet Explorer, you will get the **v4mysite.com** website on HTTPS. Now you have to press the *F12*. You will get the developer window. Refresh the website. Now you should be able to see that under the Network tab, the protocol highlighted is HTTP/2.

7. Let's open the `http://v4mysite.com:80` website from the **Browse website** option:

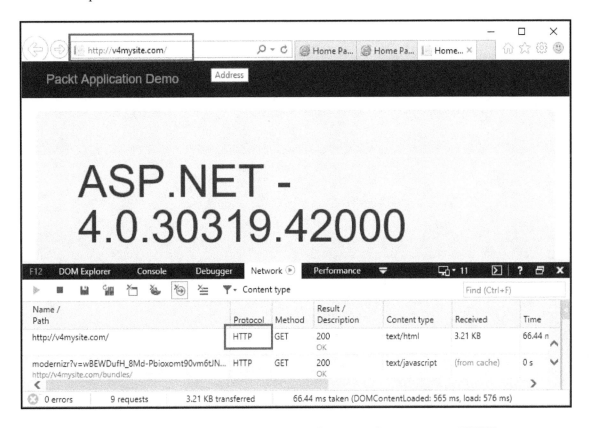

8. Here we can see that we are browsing the **v4mysite.com** using **HTTP**.

How it works...

In this recipe, we first opened IIS Manager and reviewed two different type of website browsing options. We tested the HTTPS version of v4mysite.com and saw that it was functional over HTTP/2.

We also tested it with HTTP and successfully used v4mysite.com using the protocol.

6
Getting Your Wildcard Host Up and Running

In this chapter, we will cover the following recipes:

- Understanding wildcard hosts
- Creating a wildcard host
- Configuring a wildcard host
- Uploading .NET web pages to a wildcard host
- Testing uploaded web pages

Introduction

A wildcard host or subdomain is a domain that is a part of a top-level domain under the DNS hierarchy. It is used as an easy way to create many unique web addresses for specific purposes.

For example, it could make it easier for users to remember and navigate to the demo of a product's site by placing it at the address `demo.v2mysite.com`. In this case, the subdomain is `demo.v2mysite.com`, whereas the main domain is `mysite.com`.

A wildcard host or subdomain is also known as a child domain. We have a parent domain, v2mysite.com, and I'm about to show you how to create a subdomain demo prefixed with the main domain, like `demo.v2mysite.com`. We can have different names and unlimited wildcard hosts for our parent domain. A wildcard host or subdomain website host doesn't require any separate payment or registration. The purpose of a subdomain is to have a separate URL of for products or training either for internal or external use. You can create unlimited wildcard hosts based on the primary domain, which requires registration, and you have to pay for an annual or quarterly subscription.

Here, you can see a few examples of wildcard hosts:

Wildcard	Host name	Primary domain
demo	`v2mysite.com`	`demo.v2mysite.com`
India	`v2mysite.com`	`india.v2mysite.com`
Delhi	`v2mysite.com`	`delhi.v2mysite.com`

Understanding wildcard hosts

In this recipe, we are going to understand wildcard hosts. We will create a few to demonstrate wildcard host websites and get an overview of it.

Let's understand wildcard DNS in detail.

Getting ready

To step through this recipe , you will need a running IIS 10.0 instance.

How to do it...

1. Open Internet Explorer on your Windows 10 PC or Windows Server 2016. I am using a Windows 10 PC.

2. Go to the address bar of any browser and type the URL `http://learningpoint.co.in`. You will be redirected to the default home page of `learningpoint.co.in`:

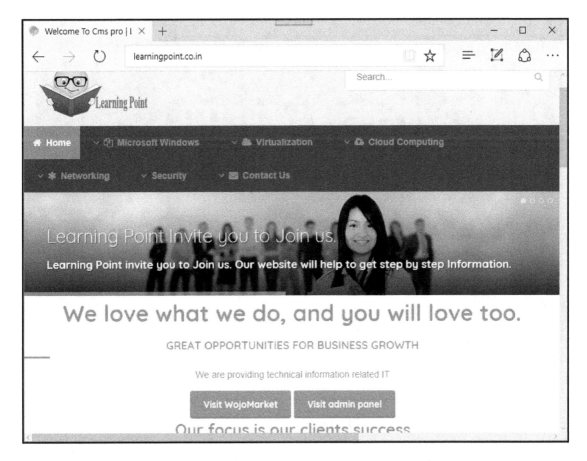

http://learningpoint.co.in/

3. The website's domain name is `learningpoint.co.in`, whose DNS record is present on a DNS registration server and points to a web hosting server such as IIS 10.0. Once you access the website's domain name, the DNS server will translate the name to an IP and forward the request to the web server (IIS 10.0 or similar). Then, you will see the website's home page displayed.

4. Now, open the `http://demo.learningpoint.co.in` website:

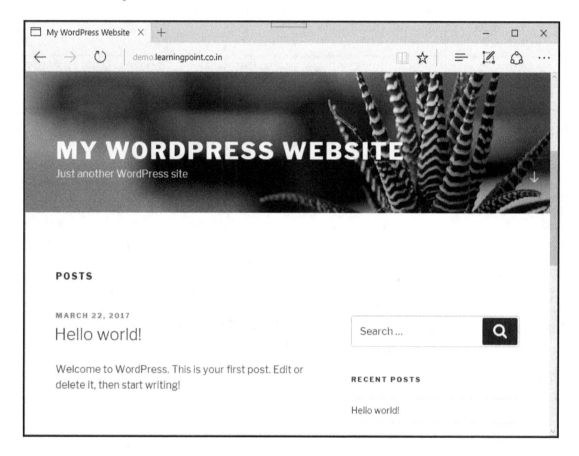

Here, we are accessing the subdomain `demo`, and the main, or parent, domain is `learningpoint.co.in`. It has been created for demonstration purposes; the subdomain site may later be removed by the owner, in general, there is no guarantee that a subdomain will stay forever for reader access.

For example, consider a company that has several branches over the world. The company doesn't want to change the main domain name, so they decide to create a wildcard host or subdomain or child domain of the main domain. Let's see how we can use the main domain and subdomain.

The company name is **Learningpoint.co.in**. The main domain for the demo of the product section we have created is `demo.learningpoint.co.in`. For the UAE office, we can add the subdomain `uae.learningpoint.co.in`.

Wildcard hosts can be used in several ways, as per the company's requirements.

In the next recipe, we will learn how to create a wildcard host on IIS 10.0.

How it works...

In this recipe, we has an overview of wildcard hosts, also called subdomains or child domains. We have a parent domain called `learnignpoint.co.in`, and we created `demo.learningpoint.co.in`. We can use different names and create unlimited wildcard hosts for our parent domain. For a wildcard host, there is no need to pay any extra fees for perform registration. If you have a parent domain, you can create unlimited wildcard hosts.

We launched the URL `http://learningpoint.co.in`. We then got redirected to the home page of `learningpoint.co.in`. Next, we opened the URL `http://demo.learningpoint.co.in`. We were redirected to the home page of `demo.learningpoint.co.in`.

We also discussed the basics of DNS.

Creating a wildcard host

In this recipe, we are going to create a wildcard host step by step on IIS 10.0. We will also create an HTTPS wildcard host and add an SSL certificate on it. We will edit the `hosts` file and make an entry for the created wildcard host.

Let's move to the following sections, where we will be covering this in detail.

Getting ready

To step through this recipe, you will need a running IIS 10.0 instance. You should also have administrative privileges.

How to do it...

1. Open Server Manager on Windows Server 2016. Click on the **Tools** menu and open IIS Manager.
2. Expand the IIS server (**WIN2016IIS**). We then get the **Application Pools** and **Sites** listed.
3. Expand the **Sites** option. You will get the list of existing websites: **mysite.com**, **v2mysite.com**, and **v4mysite.com**.

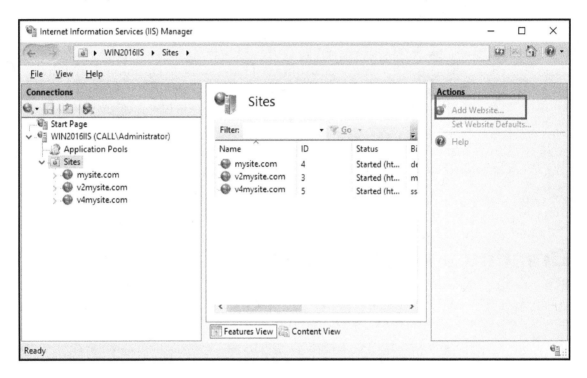

4. Click on the **Sites** folder, go to the **Actions** panel, and you will get the **Add Website...** option. You can see this highlighted in the previous figure.

5. Click on **Add Website**. You will get the **Add website** window:

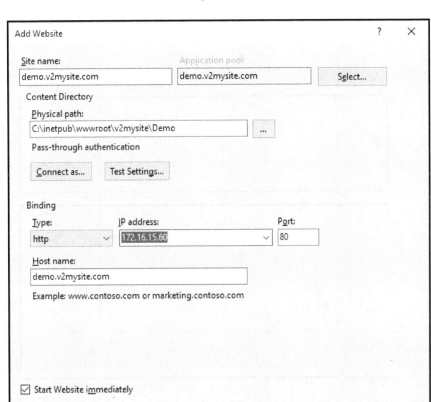

6. We already have a website called v2mysite.com, so let's create a wildcard host for it. In the **Add Website** window, we have already filled the details of the wildcard host and the site name, demo.v2mysite.com. The application pool has also been created by itself and has the same name as the the the site. The site name is just a name you are using to identify it in a list of IIS 10.0 sites.

7. Now move to content directory. You will get the physical path of the wildcard host. I've created a folder called `Demo` in `c:\inetpub\wwwroot\v2mysite\`, as shown here.

8. Set pass-through authentication as the default. In the **Bindings** section, select type **http** and enter IP `172.16.15.60`. This is our server IP associated with `v2mysite.com`. Leave the default port at `80` and move to the host header. The host header is your website's name, also known as domain name or host name. We are adding our wildcard host name, `demo.v2mysite.com`. Click on the **OK** button.

9. Let's add one more wildcard host, `SSL.v2mysite.com`. We will use the HTTPS protocol to access this wildcard host.

10. Go to IIS Manager, click on the **Sites** folder, and go to the **Actions** pane.

11. Click on **Add Website**. You will get the **Add New Website** window. We've added the details of the site name, `SSL.v2mysite.com`. Keep the application pool at the default, `SSL.v2mysite.com`.

12. Set pass-through authentication as the default. In the **Bindings** section, select type **http** and enter IP `172.16.15.60`. This is our server IP associated with `v2mysite.com`, but in your case the IP address should be different. Leave the default port at `443` and come to the host header. The host header is your website's name. We will set it to our wildcard host name, `ssl.v2mysite.com`. We've already created the SSL certificate wildcard.

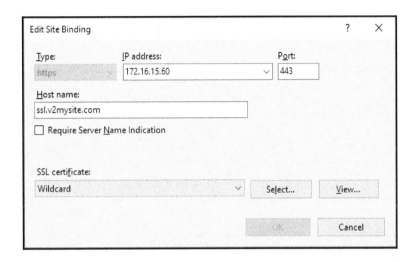

13. Click on the **OK** button. Now come to IIS Manager, and you will see in the **Sites** folder that there are two wildcard hosts created.

14. Now, you have to make one more setting in the `hosts` file. While we are not using the DNS for host names or domain names of websites, we will make the domain name or host name entry in the `hosts` file, which is located in `C:\windows\system32\drivers\etc`. The `hosts` file also converts the domain name to an IP for the local server:

15. Open the `hosts` file in Notepad using administrator rights. Make the entry highlighted in the following screenshot:

```
hosts - Notepad                                                              —   □   ×

File  Edit  Format  View  Help
# Copyright (c) 1993-2009 Microsoft Corp.
#
# This is a sample HOSTS file used by Microsoft TCP/IP for Windows.
#
# This file contains the mappings of IP addresses to host names. Each
# entry should be kept on an individual line. The IP address should
# be placed in the first column followed by the corresponding host name.
# The IP address and the host name should be separated by at least one
# space.
#
# Additionally, comments (such as these) may be inserted on individual
# lines or following the machine name denoted by a '#' symbol.
#
# For example:
#
#      102.54.94.97     rhino.acme.com          # source server
#       38.25.63.10     x.acme.com              # x client host

# localhost name resolution is handled within DNS itself.
#       127.0.0.1       localhost
#        ::1            localhost

172.16.15.60     mysite.com
172.16.15.60     v2mysite.com
172.16.15.61     v4mysite.com
172.16.15.60     Yobooking.com
172.16.15.60     SSL.v2mysite.com
172.16.15.60     demo.v2mysite.com
```

16. Now you are done with all the required entries for the domain `SSL.v2mysite.com` and IP `172.16.15.60`. Press the *Tab* button and type the domain name `SSL.v2mysite.com` and one more entries for domain `demo.v2mysite.com` and IP `172.16.15.60`.

How it works...

In this recipe, we added a wildcard host called `http://demo.v2mysite.com`. Also, we added one more wildcard host with the HTTPS protocol, `https://ssl.v2mysiste.com`. We then assigned it to the `https://ssl.v2mysite.com` wildcard host.

Configuring a wildcard host

In this recipe, we are going to configure the wildcard host `SSL.v2mysite.com` for an application pool. We will implement the **Default Document** settings of the wildcard host, with the permissions of that wildcard host. We will also implement the basic and advanced settings of the wildcard host.

Getting ready

To step through this recipe, you need a running IIS 10.0 instance. You should have already created wildcard hosts. You should also have administrative privileges.

How to do it...

1. Log in to Windows Server 2016 and go to Server Manager.
2. Click on the **Tools** menu and open IIS Manager.
3. Expand the IIS server (**WIN2016IIS**) from the **Connections** panel. We get the listed **Application Pools** and **Sites**.

4. Expand the **Sites** folder, and you will see the listed sites--**mysite.com**, **v2mysite.com**, **v4mysite.com**--and you will get the wildcard hosts, **ssl.v2mysite.com** and **demo.v2mysite.com**:

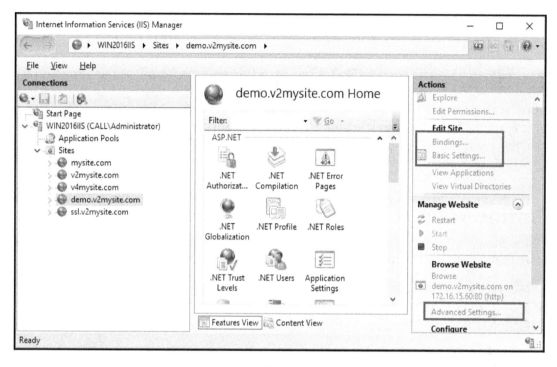

5. Select **demo.v2mysite.com** to get the properties of the **demo.v2mysite.com** wildcard host from the **Actions** panel.

6. Go to the **Actions** panel, and you will see **Edit Permissions**. This is used to provide or deny access to your wildcard host's content directory. You can manage this permission from the **Actions** pane. You can go to the wildcard host's content directory and right-click on the directory to open the property's pop-up window and select the **Security** tab. Here, you can edit the access level and deny permission as well.

7. Now, we have the **Bindings** option; we already know how to change the bindings of any website. The following actions can be performed through the binding option: adding, removing, and editing the IP, port, protocol, host name, and SSL certificate binding for any website or wildcard host.

8. **Basic Settings...** is also the same as a website's basic settings, because a wildcard host is also a child website for the main website. Here, you can find more clear information about basic settings:

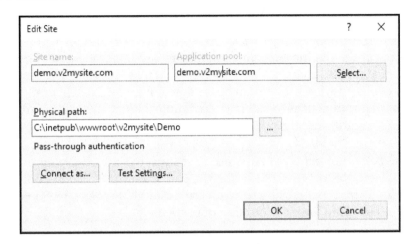

9. As shown in the previous screenshot, we have the **Site name**, **Application pool**, and **Physical path** of the wildcard host **demo.v2mysite.com.** We can set any directory as the physical path.

10. Let's have a look at the **Advanced Settings** now:

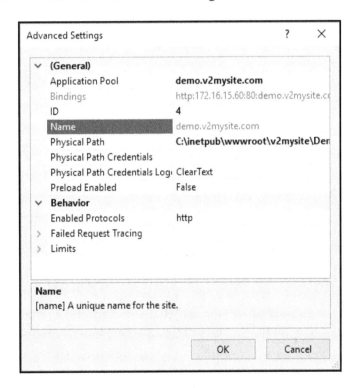

11. In **Advanced Settings**, just like the website settings, we have the application pool, website ID (number of websites you've created, also known as the unique order number of the site index), name of the wildcard host, physical path, and physical path credentials (if you have set them). We'll leave it at the defaults. The physical path credentials logon type can be clear text, network, batch, or interactive as per our configuration of physical path credentials. We are not using any credentials, so we'll use the default settings. **Preload Enabled** is used to keep the application pool always running.

12. In the **Behavior** section of **Advanced settings**, we have **Enabled protocols**, with the default option type **HTTP**, and the **Failed Request Tracing** option, which enables us to trace websites or wildcard host tracking logs. In **Limits**, we can apply settings to limit the number of users that can access a wildcard host at one time.

13. Let's move to the wildcard host, **ssl.v2mysite.com**. We've already configured bindings for it: HTTPS protocol and SSL certificate.

14. Go to IIS Manager and click on **ssl.v2mysite.com**. Go to the **Actions** panel and click on **Basic Settings...** You will get the **Basic Settings** window:

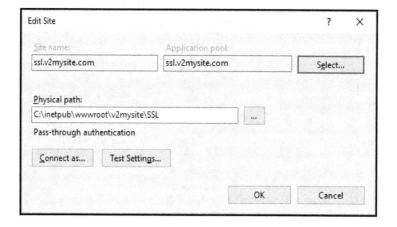

15. Let's verify the site application pool and wildcard host (subdomain) settings of **ssl.v2mysite.com**. The application pool is the same as the site name, as seen in the previous figure.

It's my recommendation to verify the application pool manually for the .NET CLR version according to the hosted website's framework version.

16. Click on the **Select** button. You will get the application pool properties:

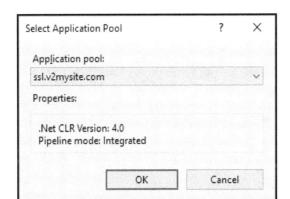

17. You can see that the **ssl.v2mysite.com** application pool version is 4.0. We can also select any other type of application pool available in IIS 10.0 on Windows Server 2016. You can check the list of available application pools by clicking on the **Application pool** dropdown, and you will get the list of application pools created in IIS 10.0.

18. Let's move further to check the **Default Document** settings. Click on any of the wildcard hosts we've created and go to the **Features View**. Find the default document, double-click on it to open it, and check for the filename `default.aspx`, which we are going to access in the wildcard **ssl.v2mysite.com**.

19. Optionally, select a **Default Document** in the list, and in the **Actions** pane, click on **Move Up** or **Move Down** to change the file's precedence.

How it works...

In this recipe, we configured the wildcard host `ssl.v2mysite.com` for application pool version 4.0 and had an overview of the permissions of wildcard hosts and content directory folder. We implemented the basic and advanced settings of wildcard hosts. Finally, we implemented the **Default Document** settings of wildcard hosts.

Uploading .NET web pages to a wildcard host

In this recipe, we are going to upload website application pages for the `ssl.v2mysite.com` wildcard host site. The website application pages have been developed in .NET framework version 4.0.

We are going to upload simple HTML website pages as well to the `demo.v2mysite.com` wildcard host for demonstration.

Getting ready

To step through this recipe, you will need a running IIS 10.0. You should have already created and configured the ssl.v2mysite.com and `demo.v2mysite.com` wildcard hosts. You should also have administrative privileges.

How to do it...

1. Log in to **Windows Server** 2016, and go to **Server Manager**.
2. Open Server Manager on Windows Server 2016. Click on the **Tools** menu and open IIS Manager.
3. Expand the IIS Server (**WIN2016IIS**). We get the listed **Application Pools** and **Sites**. You will get three websites listed in the sites folder--**mysite.com**, **v2mysite.com**, and **v4mysite.com**--and two wildcard hosts, **ssl.v2mysite.com** and **demo.v2mysite.com**. Now, we are going to upload the webpages for the **ssl.v2mysite.com** and **demo.v2mysite.com** wildcard host sites.
4. Click on the wildcard host **ssl.v2mysite.com**, go to the right-hand side of the IIS Manager console, and you will get the **Actions** panel. In the **Actions** panel, there is an option called **Explore**:

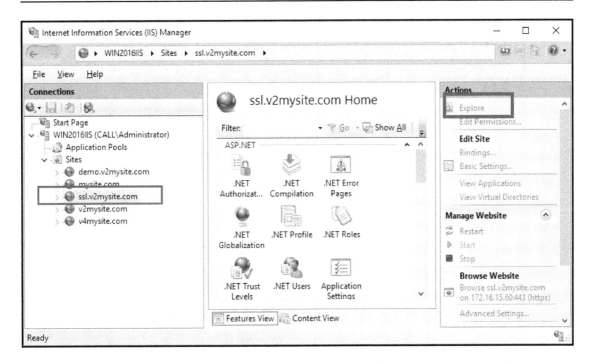

5. Click on the **Explore** option; it will open the content directory of the selected wildcard, **ssl.v2mysitecom**, or you can mention the physical folder path of the wildcard host folder, as shown here:

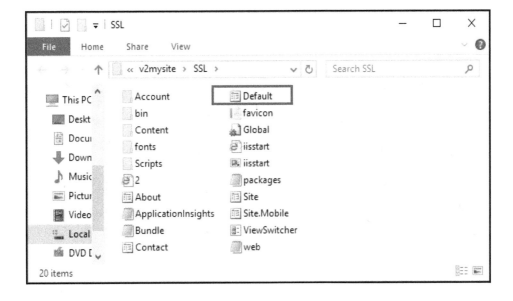

6. We have already created a website application page in ASP.NET version 4.0 and pasted it in the content directory of **ssl.v2mysite.com.**

7. Right-click on the default file, and select open the property sheet of the default page:

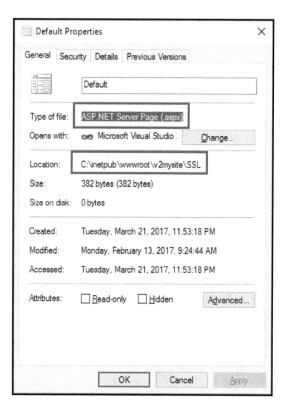

8. Now let's have a look at the extension details of the default application page. As you can see in the previous figure, the **Type of file** is ASP.NET server page (.aspx). Notice that the default file extension is .aspx and file name is default.aspx.

9. Let's upload some of HTML files to **demo.v2mysite.com**. Follow the same steps for **ssl.v2mysite.com** and paste it in an HTML file under the appropriate directory. We'll paste the iisstart.html and iisstart.png files in our case. Both are default files available in the default website, created when you install IIS Server. Let's use the same iisstart.html and iisstart.png files for testing, but you can use any HTML file or a complete website.

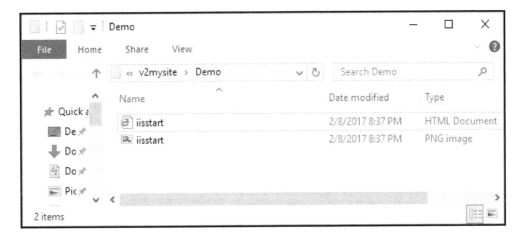

10. Now close the folder. We are using two types of wildcard hosts. The **ssl.v2mysite.com** host is an application wildcard host, and the second is **demo.v2mysite.com**, which is a simple website-type wildcard host.

How it works...

In this recipe, we uploaded website application pages written in ASP.NET to the wildcard host **ssl.v2mysite.com**. We checked the properties of the **default.aspx** application page.

We also uploaded simple HTML website pages to the wildcard host **demo.v2mysite.com**.

Testing uploaded website pages

In this recipe, before starting to test these sites, it's important to verify the Default Document settings of the wildcard hosts **ssl.v2mysite.com** and **demo.v2mysite.com**. We are going to test web application pages developed in framework version 4 and upload them to wildcard host **ssl.v2mysite.com**. We will also test our HTML web page with wildcard host **demo.v2mysite.com**, which has already been uploaded.

Getting ready

To step through this recipe, you will need a running IIS 10.0 instance. You should have already created, configured, and uploaded web pages for wildcard hosts **ssl.v2mysite.com** and **demo.v2mysite.com**. You must have administrative privileges.

How to do it...

1. Log in to Windows Server 2016, and go to **Server Manager**.
2. Click on the **Tools** menu and open IIS Manager.
3. Expand the IIS Server (**WIN2016IIS**). You will get the listed **Application Pools** and **Sites**. You will get three websites listed in the Sites folder--**foldermysite.com**, **v2mysite.com**, and **v4mysite.com**--and two wildcard hosts, **ssl.v2mysite.com** and **demo.v2mysite.com**, which we have already created.
4. Click on the wildcard host **demo.v2mysite.com**, go to the right-hand side of the IIS Manager console. You will see the **Features View.** Inside the **Features View**, we have the **Default Document** settings:

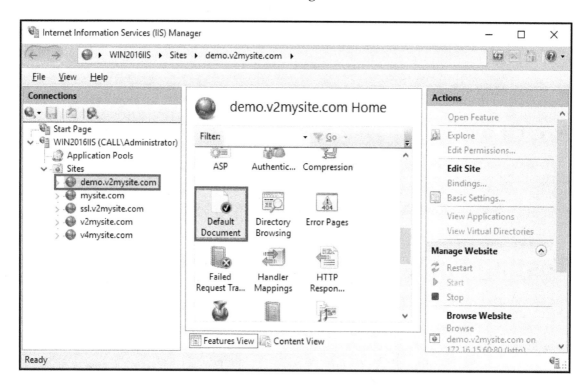

5. Open the **Default Document** settings, and check whether **isstart.hmt** is available:

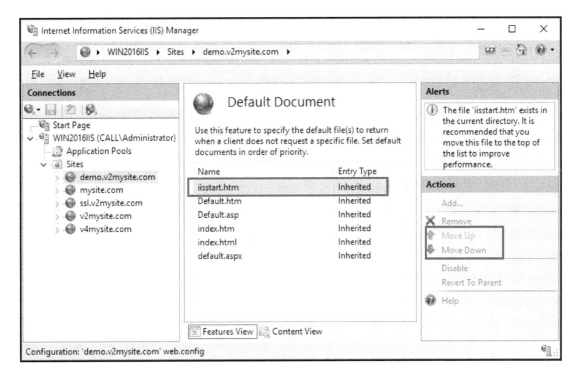

6. We'll next cross-check the **Default Document** settings and verify whether everything is perfect for testing the wildcard host URLs **demo.v2mysite.com** and **ssl.v2mysite.com**. Here, we have the entry for **iisstart.htm** at the top of the list. This is the file name of the **demo.v2mysite.com** wildcard host's web page, **iisstart.htm**. The Default Document has to be defined in the default document settings for our website's default page name, with an extension.

7. Let's move to the **Default Document** settings of wildcard host **ssl.v2mysite.com**. We find that **default.aspx** is already there and at the top of the list:

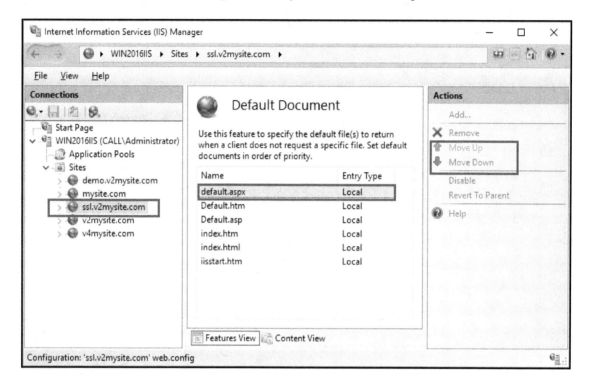

8. Close IIS Manager, open Internet Explorer, and type the wildcard host URL `demo.v2mysite.com`, as shown here:

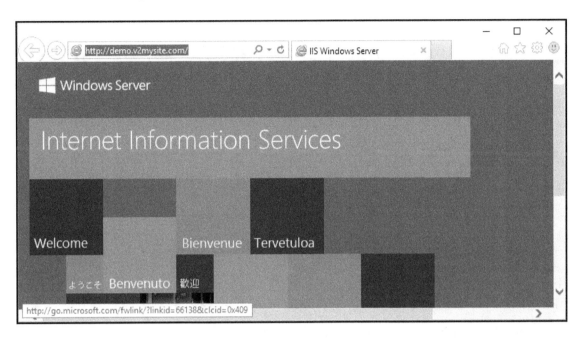

9. You can see that the wildcard host **demo.v2mysite.com** is running perfectly.

10. Now, open the wildcard host URL in Internet Explorer and check the results:

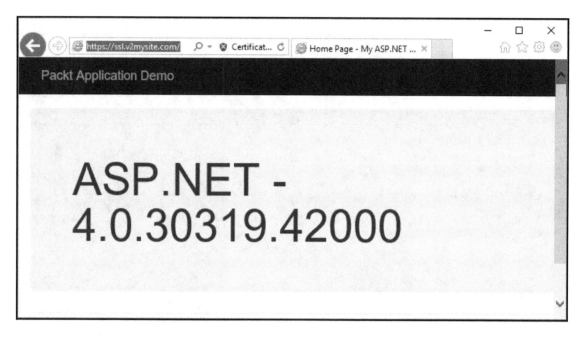

9. The wildcard host ss.v2mysite.com is also running perfectly. You can host multiple wildcard hosts with your own parent domain name with different application pools for different types of websites.

How it works...

First, we checked the Default Document settings of the wildcard hosts `ssl.v2mysite.com` and `demo.v2mysite.com`. We tested web application pages developed in framework version 4 and uploaded to wildcard host `ssl.v2mysite.com`. We also tested with an HTML web page for the wildcard host `demo.v2mysite.com`.

7
Deploying IIS 10.0 on Nano Server

In this chapter, we will cover the following recipes:

- Understanding IIS 10.0 on Nano Server
- Installing IIS 10.0 on Nano Server
- Managing IIS 10.0 on Nano Server
- Creating an IIS 10.0 website on Nano Server
- Configuring an IIS 10.0 website on Nano Server
- Uploading website pages
- Testing uploaded web pages

Introduction

Nano Server is a remotely administrated server operating system, optimized for private clouds and local or remote datacenters. Nano Server is similar to the Windows Server core mode operating system. It doesn't have any GUI interface, and it is smaller than Windows Server's core mode.

Nano Server has no local login capability. It only supports 64-bit applications, tools, and agents.

Nano Server takes up very less disk space, is installed quickly, needs fewer updates and less time to restart than Windows Server.

Nano Server can be used as a:

- Hyper-V virtual machine with or without clusters
- File server
- DNS server
- Internet Information Services (IIS) server

It can also be used to run cloud application patterns or run in a container or as a VM guest operating system.

You can install Nano Server on a physical host (server) or as a virtual server. Nano Server installation can be installed on the Standard and Datacenter editions of Windows Server 2016.

In this chapter, will use IIS 10.0 on Nano Server.

Understanding IIS 10.0 on Nano Server

In this recipe, we will have an overview of Nano Server. We will overview its IP configuration and access it from Nano Server. We'll use Nano Server 2016 on a Microsoft Hyper-V host.

Getting ready

In this recipe, you require an up and running IIS 10.0 on Nano Server and you also require Microsoft Hyper-V host. You must have administrative privileges.

How to do it...

1. Let's get the remote desktop access to the Microsoft Hyper-V host `172.16.15.181`, on which you should have already installed a Nano Server 2016 VM.
2. Log in to the Hyper-V host server with an administrator account. Open **Server Manager**, go to the **Tools** menu, and open the **Hyper-V Manager**, as shown here:

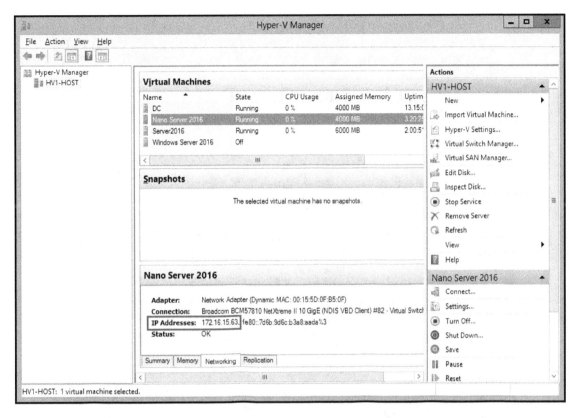

3. Under **Hyper-V manager**, we have four virtual machines: **DC**, which is the domain controller; **Nano Server 2016**; **Server 2016**, which is our IIS Server; and **Windows Server 2016**.

4. We've selected **Nano Server 2016**. You can see that the server has **4000 MB** RAM under the **Assigned Memory** header of the VM machine list, and the VM machine status is **Running**.

5. **Nano Server 2016** is the display name of the Nano Server virtual machine, the server's name is **Nano**, and its IP address is `172.16.15.63`, which is highlighted in the previous figure. This is in my case, but in your case, the IP could be different. This needs to be taken care of.

6. Select the **Nano Server 2016** virtual machine. Go to the **Actions panel** in **Hyper-V Manager**, and you will find two types of property: the **HV1-Host** property, where you can make changes to the Hyper-V host server, and **Nano Server 2016**, where you can make changes to the Nano Server virtual machine's properties. In the Nano Server 2016 **Actions** pane, click on **Connect** under the right-hand side panel just below the selected server name, and you will get **Open the Nano Server 2016** console:

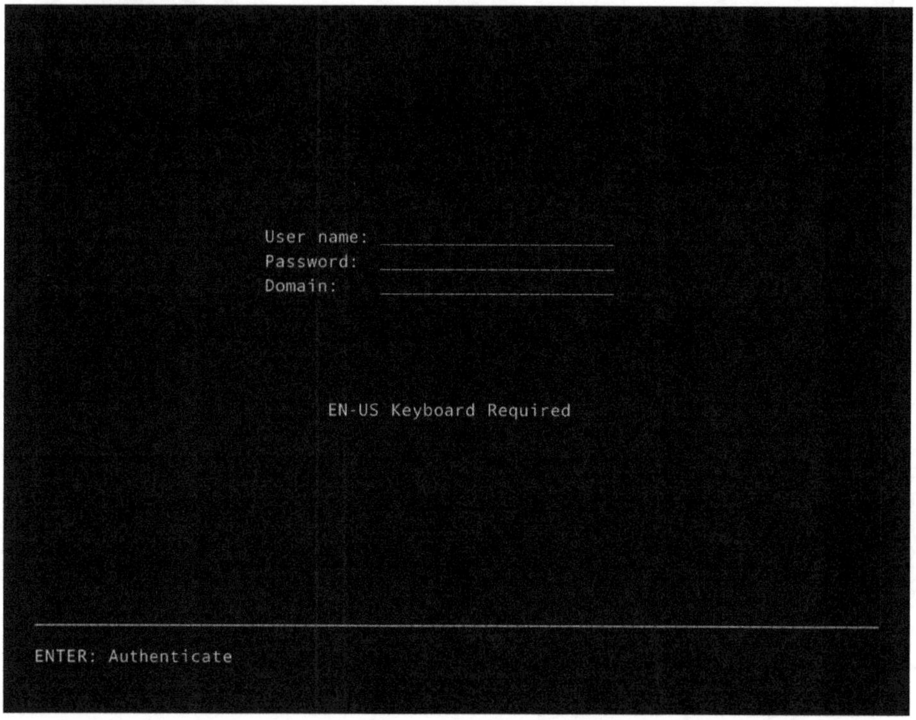

```
User name: _____
Password:  _____
Domain:    _____



                EN-US Keyboard Required



_____

ENTER: Authenticate
```

7. As shown in the screenshot, you can see the login screen of Nano Server. We have already installed IIS 10.0 on Nano server 2016, and we've checked whether the IP address 172.16.15.63 is assigned to Nano Server 2016.

8. Let's open the default IIS web page on Nano Server 2016.

9. Go to Internet Explorer, type http://172.16.15.63 (Nano Server IP), and press *Enter*. If you've already installed IIS on Nano Server 2016, it will display the IIS default home page, as shown here:

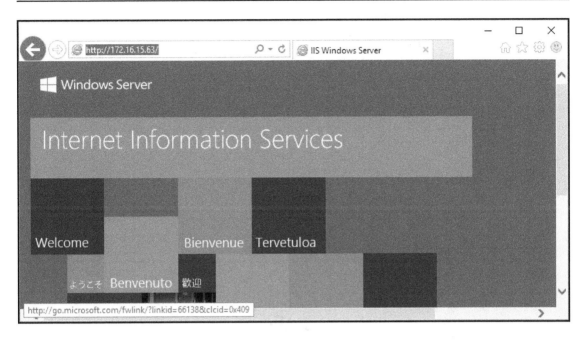

10. Now you can see that the default IIS welcome web page is displayed.

How it works...

In this recipe, we had an overview of Nano Server. We took a look at the Nano Server home screen. We checked the IP address assigned to it. We accessed the default IIS 10.0 website to check whether IIS 10.0 has been installed on Nano Server. We also got Nano Server 2016 running on a Microsoft Hyper-V host.

Installing IIS 10.0 on Nano Server

In this recipe, we are going to install IIS 10.0 on Nano Server. We will create a Nano Server 2016 virtual machine by using PowerShell, which will be attached to our Hyper-V host server. We can use PowerShell commands to install IIS on Nano Server 2016.

Getting ready

To step through this recipe, we are going to create a Nano Server instance with IIS 10.0 using PowerShell commands. You will need a Windows Server 2016 virtual instance or a physical one of Nano Server 2016, and you also need Windows Server 2016 media. You already have a Hyper-V Host ready, where you have to attach your virtual machine. For the installation and configuration, you should have administrative privileges.

How to do it...

1. Log in to Windows Server 2016. The IP of our Windows Server 2016 instance is 172.16.15.60 and the name is **WIN2016IIS**, as shown in figure.

2. Mount the Windows Server 2016 media ISO on a CD drive. Open the CD drive, and you will find the NanoServer folder:

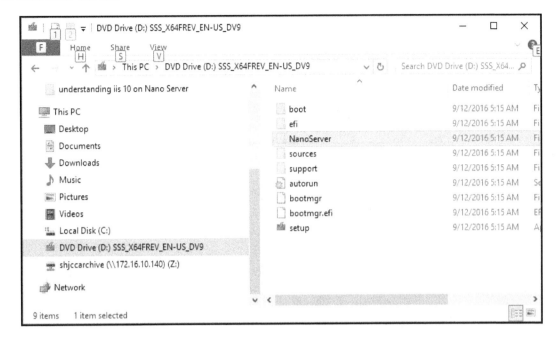

3. Copy the `NanoServer` folder from from the DVD/CD drive (`D:` in this case), and paste it into the `C:` local disk drive:

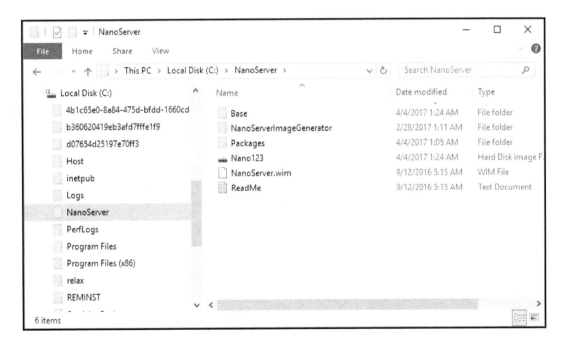

4. You can see in the figure that inside the `NanoServer` folder, you should have the following folders and files: `Base`, `NanoServerImageGenrator`, `Packages`, `NanoServer.wim`, and `Nano123.vhd`. Now you can close the `NanoServer` folder.

5. Next, you have to open PowerShell with administrator rights. Press *Windows + R* key from the keyboard. You will get the **Run** window:

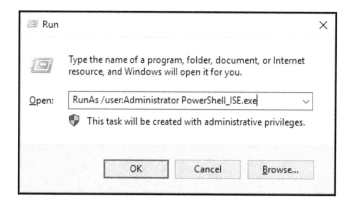

6. Type the command `RunAs /user:Administrator PowerShell_ISE.exe` and press **OK**. Now it will ask you the administrator password. Type the administrator password and press *Enter*. You will get the PowerShell command window:

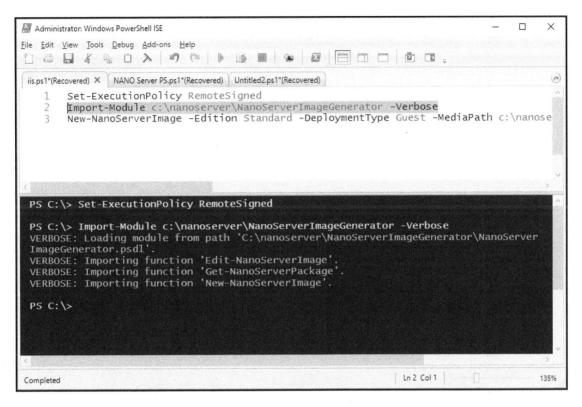

7. You have to first set the execution policy to RemoteSigned. Type into the PowerShell command prompt Set-ExecutionPolicy RemoeSigned and press *Enter*. The **Execution policy** window will pop up. Press **Yes** or **Yes to all**.

8. Next, you have to import the NanoServerImageGenerator module. Type into the PowerShell command prompt Import-Module C:\nanoserver\NanoServerImageGenerator and press *Enter*. Your selected folder's files are imported into the module.

9. Next, we set the RemoteSigned policy and import the module for NanoServerImageGenerator.

10. Let's create the Nano Server image with our IIS module. Type the following command in PowerShell:

```
New-NanoServerImage -Edition Standard -DeploymentType Guest -
MediaPath c: -BasePath .Base -TargetPath c:\nanoserver\Nano.vhd -
ComputerName Nano -Package Microsoft-NanoServer-IIS-Package
```

11. With this command, we are creating a VHD from the `NanoServer` folder, which is available in `C:`. When creating the VHD, it will use a folder called **Base** in the same directory where you run `New-NanoServerImage`: it will place the VHD (called `Nano.vhd`) in a folder in `C:\NanoServer`. The computer name will be `Nano`. The resulting VHD will contain the Standard edition of Windows Server 2016 and will be suitable for Hyper-V virtual machine deployment. Offline installation of IIS on Nano Server is recommended by Microsoft. We will use the `-Package` parameter to add the package while we create the new Nano Server.

12. Run the command `New-NanoServerImage -Edition Standard -DeploymentType Guest -MediaPath c:\ -BasePath .\Base -TargetPath c:\nanoserver\Nano.vhd -ComputerName Nano -Package Microsoft-NanoServer-IIS-Package` in PowerShell. You have to the set the administrator password for Nano Server, as shown in the following screenshot. This password will be required in the future to use Nano Server.

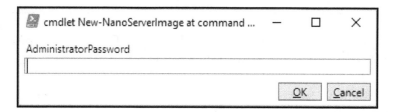

13. You can choose your own password for Nano Server 2016. Press the **OK** button, and you will get the process window, as shown here:

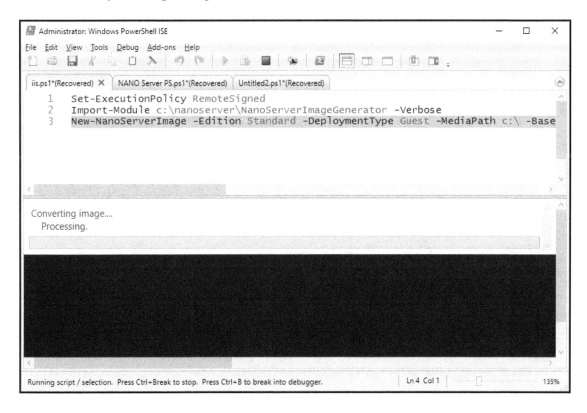

14. Once the processing for `New-NanoServerImage` is complete, you will get the `Nano.vhd` file under the `C:\NanoServer` folder. That's it! We get a message in PowerShell saying **Done**. The log is at `C:\BaseLogs2017-04-08_23-12-34-41`. Let's go to the `C:\NanoServer` folder and check whether `Nano.vhd` is available:

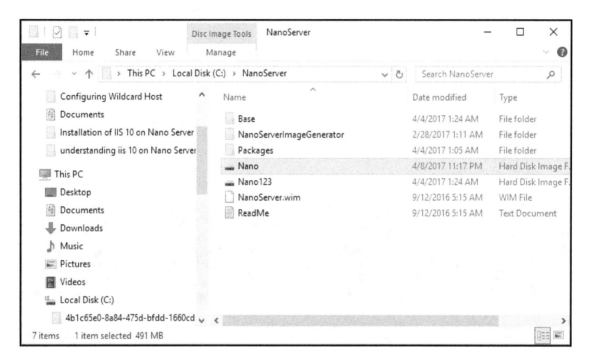

15. Copy the `Nano.vhd` file from the `C:\NanoServer` folder and paste it into the Hyper-V host (`IP 172.16.15.181`) server's `D:\vhdx` folder. We've created a virtual machine and attached `Nano.vhd` to the Nano Server 2016 virtual machine:

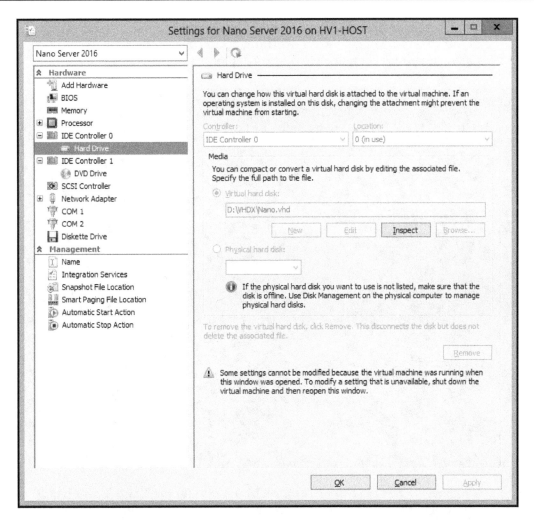

16. Click on **OK** to close the **Nano Server 2016** settings window.

17. Go to the HV1-Host (172.16.15.181) server, open **Hyper-V Manager**, go to the **Virtual Machines** pane, and select the Nano server 2016 VM. Go to the Nano Server 2016 **Actions** pane, and power on **Nano server 2016**. Next, you have to click on **Connect** to view the server login screen. Type the admin username and password (your own password you set while creating the Nano Server instance), press *Enter*, and you will be logged in.

18. Now, you have to set the IP address for Nano Server. Once you have logged in to the server, you will get the **Networking** option. Select the network and press *Enter*, and you will get the **Network Adapter** property window:

```
                          Network Adapter Settings
================================================================================
Ethernet
Microsoft Hyper-V Network Adapter
--------------------------------------------------------------------------------

State           Started
MAC Address     00-15-5D-0F-B5-0F

Interface
DHCP            Disabled
IPv4 Address    172.16.15.63
Subnet mask     255.255.255.0
Prefix Origin   Manual
Suffix Origin   Manual

Interface
DHCP            Enabled
IPv6 Address    fe80::7d6b:9d6c:b3a8:aada
Prefix Length   64
Prefix Origin   Well Known
Suffix Origin   Link

_____

Up/Dn: Scroll | ESC: Back | F4: Toggle | F10: Routing Table
F11: IPv4 Settings | F12: IPv6 Settings
```

19. You have to press *F11* to set up IPv4. You can enter the Nano Server IP address, gateway, and subnet; I've made entries for IP as 172.16.15.63, gateway as 172.16.15.254, and subnet as 255.255.255.0. You can set an IP address as per your network configuration.

20. Press *Esc* and close Nano Server. Once we've installed the IIS package, a default rule will be created in the Nano server firewall to allow ports 80 and 443.

21. Next, come to the **WIN2016IIS** server, open Internet Explorer, type the IP address of our Nano Server instance (172.16.15.63), and press *Enter*. You will see **Open the IIS default page**. We have already checked it out in this chapter.

How it works...

In this recipe, we installed IIS 10.0 on Nano Server and created a Nano Server 2016 virtual machine, which we attached to our Hyper-V host server. We set up the 172.16.15.63 IP address for Nano Server. We used PowerShell to install IIS on Nano Server 2016 and also modified the execution policy and set it to RemoteSigned. We then imported the NanoServerImageGenrator module to create a Nano Server instance through PowerShell. We also discussed how to create a new image through PowerShell commands.

Managing IIS 10.0 on Nano Server

In this recipe, we will remotely connect via PowerShell to Nano Server, and we will check out the default website. We will start up and stop website services of the default website.

Getting ready

To step through this recipe, we are going to manage IIS 10.0 on Nano Server 2016 through PowerShell. IIS 10.0 on Nano Server can only be managed using PowerShell. You will need a Nano Server 2016 instance. For all this installation and configuration work, you should have administrative privileges.

How to do it...

1. Go to the WIN2016IIS server. To connect Nano Server 2016 through PowerShell, we have to first log in to the **WIN2016IIS** server (any Windows Server 2016 or Windows 10 machine will do). We will use PowerShell to remotely connect to Nano Server at 172.16.15.63.

2. Open PowerShell with administrative rights on the **WIN2016IIS** server, press *Windows* + *R*, and you will get the **Run** window, like in the previous chapter.

3. Type the command `RunAs /user:Administrator PowerShell_ISE.exe` and press the **OK** button. Now, it will ask you the administrator password to **WIN2016IIS.** Type the administrator password and press *Enter*. PowerShell will open with administrative rights:

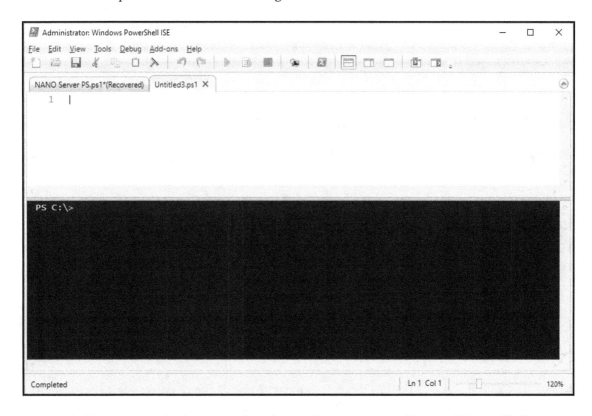

4. You see now in the screenshot that we have a script editor and PowerShell command prompt. Let's connect to Nano Server at `172.16.15.63`. We have to first set up a Nano Server instance as the trusted host for the **WIN2016IIS** server. Execute the PowerShell command `Set-Item WSMan:localhostClientTrustedHosts -Value 172.16.15.63 -Concatenate`, and you will get a popup to confirm the trusted host with options **Yes, Yes to all,** and **No.** We will click on the **Yes** button. With this, you have finished the trusted host setup.

5. Let's move to connecting the Nano Server instance. Write the PowerShell command `Enter-PSSession -ComputerName "172.16.15.63" - Credential ~Administraton` to connect Nano Server. Then press **Enter** and run the command. A popup for the Nano Server administrator password will come up, and you have to provide your Nano server password and press **Enter**. You will get logged in through PowerShell remotely:

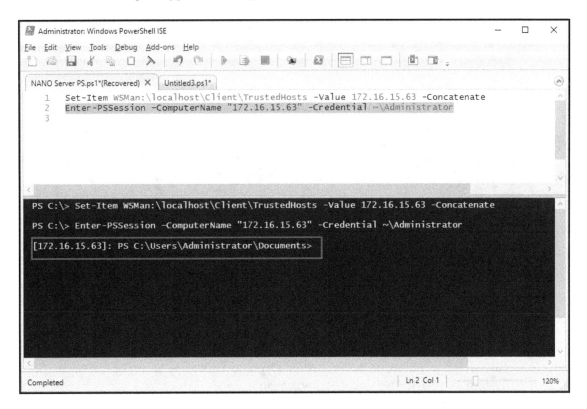

6. After getting connected to Nano Server, we have to check the default listed website in IIS. First, we have to import the IIS module with the PowerShell command `Import-module iisadministration` and then write the command `Import-module iisadministration` in PowerShell . This will import the `IISAdministration` module.

7. Execute the command `Get-IISSite` in PowerShell, and you will get all the websites listed inside your IIS instance:

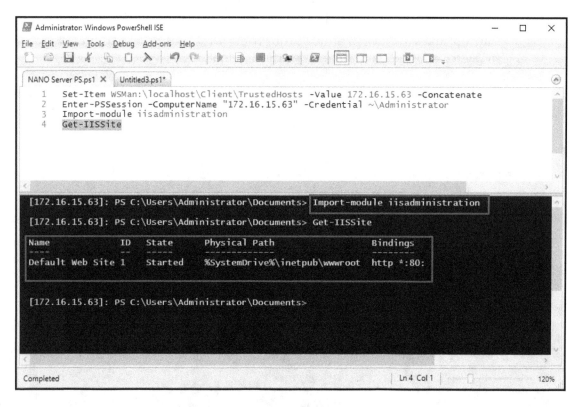

8. You can see in the figure that we only have one default website, **Default Web Site** which has **State** as **Started** and a **Physical Path** of `%SystemDrive%=C:`. The system drive is the default operating system drive, `%SystemDrive%\inetpub\wwwroot`, and the binding is `http *:80:`, which means any IP available on Nano Server.

9. You can stop and start the website with the PowerShell commands `Stop-IISSite -Name "Default Web Site"` and `Start-IISSite -Name "Default Web Site"`, respectively.

10. You can do many more things in IIS through PowerShell; for more reference, you can use the URL `https://technet.microsoft.com/itpro/powershell/windows /iisadministration/iisadministration`.

How it works...

In this recipe, we performed some management tasks for IIS 10.0 on Nano Server. We added the Nano Server IP `172.16.15.63` as a trusted host for the WIN2016IIS server and connected Nano Server using a remote PowerShell command. We also checked the listed default website on IIS server. We used PowerShell commands to start and stop the website's default website services.

Creating an IIS 10.0 website on Nano Server

In this recipe, we'll use PowerShell commands to connect to our Nano Server instance. We will import the IIS administration module and create a website. Finally, we will check the website's status.

Getting ready

To step through this recipe, we are going to create a website in IIS 10.0 on Nano Server 2016 through PowerShell. IIS 10.0 on Nano Server can only be managed using PowerShell. You will need Nano Server 2016 with the IIS package installed. For all this installation and configuration work, you should have administrative privileges.

How to do it...

1. Go to the **WIN2016IIS** server to connect to Nano Server 2016 through PowerShell. We have to first log in to the **WIN2016IIS** server or (a Windows Server 2016 or Windows 10 machine will do). We will use PowerShell to remotely connect to Nano Server `172.16.15.63`. This is the IP in my case, but it can be different in yours.

2. Open PowerShell with administrative rights on the **WIN2016IIS** server. Press *Windows + R* key from your keyboard. You will get the **Run** window.

3. Type the command `RunAs /user:Administrator PowerShell_ISE.exE` in the **Run** window and click on **OK**. Now it will ask you the administrator password of **WIN2016IIS**, so type in the password for **WIN2016IIS** and press *Enter*. You will see PowerShell open with administrative rights.

Have a look at the *Installing IIS 10.0 on Nano Server* recipe to learn how to run PowerShell.

4. Let's connect to Nano Server on `172.16.15.63`. We have to first set up our Nano Server instance as the trusted host for **WIN2016IIS** server. We will write the PowerShell command `Set-Item WSMan:localhostClientTrustedHosts -Value 172.16.15.63 -Concatenate` and press *Enter*. You will get a pop-up to confirm the trusted host. Click on **Yes.** You have now finished the trusted host setup for Nano Server.

5. Let's now connect Nano Server. Run the PowerShell command `Enter-PSSession -ComputerName "172.16.15.63" -Credential ~Administrator` to connect Nano Server. You will get the popup for the Nano Server administrator password, as shown here:

In the command `-ComputerName "172.16.15.63"`, substitute your IP address.

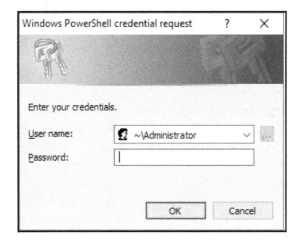

6. You have to provide your Nano server password and press *Enter*. You will be logged in through PowerShell remotely.

7. You are now connected to Nano Server through PowerShell. First, we have to run `Import-module iisadministration` and run the `Import-module iisadministration` command in PowerShell. It will import the `iisadministrator` module. This `iisadministration` module will provide us the full administration options of IIS Server.

8. I am going to create a separate website directory called `nonosite`. This directory will be created inside `C:\inetpubwwwroot`.

9. Open the file explorer on the **WIN2016IIS** server, type `172.16.15.63c$` in the address bar. This is nothing but the Nano server IP address and the `C:` drive's hidden default share, `c$`. You will get the Nano Server `C:` drive, as shown here:

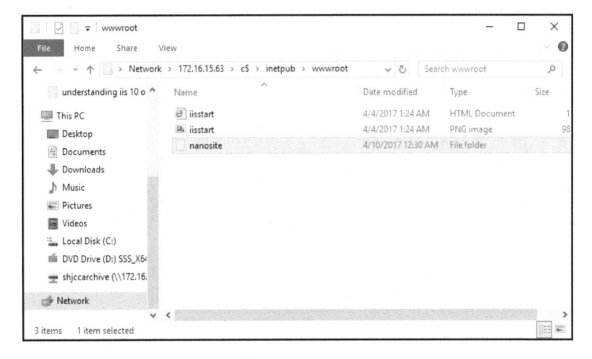

10. We go to `C:\intepubwwwroot` and create a folder called `nanosite`. If you are facing problems accessing the `C:` drive of Nano Server, you should check the firewall file and print share settings on Nano Server; you can use the PowerShell command to create a folder inside `C:\inetpubwwwroot`.

11. Now we are going to create a website called `nanosite.com`. Go to the PowerShell command prompt and run `New-IISSite -Name nanosite.com -BindingInformation "*:8080:" -PhysicalPath` `c:\inetpub\wwwroot\nanosite`. The `nanosite.com` website will be created.

12. We can check whether the website has been created or not. Open the PowerShell command prompt and run `Get-IISSite`, as shown here:

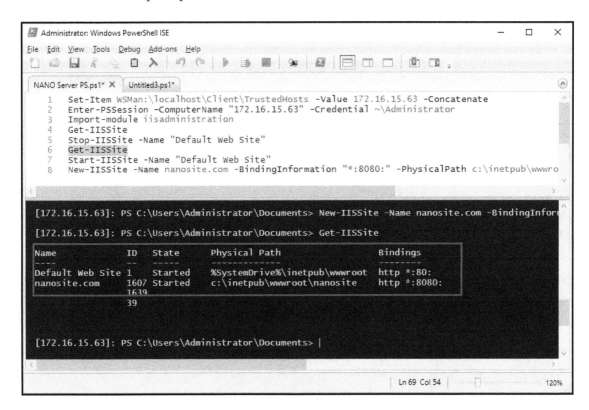

13. Once you run the Get-IISSite command in PowerShell, you will get all the listed websites available in the IIS server. Now we have two websites created in our IIS Server instance: **Default Web Site** and **nanosite.com**.

How it works...

In this recipe, we used PowerShell commands to connect to Nano Server. We imported the IISadministration module and created a separate Nanosite folder inside `C:\inetpub\wwwroot`. We also created a website with PowerShell commands and checked the listed website's details.

Configuring an IIS 10.0 website on Nano Server

In this recipe, we are going to configure a website `nanosite.com` in IIS 10.0 on Nano Server 2016 through PowerShell. We will set up the `nanosite.com` website IP binding and also get an overview of modifying the physical path of `nanosite.com`.

Getting ready

IIS 10.0 on Nano Server can be only managed with PowerShell; you will need a Nano Server 2016 instance with the IIS package installed. For all the installation and configuration work, you should have administrative privileges.

How to do it...

1. Let's modify the website's properties. We have a direct editing method we can use and modify `nanosite.com`.

2. Go to the **WIN2016IIS** server. To access Nano Server 2016, we have to first log in to the **WIN2016IIS** server (any Windows Server 2016 or Windows 10 machine will do), and we will use our **WIN2016IIS** server to remotely connect with Nano Server at `172.16.15.63`. Before going to access the Nano Server's `c$` share, you should configure the firewall on Nano Server to allow the file and print services options.

3. Open the file explorer on the **WIN2016IIS** server, and type `172.16.15.63\c$\Windows\System32\inetsrv\config` in the address bar of your browser. We are going to access the `C:` drive of Nano Server on the default hidden share, `c$`. It will prompt you for the administrator password. Once you've provide the correct password for Nano Server, you will get Nano Server to open to `172.16.15.63\c$\Windows\System32\inetsrv\config`, as shown here:

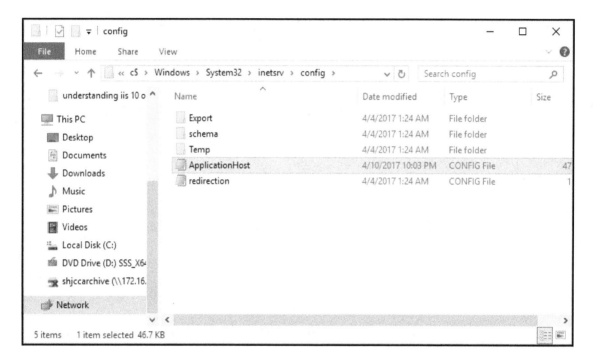

4. You have to make some changes in `ApplicationHost.config`. Open it in Notepad:

Make the changes carefully. It's better to keep a backup file in a safe place before editing the original one!

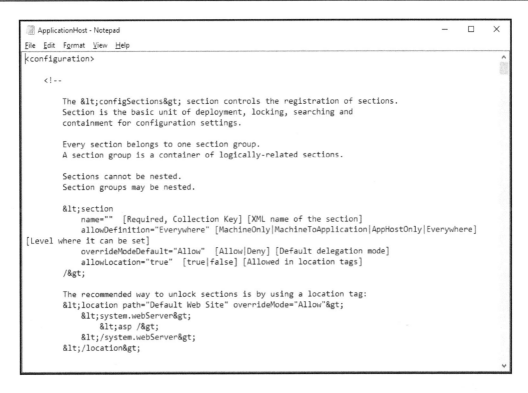

5. The `ApplicationHost.config` file has all the IIS website-related property configuration options. Make sure you're changing the `ApplicationHost.config` file and not something else. You'll find `nanosite.com`, as shown here:

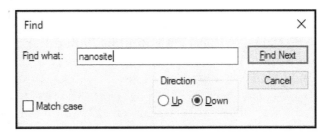

6. Click on **Find**, and it will take you inside `applicationHost.config`, where the **nanosite.com** details are available:

```
ApplicationHost - Notepad                                          —   □   ×
File  Edit  Format  View  Help
        </listenerAdapters>

        <log>
            <centralBinaryLogFile enabled="true" directory="%SystemDrive%\inetpub\logs
\LogFiles"></centralBinaryLogFile>
            <centralW3CLogFile enabled="true" directory="%SystemDrive%\inetpub\logs
\LogFiles"></centralW3CLogFile>
        </log>

        <sites>
            <site name="Default Web Site" id="1">
                <application path="/">
                    <virtualDirectory path="/" physicalPath="%SystemDrive%\inetpub
\wwwroot"></virtualDirectory>
                </application>
                <bindings>
                    <binding protocol="http" bindingInformation="*:801:"></binding>
                </bindings>
            </site>
            <site name="nanosite.com" id="1607163939">
                <application path="/">
                    <virtualDirectory path="/" physicalPath="c:\inetpub\wwwroot\nanosite" />
                </application>
                <bindings>
                    <binding protocol="http" bindingInformation="*:8080:" />
                </bindings>
            </site>
            <siteDefaults>
                <logFile logFormat="W3C" directory="%SystemDrive%\inetpub\logs\LogFiles"></logFile>
```

7. As shown in the screenshot, we've selected the `site` property. Here, you can change the **Site Name**, **Physical Path**, **Binding Protocol**, and **Binding Information.** We will change only the `nanosite.com` IP address and port number. You can see in screenshot the code `bindingInformation="172.16.15.63*:8080:"` `*`. This will used any available IP, but we will assign Nano Server's `172.16.15.63` and we change the port to `8081`, as shown here:

```
ApplicationHost - Notepad                                              —    □    ×
File  Edit  Format  View  Help
            </listenerAdapters>

            <log>
                <centralBinaryLogFile enabled="true" directory="%SystemDrive%\inetpub\logs
\LogFiles"></centralBinaryLogFile>
                <centralW3CLogFile enabled="true" directory="%SystemDrive%\inetpub\logs
\LogFiles"></centralW3CLogFile>
            </log>

            <sites>
                <site name="Default Web Site" id="1">
                    <application path="/">
                        <virtualDirectory path="/" physicalPath="%SystemDrive%\inetpub
\wwwroot"></virtualDirectory>
                    </application>
                    <bindings>
                        <binding protocol="http" bindingInformation="*:801:"></binding>
                    </bindings>
                </site>
                <site name="nanosite.com" id="1607163939">
                    <application path="/">
                        <virtualDirectory path="/" physicalPath="c:\inetpub\wwwroot\nanosite" />
                    </application>
                    <bindings>
                        <binding protocol="http" bindingInformation="172.16.15.63:8081:" />
                    </bindings>
                </site>
                <siteDefaults>
                    <logFile logFormat="W3C" directory="%SystemDrive%\inetpub\logs\LogFiles"></logFile>
```

8. If you want to change the physical path of `nanosite.com`, you can edit the path as you want. Now you can **Save** the `applicationHost.config` file and close it.

9. Let's check the modified `nanosite.com` binding information through PowerShell. On the **WIN2016IIS** server, open the Run prompt and execute `RunAs /user:Administrator PowerShell_ISE.exe`. It will ask you for the administrator password of **WIN2016IIS**; type it in and press *Enter*. You will get PowerShell open with administrative rights.

10. We need to first set up a Nano Server instance that is the trusted host for the **WIN2016IIS** server. Run the command `Set-Item WSMan:\localhost\client\trustedhosts -Value 172.16.15.63 -Concatenate`. You will get a popup to confirm the trusted host. Click on **Yes**.

11. We need to run this PowerShell command to connect Nano Server to PowerShell: `Enter-PSSession -ComputerName "172.16.15.63" -Credential ~Administrator`. You will get a popup for the Nano Server administrator password. Enter the administrator password and press **OK**.

12. Now you need to run the PowerShell command `Import-module iisadministration`. This will import the IIS administration module. Now, to get the site details, run `Get-IISSite`. You will get the site information, as shown here:

13. In the figure, we have the updated binding information. You can see that the `nanosite.com` IP is `172.16.15.63` and port `8081`.

How it works...

In this recipe, we edited the `ApplicationHost.config` file to change the `nanosite.com` binding information. We configured `nanosite.com` with a new port, `8081`. We set the binding of `nanosite.com` to the IP `172.16.15.63`, and we had an overview of modifying the physical path of `nanosite.com`. We checked the website's functioning and made changes through PowerShell.

Uploading website pages

In this recipe, we are going to upload website pages to `nanosite.com`; we will create the `default.htm` file using PowerShell.

Getting ready

To step through this recipe, you will need a Nano Server 2016 instance with the IIS package installed. For all this installation and configuration work, you should have administrative privileges.

How to do it...

1. Go to the **WIN2016IIS** server. To access Nano Server 2016, we have to first log in to the **WIN2016IIS** server (any Windows Server 2016 or Windows 10 machine will do); we will use our **WIN2016IIS** server to remotely connect with Nano Server `172.16.15.63`. Before going to access the Nano Server `c$` share, you should configure the firewall on Nano Server to allow file and print service options.

2. Open the file explorer on **WIN2016IIS** server, and type `172.16.15.63\c$\inetpub\wwwroot\nanosite` in the address bar. It will prompt you for the administrator password of your Nano Server instance. Once you provide the correct password, the Nano Server instance will open to `172.16.15.63\c$\inetpub\wwwroot\nanosite`.

3. Copy the default IIS Server `IISStart.htm` and `IISSstart.png` files from `c:\inetpub\wwwroot` and paste them in the physical Nanosite website folder, `172.16.15.63\c$\inetpub\wwwroot\nanosite`. This is one option we can use to upload website pages. I will show you a much easier option to create a simple web page for testing purposes.

4. Connect to Nano Server through PowerShell with administrator rights.

5. Run `Import-module iisadministration`. After this, you can create a web page through PowerShell using the following commands:

```
"Welcome to IIS on Nano Server by Ashraf Khan This
Nanosite.com" | Out-File -PSPath
"c:\inetpub\wwwroot\nanosite\Default.htm"
```

> "Welcome to IIS on Nano Server by Ashraf Khan This Nanosite.com" is the text that will be displayed on the web page, and `Out-file -PSPath` is used to define the type of file and physical path of your website. You can see this in the following screenshot:

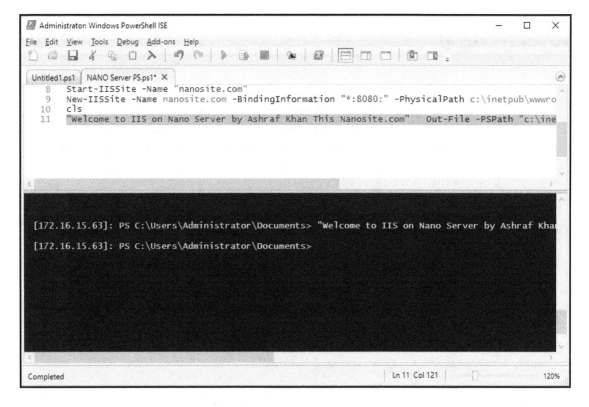

6. So we've just written a single line of easy code to create an HTML webpage. Let's check the `nanosite` folder and see whether the file has been created.

7. Open `172.16.15.63\c$\inetpub\wwwroot\nanosite`. As shown in this screenshot, the `default.htm` file has been created:

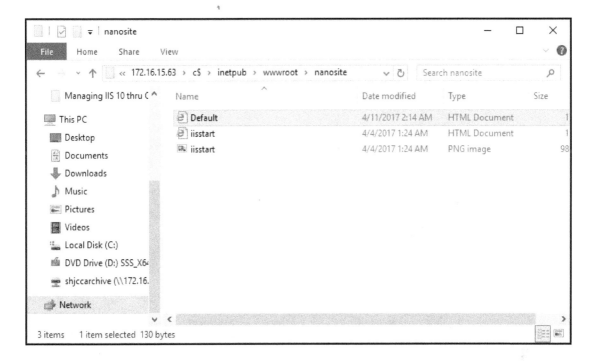

How it works...

In this recipe, we uploaded default IIS website pages `IISStart.htm` and `IISStart.png` to the `nanosite` folder, which is located in the Nano Server `C:\inetpub\wwwroot\nanosite` folder. We created the `default.htm` file through PowerShell and verified that the file was created in the folder.

Testing uploaded web pages

In this recipe, we will open the firewall port for Nano Server. We've already modified the port `8081` binding information for `nanosite.com`. We need to open the firewall port `8081` in Nano Server, which will allow us to access the website with port `8081`. We will open the `default.htm` page, which we created through PowerShell.

Getting ready

To step through this recipe, you will need a Nano Server 2016 instance with the IIS package installed. For all this installation and configuration work, you should have administrative privileges.

How to do it...

1. Go to the **WIN2016IIS** server to access Nano Server 2016. We have to first log in to the **WIN2016IIS** server with any Windows 2016 Server or Windows 10 machine. We will use the **WIN2016IIS** server to remotely connect to Nano Server on `172.16.15.63`.

2. Let's first create the firewall rule to allow port `8081` on Nano Server. Execute `RunAs /user:Administrator PowerShell_ISE.exe` in the Run window on the **WIN2016IIS** server. It will ask you for the administrator password of **WIN2016IIS.** Type the administrator password and press *Enter*. You will get PowerShell to open with administrative rights.

3. Next, we will write the PowerShell command `Set-Item WSMan:localhost\Client\TrustedHosts -Value 172.16.15.63 -Concatenate` and press the *Enter* button. You will get a popup for confirmation of the trusted host option. Click on **Yes**.

4. Now we have to execute a PowerShell command to connect to Nano Server: `Enter-PSSession -ComputerName "172.16.15.63" -Credential ~Administrator`. You will get the popup for the Nano Server administrator password. Enter the password and press **OK**.

5. Once Nano Server is connected to, we have to write a PowerShell command for the firewall: we will add a firewall rule to allow port `8081`. Type the command `New-NetFirewallRule -DisplayName "Allow Inbound Port 8081" -Direction Inbound -LocalPort 8081 -Protocol TCP -Action Allow` in the PowerShell command prompt:

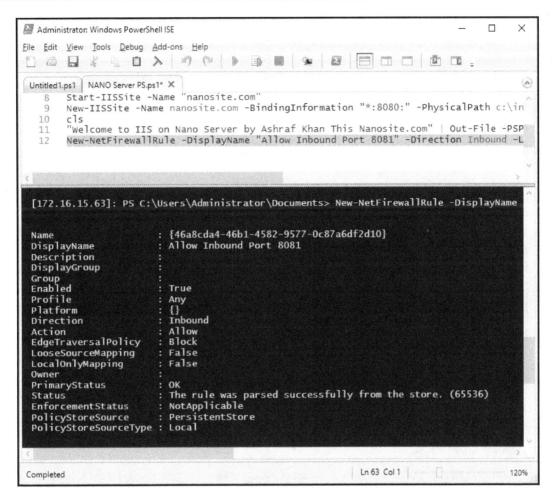

6. You can see in the screenshot that the firewall Allow rule has been created. Now let's test `nanosite.com:8081` to check whether it's working or not.

7. Open Internet Explorer on the **WIN2016IIS** server, type the **nanosite.com** IP address, 172.16.15.63, along with the port number, 8081:

8. As you can see, we have access nanosite.com using its IP address. If you configure the DNS, you can use the website domain name, nanosite.com.

How it works...

In this recipe, we set up a firewall rule to allow port 8081 on Nano Server. We opened the firewall port 8081 on Nano Server through PowerShell, which allows us to access the nanosite.com on port 8081. We opened the default.htm page, which we had created using PowerShell.

8
Configuring IIS Administration with PowerShell Cmdlets

In this chapter, we will cover the following recipes:

- IIS administration with PowerShell cmdlets
- Creating an advanced IIS 10.0 website on Nano Server
- Configuring IIS 10.0 websites on Nano Server
- Uploading IIS 10.0 websites to Nano Server
- Testing uploaded web pages

Introduction

PowerShell is an automation platform and scripting language for Windows and Windows Server that allows you to simplify the management of your systems. Unlike other text-based shells, PowerShell harnesses the power of the .NET Framework, providing rich objects and a massive set of built-in functionality for taking control of your Windows environment.

We can use PowerShell scripts in two ways, PowerShell Desired State Configuration (DSC) and PowerShell Integrated Scripting Environment (ISE).

PowerShell DSC:

PowerShell DSC is a platform for testing and ensuring the declarative state of a system. DSC allows you to scale complex deployments across environments, enables collaboration of management, and corrects for configuration drift.

PowerShell ISE:

PowerShell Integrated Scripting Environment (ISE) is a Windows application that supports enhanced usage of PowerShell for beginners and experts alike. ISE's many features include:

- A built-in editor for writing, testing, and debugging scripts
- Full IntelliSense tab completion, syntax highlighting, and context-sensitive help
- A myriad of keyboard shortcuts
- Support for right-to-left languages
- Extensible add-ons

For more information, you can refer to `https://msdn.microsoft.com/en-us/powershell/mt173057.aspx`.

IIS administration with PowerShell cmdlets

In this recipe, we will log in to the different PowerShell remote-management modules for Nano Server to manage IIS Server. We will log in through Server Manager to PowerShell, and we will also review the PowerShell remote script.

Getting ready

In this recipe, we are going to access Nano Server through PowerShell and the IISAdministrator module. You will need a Windows Server 2016 virtual or physical instance for remote PowerShell management of Nano Server 2016. For all this installation and configuration work, you should have administrative privileges.

How to do it...

1. Log in to Windows Server 2016 at the IP `172.16.15.60` and on the server named **WIN2016IIS**.

2. Open Server Manager and click on **All Servers**:

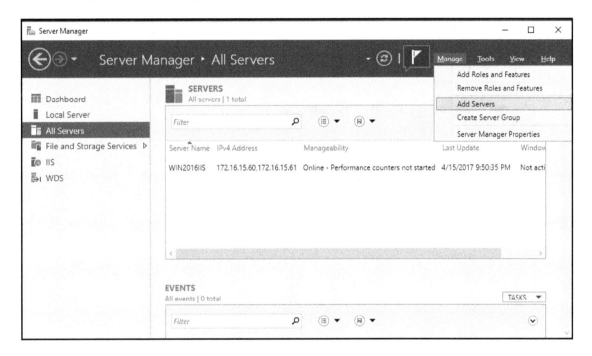

3. Go to the **Manage** menu in Server Manager and open **Add servers.** The **Add servers** option will add your remote server and can be managed with Windows Server 2016 Server Manager. Once we click on **Add Servers**, you will get the **Add Servers** window:

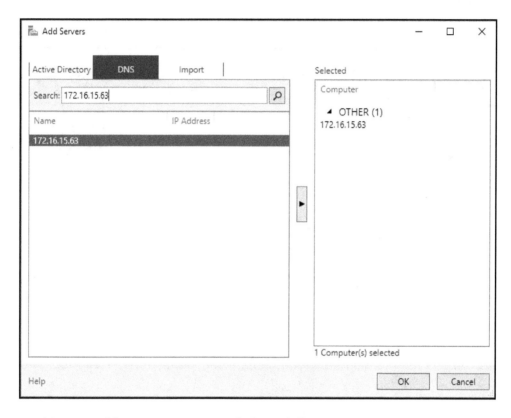

4. You can add a remote server with three different options. **Active Directory** searches for the computer name and **DNS** searches for either the name or IP address and Imports the computer (server) name and IP if you have one or more than one server. Select the **DNS** tab and add the Nano Server IP. If you have DNS set up, it will get resolved to the server name. If you don't have DNS settings configured in Nano Server, it will give you a warning. Ignore the warning and press **OK**, as shown here:

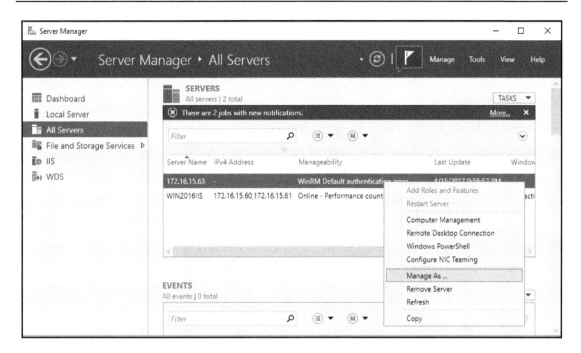

5. In the **All Servers** window, we have added the IP 172.16.15.63, which is our Nano Server 2016 IP. Now right-click on the Nano Server IP, `172.16.15.63`, and click on **Manage As....** It will open a new authentication window called **Windows Security** for Nano Server, as shown here:

6. Provide the username **localhost\administrator** and administrator password and press **OK**. I've also selected the **Remember me** option, which will remember the administrator username and password.

7. Now come back to the Server Manager page. You can see that it's authenticated with Nano Server:

8. Here you can see that we've added a server called **Nano** with IP address 172.16.15.63. Now let's move on to access PowerShell.

9. Right-click on **Nano Server**, which is listed in the **Server Manager** window. You will get a popup. Click on the PowerShell option, and it will again ask you the administrator username and password for Nano Server:

10. Type the Nano Server username and password. Click on **OK** to see PowerShell get connected with Nano Server remotely without a script:

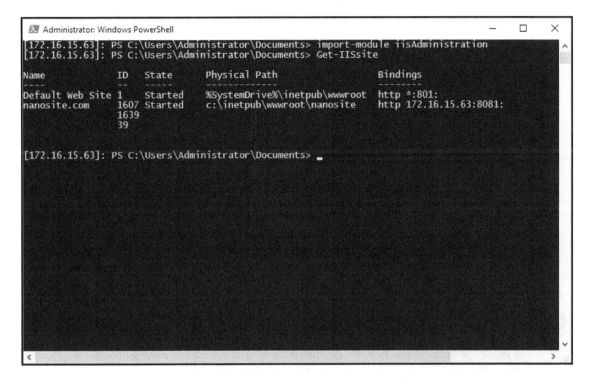

11. You get remotely connected to Nano Server PowerShell. Next, you we have to test some of the commands. We have to first use the `import-module iisAdministration` to use of IIS administration. Once the IISAdministration module is imported, we can write any IIS command and it will work.

12. Use the PowerShell command `Get-IISsite`. You can see that it will bring you all listed sites in the Nano Server IIS instance. You can write more commands through PowerShell.

13. We have one more option for the flexible use of PowerShell scripts, PowerShell ISE. Let's check how we can open it and what the benefits of it are.

14. Go to the **WIN2016IIS** server to connect to Nano Server
    2016 through PowerShell. You have to first log in to the WIN2016IIS server (any
    Windows Server 2016 or Windows 10 machine will do). We will use PowerShell
    to remotely connect to Nano Server at `172.16.15.63`.

15. Now press `Windows + R`. You will get the Run window. Open PowerShell
    ISE with administrative rights, type the command `RunAs`
    `/user:Administrator PowerShell_ISE.exe`, and press **OK**. Now it will ask
    you the administrator password for your Windows Server 2016 instance. Type
    the administrator password and press *Enter*. Now you should get the PowerShell
    window, as shown here:

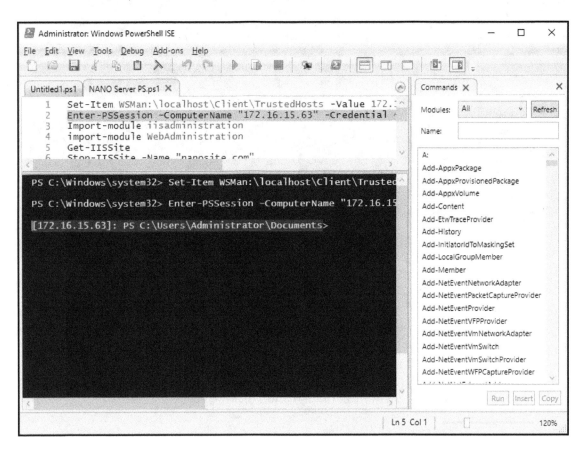

16. We performed this step earlier in `Chapter 7`, *Deploying IIS 10.0 on Nano Server*. Here we just have to recap. You can that see we have several easy options available in PowerShell ISE. Using the **Script Editor**, we can write our script and it will also show you the advanced automation writing option. You can save and use it several times. We have **Commands**, which displays available commands in PowerShell and available PowerShell module features. You can open the simple PowerShell prompt, which is available in Windows Server; if you need administrative privileges with PowerShell ISE, you'll need the administrator username and password to access PowerShell ISE. Once you are accessing Nano Server remotely, make Nano Server a trusted host, and then get connected to it with the proper username and password.

How it works...

In this recipe, we opened Server Manager on the WIN2016IIS server and added the Nano Server host to the **All Servers** list. We then authenticated Nano Server with Server Manager and opened PowerShell remote management for Nano Server to manage IIS Server. We logged in through Server Manager to PowerShell, imported the IISAdministration module, and ran the Get-Site command. Also, we reviewed the PowerShell ISE remote script.

Creating an advanced IIS 10.0 website on Nano Server

In this recipe, we will create a website with a website header (website name) and also add an application pool. We will create a separate application pool and add the application pool to our website. We will find all the available listed application pools in IIS Server.

Getting ready

We are going to remotely connect Nano Server through PowerShell and manage IIS over the IISAdministrator module. You will need a Windows Server 2016 virtual or physical server for remote PowerShell management of Nano Server 2016. For all this installation and configuration work, you should have administrative privileges.

How to do it...

1. Log in to Windows Server 2016. The IP address of Windows Server 2016 is `172.16.15.60` and the name of the server is **WIN2016IIS**.

2. Press *Windows + R* on your keyboard. You will get the **Run** window. Open PowerShell ISE with administrative rights, type `RunAs /user:Administrator PowerShell_ISE.exe` in the **Run** window, and press **OK**.

3. Now it will ask you the administrative password for you Windows Server 2016 instance (not Nano Server). Type the administrator password and press *Enter*. The PowerShell window will open.

4. Now we have to remote-connect to Nano Server 2016 on the IP `172.16.15.63`.

5. We will use the following command from PowerShell:

```
Enter-PSSession -ComputerName "172.16.15.63" -Credential ~\Administrator
```

You can use either the computer name or IP address for `-ComputerName`. We are using the IP address in this command.

6. Now you will get a pop-up window for the Nano Server administrator username and password. We will enter the Nano server administrator password and press **OK** to log in. You have connected successfully. Run the `Import-module iisAdministration` command. Press **Enter** and you will get the PowerShell module imported.

7. Let's create the website with an advanced script. We will use the following command:

```
$manager = Get-IISServerManager
$site = $manager.Sites.Add("v5mysite", "http", "*:8082:v5mysite.com",
"C:\v5mysite") $site.Id = 4
$site.Bindings.Add("*:8083:", "http")$manager.CommitChanges()"
```

8. Close PowerShell and press *Enter*. We can run the command from the
   PowerShell toolbar by clicking on the **Play** button at the top:

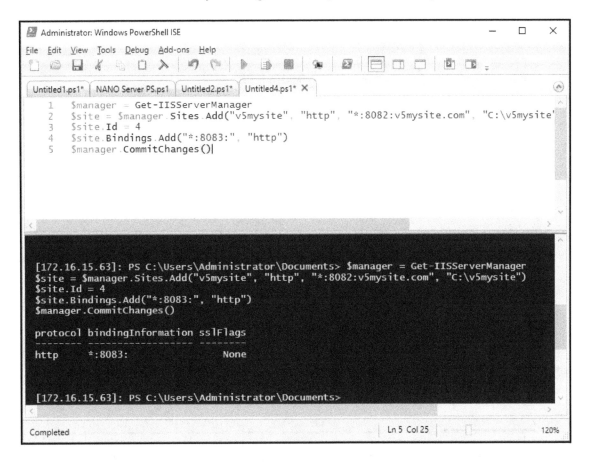

9. You can see here that we created a website called `v5mysite` with protocol
   `http`, IP `*` (all available IPs), and header `v5mysite.com`. We also set the physical
   path of `v5mysite` as `C:\v5mysite` and set the site ID as `4`.

10. Now let's check the created website, `v5mysite`. Run the command `Get-IISSite` in PowerShell:

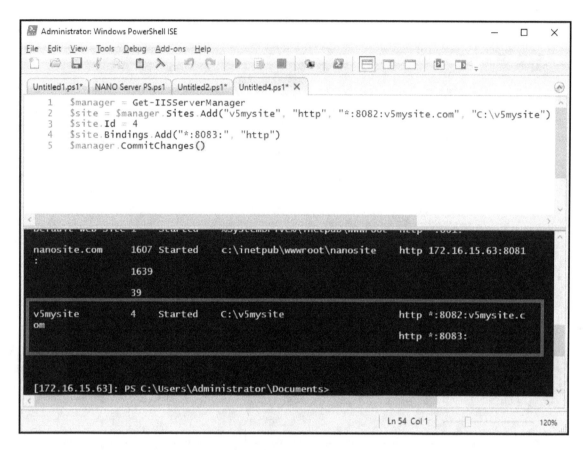

11. You'll see in the figure that it shows that you have a website called **v5mysite**, ID **4**, status `Started`, and physical path `C:\v5mysite`, and we have two pieces of binding information, one with the header and the other without.

12. Let's create the application pool in IIS 10.0 on Nano Server. Run the following command in PowerShell:

```
$manager = Get-IISServerManager $pool =
$manager.ApplicationPools.Add("NanoAPP") $pool.ManagedPipelineMode =
"Integrated" $pool.ManagedRuntimeVersion = "v4.0"
$pool.Enable32BitAppOnWin64 = $false $pool.AutoStart = $true
$pool.StartMode = "OnDemand" $pool.ProcessModel.IdentityType =
"ApplicationPoolIdentity" $manager.CommitChanges()
```

13. Next, we create an application pool called `NanoApp` and set the property of the application pool, as shown here:

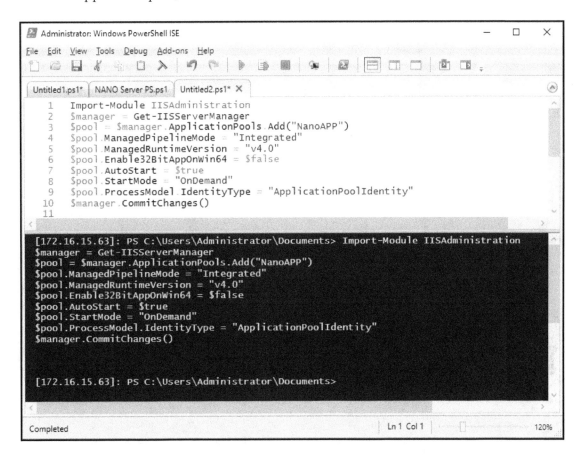

14. Once you create the application pool, you can check its status with the command `Get-IISAppPool`, as shown here:

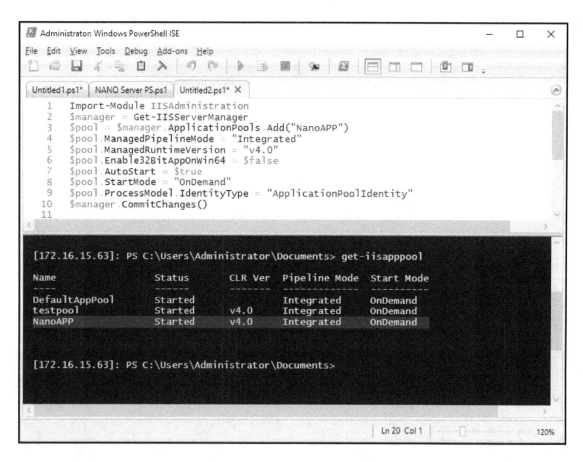

15. You can see that we have created the application pool called `NanoApp`. Let's add `NanoApp` to `v5msite.com`. Use the following command:

```
\$manager = Get-IISServerManager $website = $manager.Sites["v5mysite"]
$website.Applications["/"].ApplicationPoolName = "NanoApp"
$manager.CommitChanges()
```

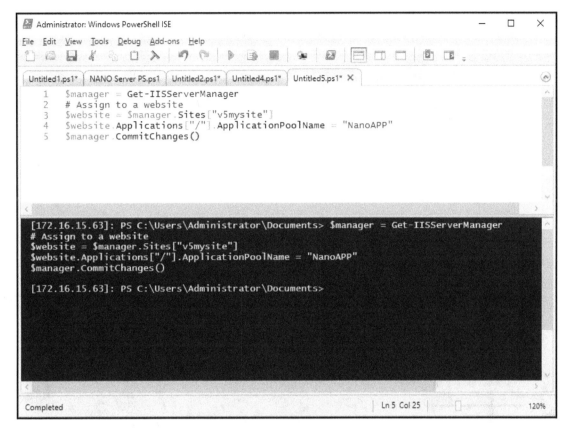

16. We assigned the application pool `NanoApp` to website `v5mysite`. Now let's check the application pool name for `v5mysite.com`.

17. Use the following command:

```
"$manager = Get-IISServerManager
$website = $manager.Sites["v5mysite"]
$website.Applications["/"].ApplicationPoolName"
```

18. You will get the application pool name as NanoAPP, as shown here:

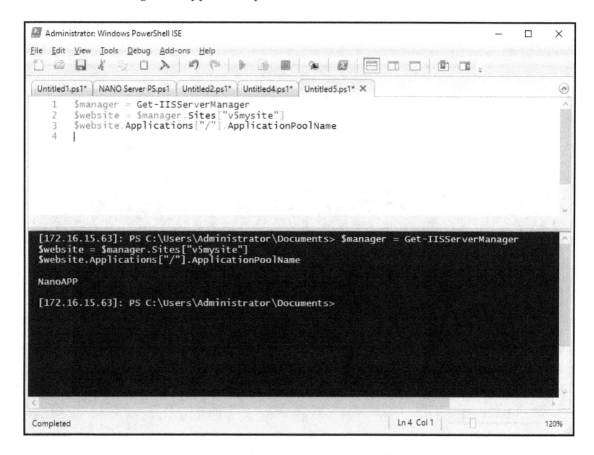

How to do it...

In this recipe, we remotely connected to Nano Server with a PowerShell command and imported the IIS module through IISAdministrator. We created the website v5mysite with website header v5mysite.com. We created a separate application pool called NanoAPP and added it to our website, v5mysite and found all the listed available application pools in IIS Server using a PowerShell command.

Configuring IIS 10.0 websites on Nano Server

In this recipe, we will use PowerShell commands to recycle the `v5mysite.com` application pool. We will check the default **Document Settings** and listed page name and add the new filename to the default document, `v5mysite.htm`. We will make the changes in the physical path of the `v5mysite.com` website.

Getting ready

In this recipe, we are going to remote connect Nano Server through PowerShell and configure our website through the `IISAdministrator` module. You will require a Windows Server 2016 virtual or physical server for remote PowerShell management for Nano Server 2016. For all this installation and configuration work, you should have administrative privileges.

How to do it...

1. Log in to Windows Server 2016 with the `172.16.15.60` and name **WIN2016IIS**. Press *Windows + R* on your keyboard, and you will get the **Run** window. Open PowerShell ISE with administrative rights, and type in the command `RunAs /user:Administrator PowerShell_ISE.exe` in the **Run** window, as shown here:

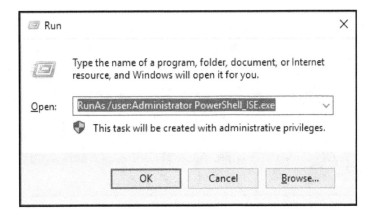

2. Press **OK.** It will ask you the administrator password of your Windows Server 2016 instance (not Nano Server). Type the administrator password and press *Enter*. Now the PowerShell window will open.

3. Now we have to remote connect to Nano Server 2016 at IP `172.16.15.63`. Write the following command in PowerShell:

```
Enter-PSSession -ComputerName "172.16.15.63" -Credential ~\Administrator
```

4. Now you will get a pop-up window for the Nano Server administrator username and password. Enter the administrator password and press **OK** to log in. You have successfully connected.

5. Now let's import the IIS Administration module. Write the command `Import-module iisAdministration` and press *Enter*. You will get the PowerShell module imported.

6. Write the command `Get-IISAppPool $sm = Get-IISServerManager $sm.ApplicationPools["NanoAPP"].Recycle()` to recycle the application pool `NanoAPP`, as shown here:

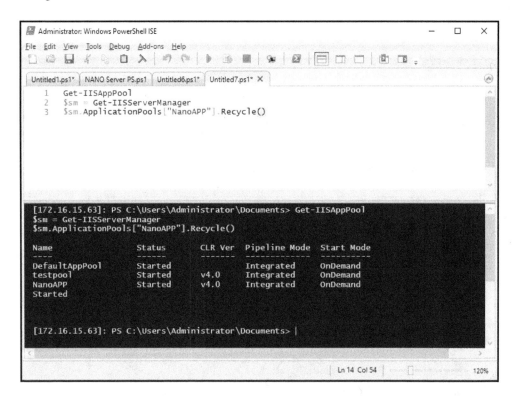

7. Once we run the command, we will get a list of application pools available in IIS on Nano Server, the PowerShell command will only recycle the application pool **NanoAPP**, and we'll get **its** status as Started. We can use the start and stop commands `$sm = Get-IISServerManager` `$sm.ApplicationPools["NanoAPP"].Stop()` and `$sm.ApplicationPools["NanoAPP"].Start()` for the application pool, respectively. We can use these commands as and when we require.

8. Now we are going to check the default document files list available in the **Default Document** settings. Write the command `Get-IISConfigSection -SectionPath "system.webServer/defaultDocument" | Get-IISConfigCollection -CollectionName "files"` in PowerShell and press *Enter*, as shown here:

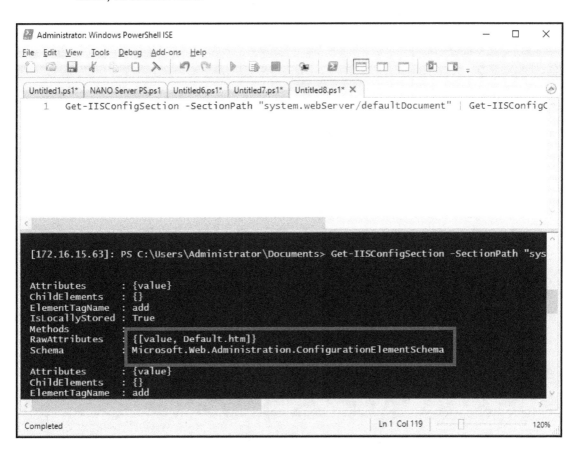

9. We can now see that we have listed all available file names in IIS Server. Marked `default.htm`.

10. Now we are going to create a file named `v5mysite.htm` in the **Default Document** settings. Write the command `Get-IISConfigSection -SectionPath "system.webServer/defaultDocument" | Get-IISConfigCollection -CollectionName "files" | New-IISConfigCollectionElement -ConfigAttribute @{"Value" = "v5mysite.htm"}` and press *Enter*, and you will get the filename `v5mysite.htm` added to the **Default Document**.

11. Now we are going to check whether `v5mysite.htm` is available in the **Default Document**. Run the command `Get-IISConfigSection -SectionPath "system.webServer/defaultDocument" | Get-IISConfigCollection -CollectionName "files"`, as shown here:

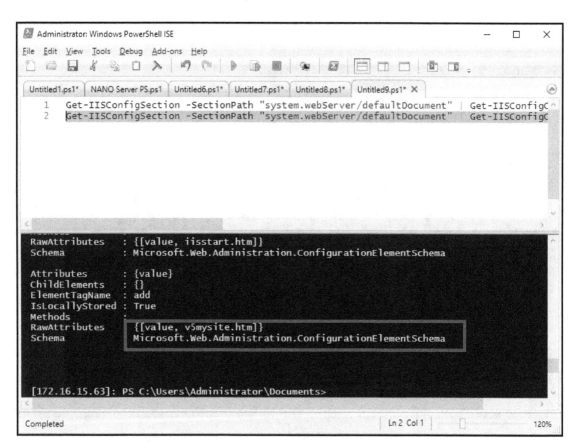

12. You can see in the figure that we have created the entry for `v5mysite.htm` entry in the **Default Document**.

13. Let's change the existing physical path, `C:\v5mysite`, of the website `v5mysite` to the new physical path, `C:\v5mysite-new`. Run the following command:

```
Get-IISsite v5mysite
$manager = Get-IISServerManager
$manager.Sites["v5mysite"].Applications["/"].VirtualDirectories["/"].Physic
alPath = "C:\v5mysite-New"Get-IISsite v5mysite
```

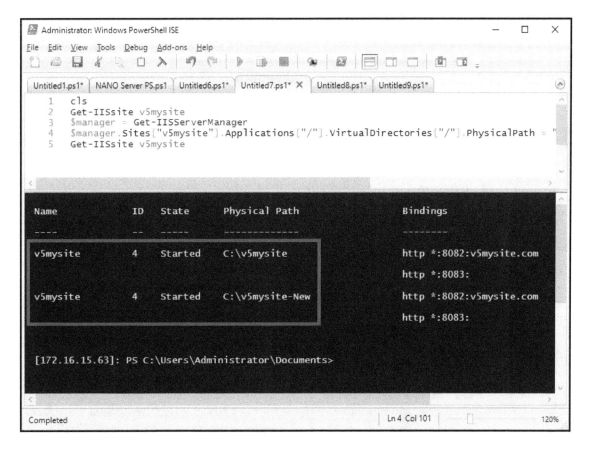

14. You can see in the figure that website `v5mysite` has the existing path `C:\v5mysite`. After running the PowerShell command, the physical path has changed to `C:\v5mysite-New`.

To recycle an application pool on demand, you may have to immediately recycle an unhealthy worker process instead of waiting for the next configured recycle. Rather than instantly stopping the worker process, which can cause service interruptions, you can use on-demand recycling specially when new settings/ changes are done that will sometimes not be replicated. After recycling, all running worker processes are restarted with the new changes of the application pool.

How it works...

In this recipe, we recycled the v5mysite.com application pool NanoAPP and checked the files listed in the **Default Document**. We added a new file called v5mysite.htm to the Default Document. We also changed the physical path of v5mysite.com.

Uploading IIS 10.0 websites to Nano Server

In this recipe, we are going to upload web pages to v5mysite.com. We will also create the index.htm and v5mysite.htm files with PowerShell commands.

Getting ready

To step through this recipe, you will need a Nano Server 2016 instance with the IIS package installed. For all this installation and configuration work, you should have administrative privileges.

How to do it...

1. Log in to Windows Server 2016. The IP of Windows Server 2016 is 172.16.15.60 and the name of the server is **WIN2016IIS**. Press *Windows + R* on your keyboard. You will get the **Run** window. We have to open PowerShell ISE with administrative rights, so type in the Run command window RunAs /user:Administrator PowerShell_ISE.exe and press **OK.**

2. Now it will ask you the administrator password for your Windows Server 2016 instance (not Nano Server). Type the administrator password and press *Enter*. You will get the PowerShell window.

3. Now we have to remote connect to Nano Server 2016 with the IP `172.16.15.63`. Run the command `Enter-PSSession -ComputerName "172.16.15.63" - Credential ~\Administrator`.

4. Now you will get a pop-up window for the Nano Server administrator account password. Enter the Nano Server administrator account password and press **OK** to log in. You have connected successfully. Now run the command `Import-module iisAdministration` in PowerShell and press *Enter*. You will get the PowerShell module imported.

5. We are going to copy `iisstart.htm` and `iisstart.png` from `C:\inetpub\wwwroot\` to v5mysite-new directory `c:\v5mysite-new`. Run `copy C:\inetpub\wwwroot\iisstart.htm C:\v5mysite-new""copy C:\inetpub\wwwroot\iisstart.png C:\v5mysite-new`, as shown here:

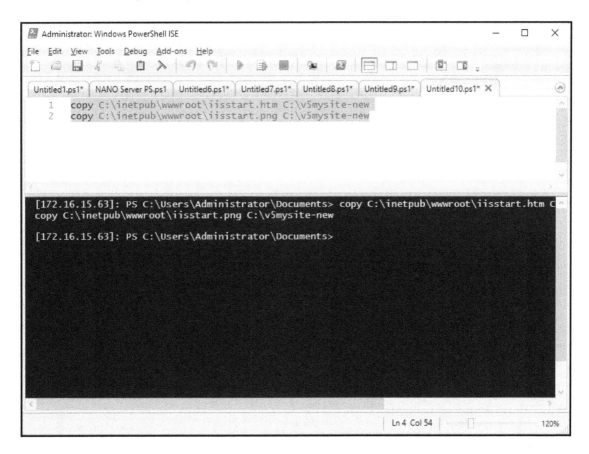

6. Write both the commands and run them. Now you have to check whether these files have been copied. Go to the `C:\v5mysite-new` folder:

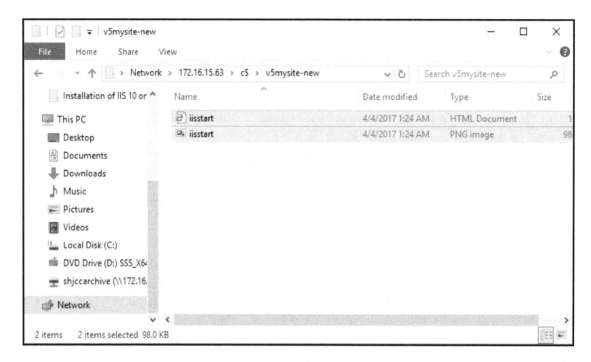

7. Here, you can see that both `iisstart.htm` and `iistart.png` have been copied. Now we have to create two more HTML files for testing. Run the following command:

```
Welcome to IIS on Nano Server by Ashraf Khan This is Index.htm page" | Out-
File -PSPath "c:\v5mysite-new\index.htm"
"Welcome to IIS on Nano Server by Ashraf Khan This is v5mysite.htm page " |
Out-File -PSPath "c:\v5mysite-new\v5mysite.htm
```

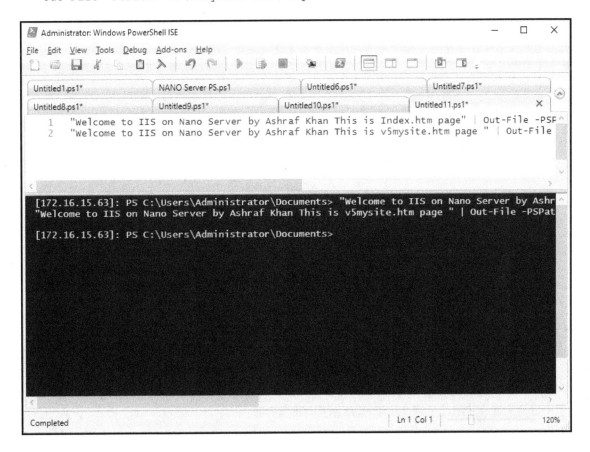

8. Run the commands one by one. Now let's check the `C:\v5mysite-new` folder:

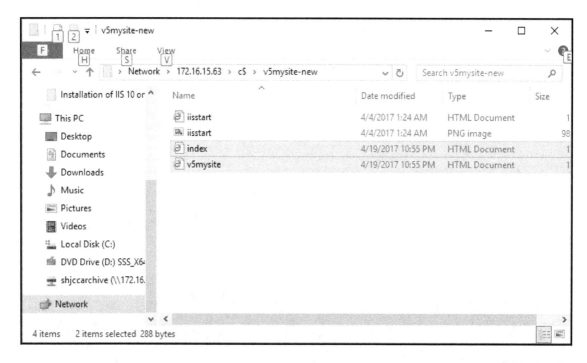

9. You can see the `C:\v5msite-new` folder has two more files created.

How it works....

In this recipe, we copied two website pages from `C:\inetpub\wwwroot` to `C:\v5mysite-new`, and we created two HTML files, `index.htm` and `v5mysite.htm`, with PowerShell commands.

Testing uploaded web pages

In this recipe, we are going to test the website v5mysite.com, which we've created and configured. We will create an Allow rule on Nano Server for port 8082 in the firewall, and we will set the default page to v5mysite.htm in the **Default Document** setting for the website v5mysite.com. We will browse v5mysite.com and verify the default page.

Getting ready

We are going to remotely connect to Nano Server through PowerShell and use the IISAdministrator module. You will need a Windows Server 2016 virtual or physical server for remote PowerShell management of Nano Server 2016. For all this installation and configuration work, you should have administrative privileges.

How to do it...

1. We have created the application pool NanoAPP and assigned it to the website v5mysite; we haven't yet made the ASP.Net configuration on IIS Server. We will test the application pool in the next chapter. Let's remove the entry of the application pool in v5mysite.

2. Log in to Windows Server 2016. The IP of Windows Server 2016 is `172.16.15.60` and the name of the server is **WIN2016IIS.** Press *Windows + R* on your keyboard, and you will get the **Run** window. Type the following address: `\\172.16.15.63\c$\Windows\System32\inetsrv\config`. When accessing the Nano Server IIS configuration folder, you will find the filename `ApplicationHost.config`, as shown here:

```
ApplicationHost - Notepad                                              —   □   ×
File  Edit  Format  View  Help
        <sites>
            <site name="Default Web Site" id="1">
                <application path="/">
                    <virtualDirectory path="/" physicalPath="%SystemDrive%\inetpub
\wwwroot"></virtualDirectory>
                </application>
                <bindings>
                    <binding protocol="http" bindingInformation="*:801:"></binding>
                </bindings>
            </site>
            <site name="nanosite.com" id="1607163939">
                <application path="/">
                    <virtualDirectory path="/" physicalPath="c:\inetpub\wwwroot
\nanosite"></virtualDirectory>
                </application>
                <bindings>
                    <binding protocol="http" bindingInformation="172.16.15.63:8081:"></binding>
                </bindings>
            </site>
            <site name="v5mysite" id="4">
                <application path="/">
                    <virtualDirectory path="/" physicalPath="C:\v5mysite" />
                </application>
                <bindings>
                    <binding protocol="http" bindingInformation="*:8082:" />
                </bindings>
            </site>
            <siteDefaults>
                <logFile logFormat="W3C" directory="%SystemDrive%\inetpub\logs\LogFiles"></logFile>
```

3. As shown in the screenshot, we removed the application name. Now you have to save the `ApplicationHost` file and close it. Let's open the PowerShell command prompt.

4. We have to open PowerShell ISE with administrative rights and run `RunAs /user:Administrator PowerShell_ISE.exe` in the **Run** command window. Now it will ask you the administrator password for your Windows Server 2016 instance (not Nano Server). Type the administrator password and press *Enter*. The PowerShell window will open.

5. Now we have to remotely connect to Nano Server 2016 on `172.16.15.63`. Run the following command: `Enter-PSSession -ComputerName "172.16.15.63" -Credential ~\Administrator`

6. Now you will get a pop-up window for the Nano Server administrator account password. Enter the Nano Server administrator password and press **OK** to log in. Now you have connected successfully.

7. Write the command `Import-module iisAdministration` in PowerShell and press *Enter*. You will get the PowerShell module imported. You have successfully finished the remote connection setup and imported the PowerShell module to Nano Server IIS.

8. You know that we have created a website called `v5mysite` with the default port number `8082`. If we try to open `v5mysite`, it will not open because the Nano Server default allowed IIS ports are 80 and `443`. So we have to first open the firewall port for `v5mysite`. Run the following command in PowerShell:

```
New-NetFirewallRule -DisplayName "Allow Inbound Port 8082" -Direction
Inbound -LocalPort 8082 -Protocol TCP -Action Allow
```

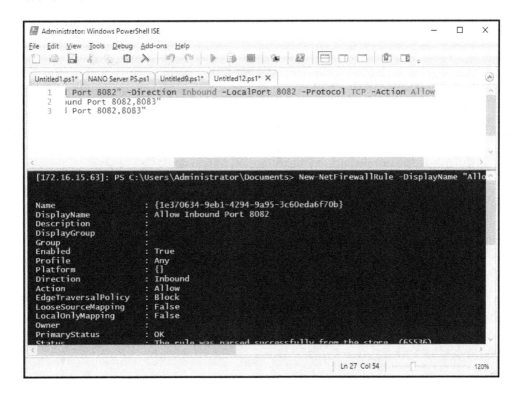

9. We've created a firewall rule called `Allow Inbound Port 8082`.

10. Open Internet Explorer and type the URL `http://172.16.15.63:8082/`, as shown here:

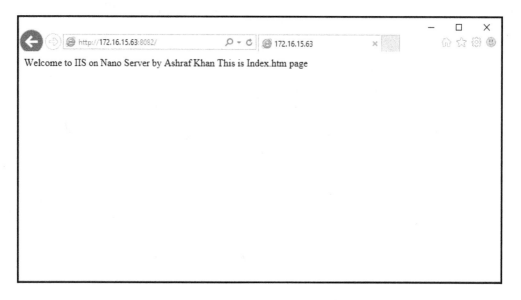

11. As you can see in the screenshot, we get the webpage `index.htm` as the default page of `v5mysite`. Now we have to set up the **Default Document** to access the default page, `v5mysite.htm`.

12. We have to remove the existing default document entry `v5mysite.htm`, which we made earlier, in order to remove the existing default document filename. Type the following command in PowerShell:

```
"Get-IISConfigSection -SectionPath "system.webServer/defaultDocument" |
Get-IISConfigCollection -CollectionName "files" | Remove-
IISConfigCollectionElement -ConfigAttribute @{value = "v5mysite.htm"}",
```

Once we run this command, a confirmation popup window will appear, as shown here:

13. Click on **Yes.** Now you have to create a new entry for v5mysite.htm in the **Default Document** settings. Type the following command in PowerShell:

```
Get-IISConfigSection -SectionPath "system.webServer/defaultDocument" | Get-
IISConfigCollection -CollectionName "files" | New-
IISConfigCollectionElement  -ConfigAttribute @{Value = "v5mysite.htm"} -
AddAt 0
```

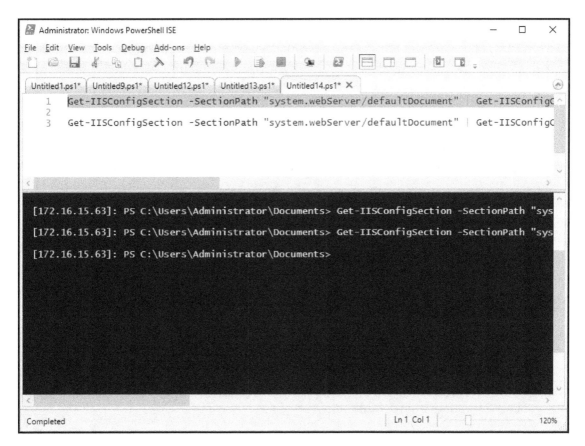

14. Let's test the website `v5mysite.com` and check the default page. Open Internet Explorer and type the URL `http://172.16.15.63:8082/`:

15. Here you can see that the website opens the default page, `v5mysite.htm`.

How it works...

In this recipe, we tested the website `v5mysite.com`, which we created and configured. We created an Allow rule on Nano Server for port `8082` in the firewall. We set up the **Default Document** settings for the default page `v5mysite.htm` of website `v5mysite.com`, and we made the default page entry for `v5mysite.htm` at the top. We browsed the website `v5mysite.com` and saw the default page.

9
Enabling ASP.NET Core with IIS on Nano Server

In this chapter, we will cover the following recipes:

- Understanding ASP.NET Core with IIS on Nano Server
- Configuring ASP.NET Core with IIS on Nano Server
- Creating an IIS 10.0 virtual directory on Nano Server
- Configuring a virtual directory in IIS 10.0
- Uploading and testing web pages in a virtual directory

Introduction

ASP.NET Core is an open source and cross-platform framework that runs on any operating system with or without an ASP.NET application pool (framework). It helps us develop and publish web-based applications independent of platforms such as macOS, Linux, or Windows Server Core. ASP.NET Core is also known as ASP.NET 5. Nano Server 2016 targets ASP.NET Core.

Once we start developing an ASP.NET Core application and publish it, it will automatically copy the all the required runtime DLLs and other files to the web application publish directory so that the core web application runs independently without requiring any framework on IIS Server.

ASP.NET 2.0 will not run on Nano.

Understanding ASP.NET Core with IIS on Nano Server

In this recipe, we will create an ASP.NET Core website application and run it on Visual Studio 2017.

Getting ready

To step through this recipe, you need Visual Studio 2017 set up. For all the installation and configuration work, you should have administrative privileges.

How to do it...

1. Log in to your Windows 10 PC or Windows Server 2016. We've already installed Visual Studio for testing, so open it.
2. Open the **File** menu, create a new project, and select **.Net Core** and application type **ASP.NET Core Web Application (.NET Core)**, as shown here:

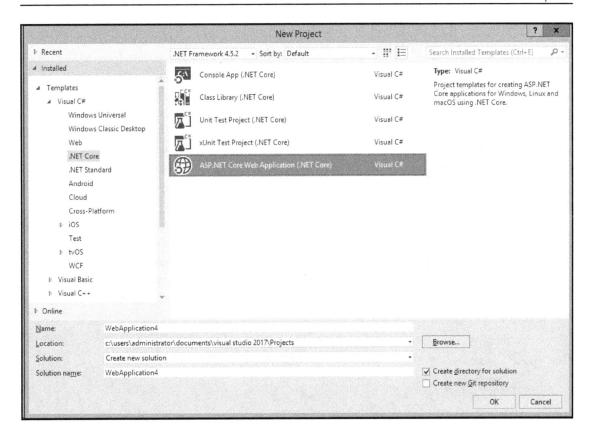

3. Click on the **OK** button. You will get a New ASP.NET Core window to select the type of ASP.NET Core application, as shown here:

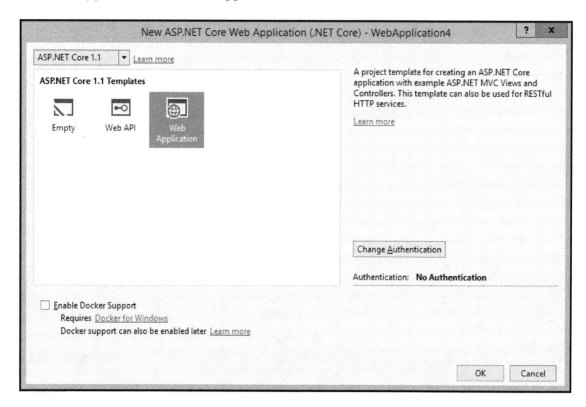

4. Now select the **Web Application** option and click on **OK**. You'll have the default ASP.NET web application created. This is just for demonstration to show you how an ASP.NET web application looks.

5. Now let's run the created project on Visual Studio 2017, and you will get the web application page, as shown in the following screenshot.

To run an application from Visual Studio, click on the "play" sign in the toolbar at the top or hit *F5*.

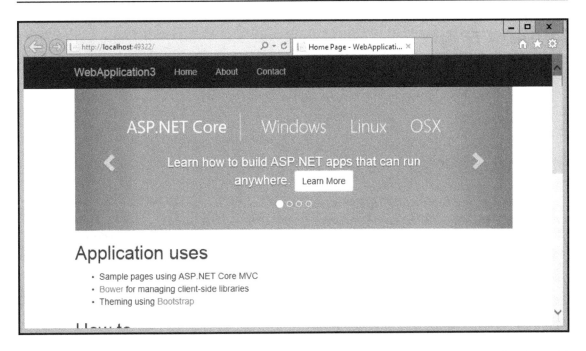

6. You can now see the default sample application, which we created with ASP.NET core.

How it works...

In this recipe, we logged in to Windows Server 2016 and opened the Visual Studio 2017 software. We also created the ASP.NET Core website application and ran it on Visual Studio 2017.

Configuring ASP.NET Core with IIS on Nano Server

In this recipe, we will install `HttpPlatformHandler` on the **WIN2016IIS** server (this is the physical server) and configure `httpPlatformHandler.dll` and `httpplatform_schema.xml` from **WIN2016IIS** to Nano Server. We will configure our ASP.NET Core application on Nano Server. We will connect Nano Server remotely through PowerShell and manage IIS over the `IISAdministrator` module and Nano Server.

Getting ready

To step through this recipe, you will need a Windows Server 2016 virtual or physical server for remote PowerShell management and installation of ASP.NET Core on Nano Server 2016. For all this installation and configuration work, you should have administrative privileges.

How to do it...

1. Log in to the **WIN2016IIS** server (this is not Nano Server, but a normal server). Open Internet Explorer and type in the address bar `http://www.iis.net/downlo ads/microsoft/httpplatformhandler` to download **HttpPlatformHandler x64**, as shown here:

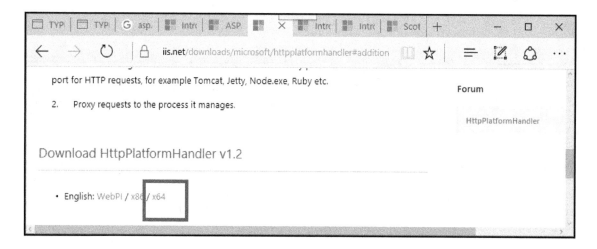

2. Click on the selected link, and it will start downloading **HttpPlatformHandler**.

3. Run **HttpPlatformHandler** on WIN2016IIS. You will get the installation page of **HttpPlatformHandler**, as shown here:

4. Click on **Next**, follow the default steps, and finish the installation of **HttpPlatformHandler**.

5. On the WIN2016IIS server, go to `C:\Windows\System32\inetsrv`, find `httpPlatformHandler.dll`, and copy it to the desktop of the **WIN2016IIS** server. I have created a folder named `ASP Net core\ASP.net`, and I will paste `httpPlatformHandler.dll` in it. Now, go to `C:\Windows\System32\inetsrv\config\schema` and copy `httpplatform_schema.xml` to `Asp Net core\ASP.net`, as shown here:

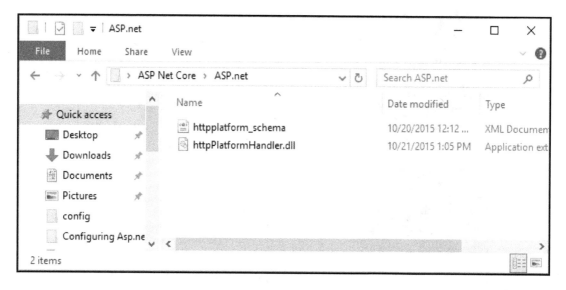

6. As shown in the screenshot, we have copied the `httpplatform_schema.xml` and `httpPlatformHandler.dll` files.

7. Copy `httpPlatformHandler.dll` from `ASP Net Core\ASP.net`, remotely access the Nano Server location `\\172.16.15.63\c$\Windows\System32\inetsrv\`, and paste it, as shown here:

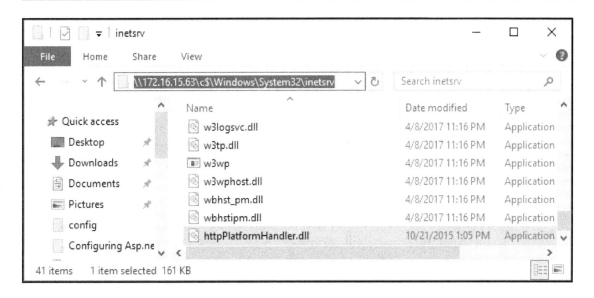

8. Copy `httpplatform_schema.xml` from `ASP Net Core\asp.net`, remotely access the Nano Server location `\\172.16.15.63\c$\Windows\System32\inetsrv\config\schema`, and paste it.

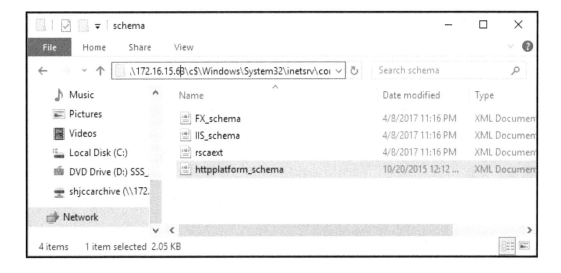

8. Log in to Windows Server 2016. The IP is `172.16.15.60` and the name of the server is **WIN2016IIS.** Press *Windows + R* on your keyboard, and you will get the *Run* window. Open PowerShell ISE with administrative rights, type in the **Run** command window
`RunAs /user:Administrator PowerShell_ISE.exe`, and press **OK.**

In this command, `Administrator` is the username for that machine; you can use any username that has administrator rights to perform the given task.

9. Now it will ask you the administrator password for your Windows Server 2016 (not Nano Server) instance. Type the administrator password and press *Enter.* You will get the PowerShell window.

10. Now you have to remotely connect to Nano Server 2016 at `172.16.15.63`. Run the command `Enter-PSSession -ComputerName "172.16.15.63" - Credential ~\Administrator`.
Now you will get a popup window for the Nano Server administrator account password. Enter the password and press **OK** to log in. You have now connected successfully. Write `Import-module iisAdministration` and press *Enter.* This will import the PowerShell module.

11. Now you need to install the Reverse Forwarders packages, which you created in the `Packages` folder in the Nano Server `C:\` drive, and copy the Nano Server Packages, as shown here:

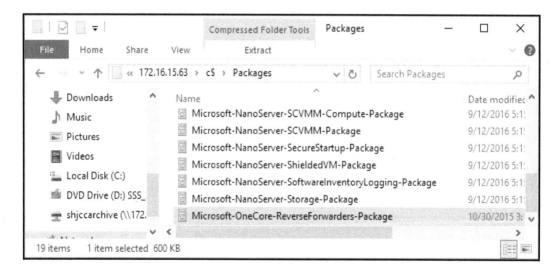

12. Type the
    `dism/online/addpackage/packagepath:c:\packages\Microsoft-OneCore-ReverseForwarders-Package.cab` and `dism /online /add-package /packagepath:c:\packages\en-us\Microsoft-OneCore-ReverseForwarders-Package.cab` DISM commands and run them, as shown here:

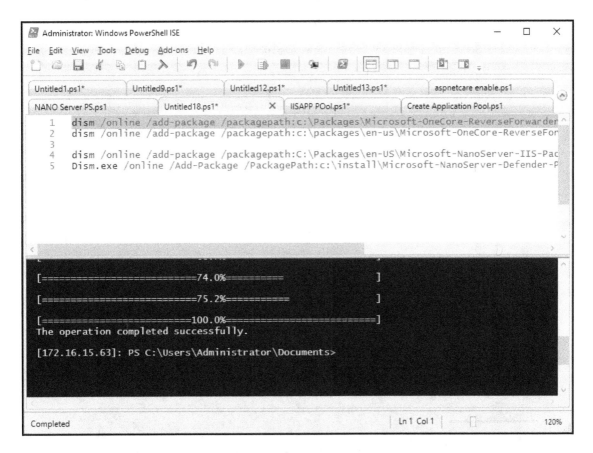

13. Let's move on to configuring ASP.NET Core. We have already copied the required DLL and XML files. Type the following commands in PowerShell:

```
$sm = Get-IISServerManager
$sm.GetApplicationHostConfiguration()
.RootSectionGroup.Sections.Add("appSettings")
$appHostconfig =
$sm.GetApplicationHostConfiguration()
$section =
```

```
$appHostconfig.GetSection
("system.webServer/handlers")
$section.OverrideMode="Allow"
$sectionHttpPlatform =
$appHostConfig.RootSectionGroup.SectionGroups
["system.webServer"].Sections.Add("httpPlatform")
$sectionHttpPlatform.OverrideModeDefault = "Allow"
$globalModules = Get-IISConfigSection
"system.webServer/globalModules" | Get-
IISConfigCollection
New-IISConfigCollectionElement $globalModules -
ConfigAttribute
@{"name"="httpPlatformHandler";
"image"="%SystemRoot%\system32\inetsrv\
 httpPlatformHandler.dll"}
 $modules = Get-IISConfigSection
"system.webServer/modules" | Get-IISConfigCollection
New-IISConfigCollectionElement
$modules -ConfigAttribute
@{"name"="httpPlatformHandler"}$sm.CommitChanges()
```

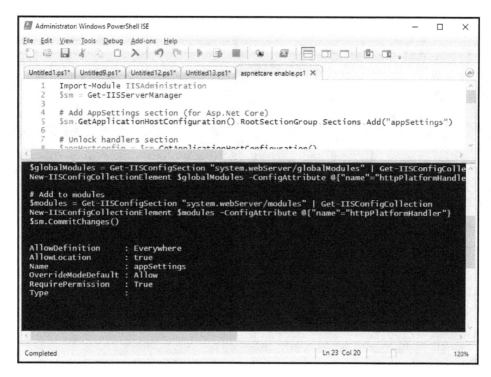

14. You can see in the screenshot that we've configured the required steps to run ASP.NET Core on Nano Server. However, you have to do a few more things in your core application and publish the code with the DNU publish command. You can find out more at `https://blogs.iis.net/davidso/nano/aspnet`.

How it works...

In this recipe, we installed HttpPlatformHandler on the WIN2016IIS server (physical server, not Nano Server). We then copied `httpPlatformHandler.dll` and `httpplatform_schema.xml` from WIN2016IIS and pasted them to Nano Server. We configured `httpPlatformHandler.dll` and `httpplatform_schema.xml` on Nano Server through PowerShell. We also configured the `ReverseForwarders` package on Nano Server.

Creating an IIS 10.0 virtual directory on Nano Server

In this recipe, we will create a website named `NanoAspnet`. We will create a virtual directory inside the website called `NanoAspnet`. We will then remotely connect to Nano Server using PowerShell and manage IIS using the `IISAdministrator` module and Nano Server.

Getting ready

To step through this recipe, you will need a Windows Server 2016 virtual or physical server for remote PowerShell management and creating the virtual directory on Nano Server 2016. For all this installation and configuration work, you should have administrative privileges.

How to do it...

1. Log in to Windows Server 2016. The IP is `172.16.15.60` and the name of the server is **WIN2016IIS**. Press *Windows + R*. You will get the **Run** window. Open PowerShell ISE with administrative rights, type `RunAs /user:Administrator PowerShell_ISE.exe`, and press **OK**.

2. Now it will ask you the administrator password for your Windows Server 2016 (not Nano Server) machine. Type it and press *Enter*. You will get the PowerShell window.

3. Now we have to remotely connect to Nano Server 2016 at IP `172.16.15.63`. Run the command `Enter-PSSession -ComputerName "172.16.15.63" - Credential ~\Administrator`. Now you will get a popup window for the Nano Server administrator account password. Enter the Nano Server administrator account password and press **OK** to log in. You have connected successfully. Now write the command `Import-module iisAdministration` and press *Enter*. This will import the PowerShell module.

4. Now let's create a website called `NanoAspnet`. Type `New-IISSite -Name "NanoAspNet" -PhysicalPath c:\inetpub\wwwroot - BindingInformation "*:8000:"` and run it. The website will be created.

5. Now let's check whether `NanoAspnet` has been created or not. Type `Get-IISsite`, as shown here:

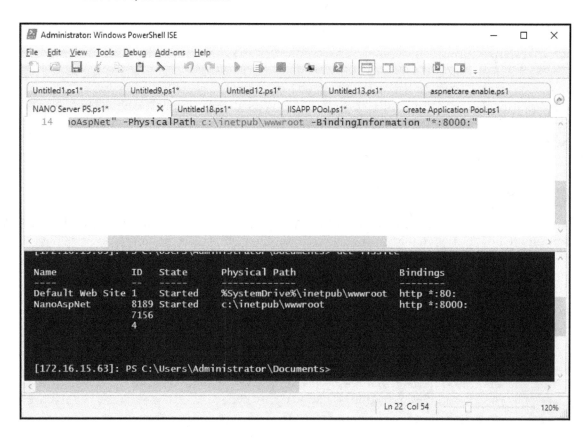

6. You can see from the screenshot that we have created the
   website `NanoAspNet` with port `8000`. Now let's create the virtual directory
   `MyApp` on `NanoAspNet`. First, we have to create a physical directory (folder on
   Nano Server) that we can use for the virtual directory. We create a directory
   called `MyApp` under `C:\inetpub\wwwroot`, as shown here:

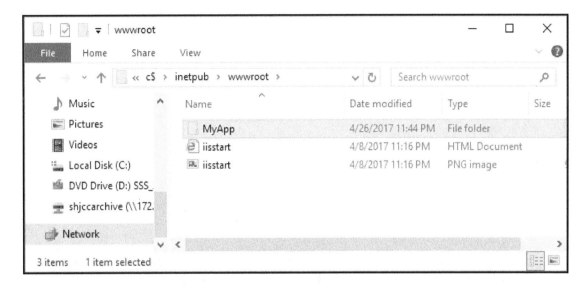

7. Now open PowerShell, which is already connected with our Nano Server instance, and type the following command to create a virtual directory:

```
$manager = Get-IISServerManager $app =
$manager.Sites["NanoAspNet"].Applications.Add
("/MyApp",
"c:\inetpub\wwwroot\MyApp") $manager.CommitChanges()
```

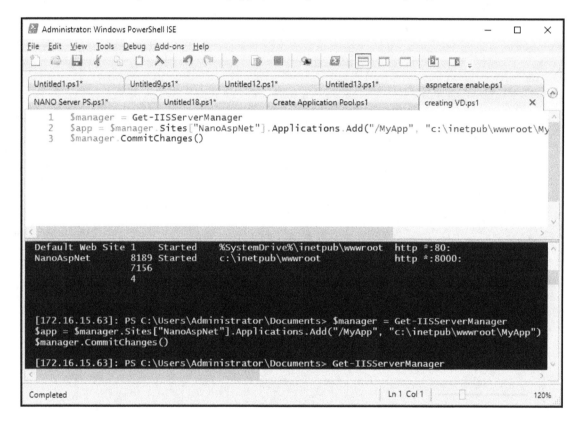

8. You have successfully created the MyApp virtual directory for NanoAspNet.

How it works...

In this recipe, we remotely connected PowerShell with Nano Server to manage IIS over the IISAdministrator module. We used a Windows Server 2016 virtual/physical server instance for remote PowerShell management and creating a virtual directory on Nano Server 2016. We also created a website named `NanoAspnet` and created a virtual directory `MyApp` inside `NanoAspNet`.

Configuring a virtual directory in IIS 10.0

In this recipe, we will create an application pool and assign it to our virtual directory, `MyApp`. We will create a firewall rule to allow inbound port `8000` for `NanoAspNet`.

Getting ready

To step through this recipe, you will need a Windows Server 2016 virtual or physical server for remote PowerShell management and configuring a virtual directory on Nano Server 2016. For all this installation and configuration, you should have administrative privileges.

How to do it...

1. Log in to Windows Server 2016. The IP is `172.16.15.60` and the name **WIN2016IIS**. Press *Windows + R* key. You will get the **Run** window. Open PowerShell ISE with administrative rights: type `RunAs /user:Administrator PowerShell_ISE.exe` and press **OK**.

2. Now, it will ask you the administrator password for your Windows Server 2016 (not Nano Server) machine. Type the password and press *Enter*. You will get the PowerShell window.

3. Now you need to remotely connect to Nano Server 2016 using the IP `172.16.15.63`. Write the command `Enter-PSSession -ComputerName "172.16.15.63" -Credential ~\Administrator`. You will get a popup window for the Nano Server administrator account password. Enter the password and press **OK**. You'll have connected successfully. Now you have to write `Import-module iisAdministration` and press *Enter*. This will import the PowerShell module.

4. Type the command `$sm = Get-IISServerManager`
   `$sm.ApplicationPools.Add("NanoAppPool")` to create the application pool
   `NanoAppPool`, as shown here:

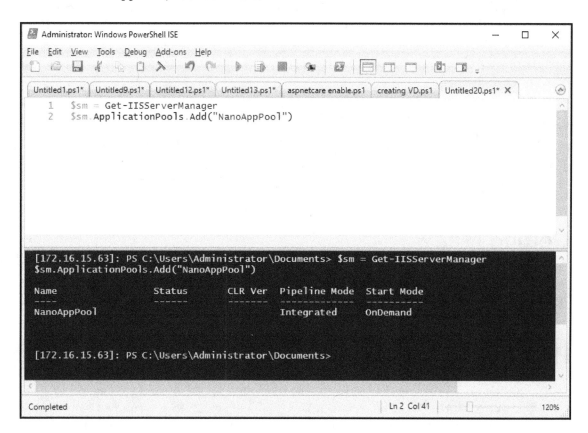

5. We have now created the `NanoAppPool` application pool. Let's move to assigning `NanoAppPool` to the `MyApp` virtual directory. Type the following command:

```
$manager = Get-IISServerManager
$website = $manager.Sites["NanoAspNet"]
$website.Applications["/MyApp"].ApplicationPoolName
= "NanoAppPool"$manager.CommitChanges()
```

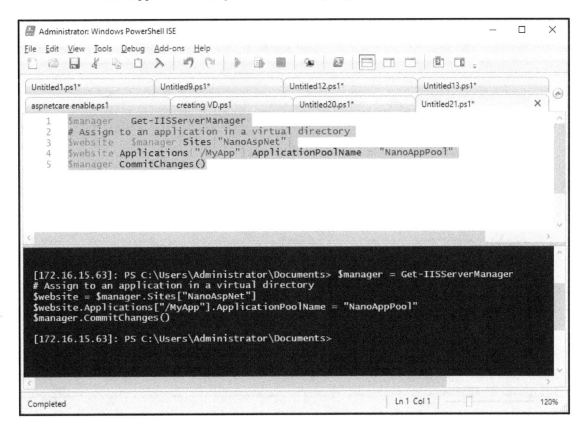

6. Let's check whether this command was successful. Access Nano Server remotely at \\172.16.15.63\c$\Windows\System32\inetsrv\config. Inside the config folder, you will get the ApplicationHost.config file. Open ApplicationHost.config and search the MyApp virtual directory, as shown here:

```
ApplicationHost - Notepad                                                    —   □   ×
File  Edit  Format  View  Help
        </log>

        <sites>
            <site name="Default Web Site" id="1">
                <application path="/">
                    <virtualDirectory path="/" physicalPath="%SystemDrive%\inetpub
\wwwroot"></virtualDirectory>
                </application>
                <bindings>
                    <binding protocol="http" bindingInformation="*:80:"></binding>
                </bindings>
            </site>
            <site name="NanoAspNet" id="818971564">
                <application path="/">
                    <virtualDirectory path="/" physicalPath="c:\inetpub\wwwroot" />
                </application>
                <application path="/MyApp" applicationPool="NanoAppPool">
                    <virtualDirectory path="/" physicalPath="c:\inetpub\wwwroot\MyApp" />
                </application>
                <bindings>
                    <binding protocol="http" bindingInformation="*:8000:" />
                </bindings>
            </site>
            <siteDefaults>
                <logFile logFormat="W3C" directory="%SystemDrive%\inetpub\logs\LogFiles"></logFile>
                <traceFailedRequestsLogging directory="%SystemDrive%\inetpub\logs
\FailedReqLogFiles"></traceFailedRequestsLogging>
            </siteDefaults>
            <applicationDefaults applicationPool="DefaultAppPool"></applicationDefaults>
```

7. Here you can see NanoAspNet website with a virtual directory MyApp and virtual directory application pool NanoAppPool.

8. We have to open the firewall port 8000 (by default, Nano Server allows IIS ports 80 and 443). Type the command New-NetFirewallRule -DisplayName "Allow Inbound Port 8000" -Direction Inbound -LocalPort 8000 - Protocol TCP -Action Allow, as shown here:

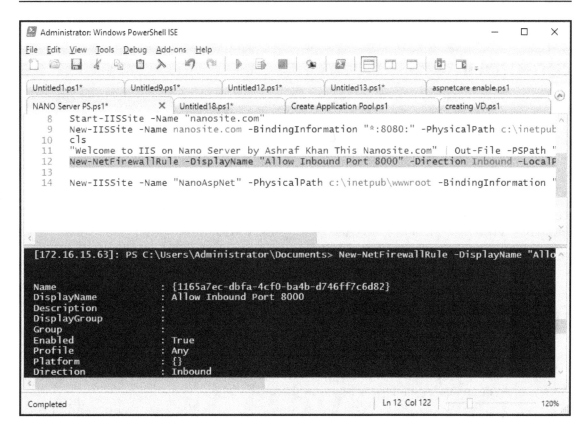

9. As you can see, the firewall allows port `8000`, and the rule has been created.

How it works...

In this recipe, we created the application pool `NanoAppPool` and assigned the application pool to `MyApp`. We checked the `MyApp` application pool, `NanoAppPool`, to the `ApplicationHost.config` file. We also created a firewall rule to allow inbound port `8000` for website `NanoAspNet`.

Uploading and testing web pages in a virtual directory

In this recipe, we will log in to Nano Server remotely. We will use PowerShell and check our created sites. We will access the Nano Server C$ share to upload our web pages. We will test the `NanoAspNet` website on port `8000` and also test the `MyApp` virtual directory.

Getting ready

To step through this recipe, you will need a Windows Server 2016 virtual or physical server for remote PowerShell management and configuring virtual directory on Nano Server 2016. For all this installation and configuration work, you should have administrative privileges.

How do to it...

1. Log in to Windows Server 2016. The IP is `172.16.15.60` and the name of the server is **WIN2016IIS.** Press *Windows + R*. You will get the **Run** window. We have to open PowerShell ISE with administrative rights. Type `RunAs /user:Administrator PowerShell_ISE.exe` in the **Run** window and press **OK.**

2. Now it will ask you the administrator password for your Windows Server 2016 (not Nano Server) machine. Type the password and press *Enter*. You will get the PowerShell window.

3. Now you have to remotely connect to Nano Server 2016 using the IP `172.16.15.63`. Run the following command in PowerShell:

   ```
   "Enter-PSSession -ComputerName "172.16.15.63" -
   Credential ~\Administrator"
   ```

4. Now you will get a popup window for the Nano Server administrator account password. Enter the password and press **OK** to log in. You'll have connected successfully.

5. Now run `Import-module iisAdministration` in PowerShell and press
   Enter. This will import the `IISAdministration` PowerShell module.

6. Run the command `Get-IISSite` on the remote-connected PowerShell window,
   as shown here:

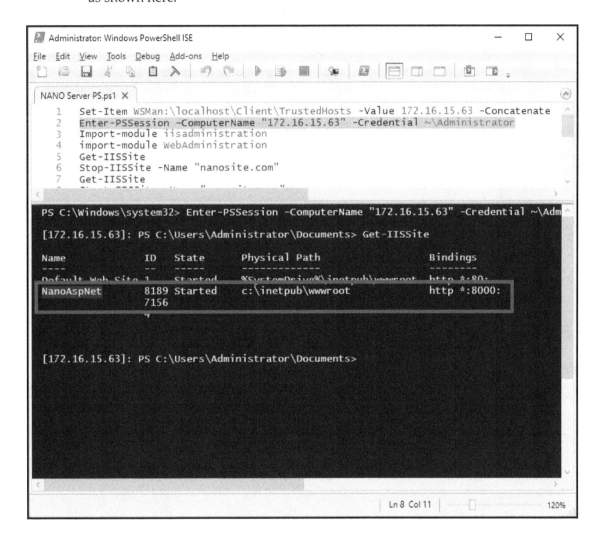

7. You can see here that we get a list of websites that we've already created in Nano Server. Let's upload the HTML web pages, which are already available.

8. Go to Windows Server 2016, Open the **Run** window, and type the UNC path of Nano Server, \\172.16.15.63\c$\inetpub\wwwroot, and press **OK**. You will get the username/password window of Nano Server. Provide the username and password and press **OK**. Now you will get the wwwroot folder of Nano Server, as shown here:

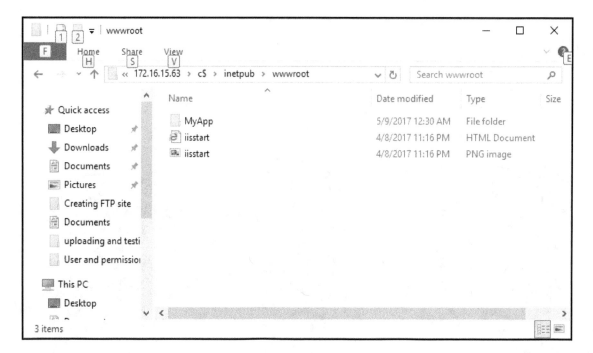

9. Inside the wwwroot folder, we have the MyApp virtual directory folder and the IISstart.htm and iisstart.png files. The iisstart files are used for NanoAspNet at http://172.16.1563:8000. Open the MyApp folder, as shown here:

10. You can see in the `MyApp` virtual directory folder that we have a file called `index.htm`:

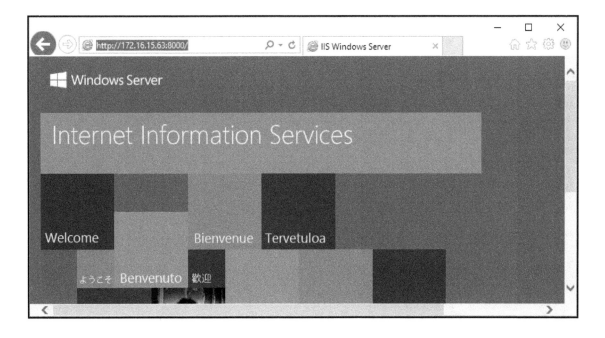

11. Let's open the virtual directory on Nano Server and browse
    to `http://172.16.15.63:8000/MyApp,` as shown here:

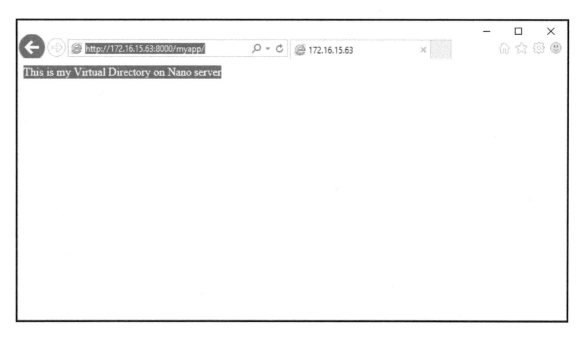

12. You can see that we get access to the virtual directory's content.

How it works...

In this recipe, we logged on to Nano Server remotely using PowerShell. We used
PowerShell to check our created sites and access the Nano Server C$ share to upload
our web pages. We tested `NanoAspNet` on port `8000`, and we tested the `MyApp` virtual
directory.

10
Installing and Configuring SSL Websites

In this chapter, we will cover the following recipes:

- Understanding SSL websites in IIS 10.0
- Installing SSL
- Creating an SSL certificate
- Configuring websites with an SSL port and certificate
- Using PowerShell commands to create SSL certificates
- Testing SSL websites

Introduction

We can build a secure infrastructure based on public-key cryptography using digital certificates with technologies such as Secure Sockets Layer (SSL).

We need two things to publish a secure website or web application:

1. HTTPS (secure) port 443
2. SSL certificate

HTTPS is a secure communications channel that is used to exchange information between a client computer and a server. It uses SSL.

To enable SSL in IIS, you must first create a certificate that is used to encrypt and decrypt the information that is transferred over the network. IIS includes its own certificate request tool that you can use to send a certificate request to a certification authority. This tool simplifies the process of obtaining a certificate.

Understanding SSL websites in IIS 10.0

In this recipe, we will open some HTTPS websites and check their SSL certificates.

Getting ready

To step through this recipe, you will need a computer and an internet connection.

How to do it...

1. Open Internet Explorer on Windows Server 2016 or Windows 10; here, we are using Windows Server 2016.
2. Go to the address bar and type `https://www.microsoft.com/en-gulf/`, as shown here:

3. At the end of the address bar, there is a padlock symbol that tells us that the website `https://www.microsoft.com/en-gulf/` is a secure website. Let's click on it and see the details:

4. You can see that **VeriSign** has identified this site as `www.microsoft.com`. Click on **View certificate**, and you will get the certificate's properties:

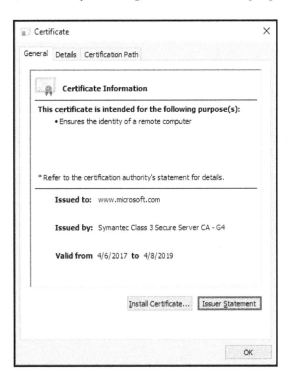

How it works...

In this recipe, we checked `www.microsoft.com` and saw it uses **Hyper Text Transfer Protocol Secure** (**HTTPS**). We also checked the SSL certificate of the website. Finally, we opened the certificate properties and saw the details of the website and certificate provider.

Installing SSL

In this recipe, we are going to open IIS Manager on the WIN2016IIS server and create a certificate request. We will also see how we can import a third-party SSL certificate.

Getting ready

To step through this recipe, we are going to create an SSL certificate request for a certificate provider. Also, we will see how we can import/install the certificate on IIS. You will need a running IIS 10.0 server and an administrator account, which will be used to make changes to IIS 10.0.

How to do it...

1. Go to **WIN2016IIS** and log in to IIS 10.0 Server. Open Server Manager and go to the **Tools** menu.
2. Open IIS Manager and click on the **WIN2016IIS** IIS server, as shown here:

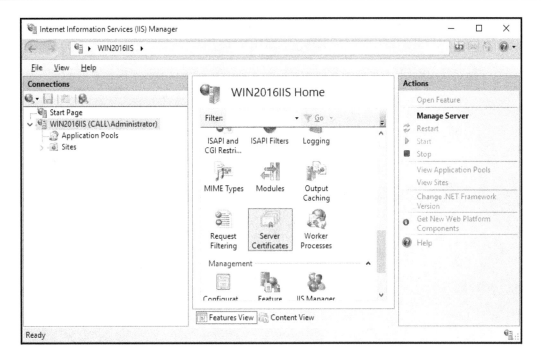

4. In the **Features** view, there is a **Server Certificates** option. Open the server
   certificate, as shown here:

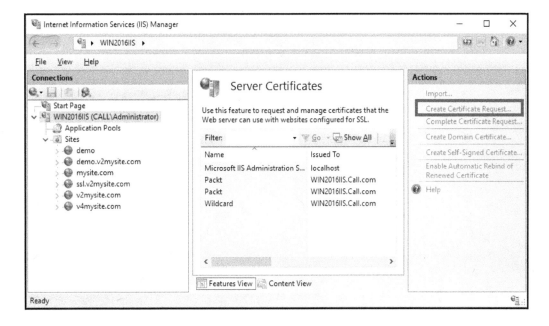

5. Go to the **Actions** pane. You can see that there is a **Create Certificate Request** option available. Click on **Create Certificate Request**, and the **Request Certificate** window will open. You have to fill in the details, as shown here:

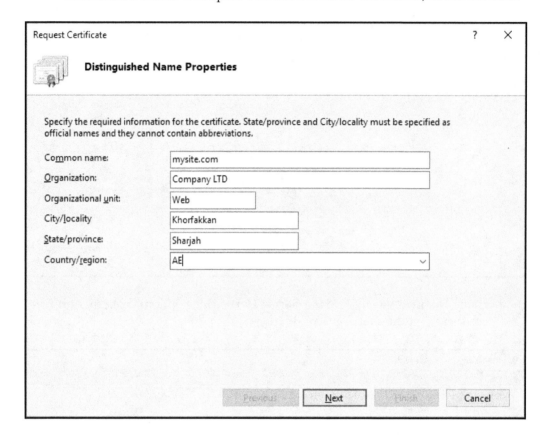

6. Here you can fill the **Common name** (website name), **Organization**, **Organizational unit** (department), **Address**, and **Country** code. Click on **Next**. You will get the **Cryptographic Service Provider Properties** window:

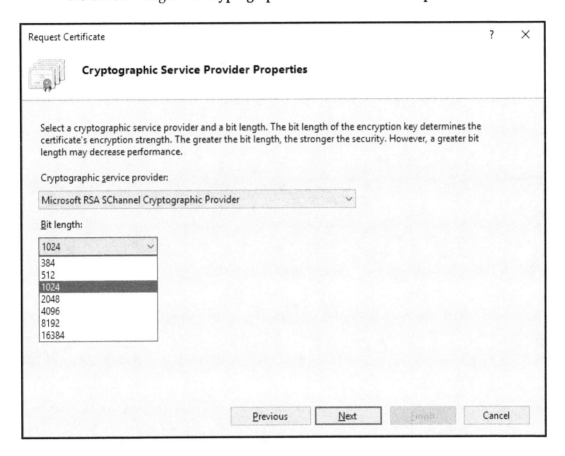

7. Select the **Bit length** of encryption you need. In my case, I have selected **1024**. Click on **Next.** Now you have to provide the local path and filename where you want to store the certificate request file:

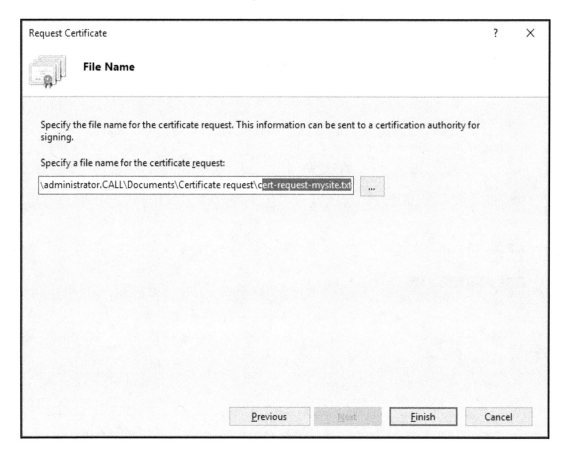

8. We are storing our certificate request file in the `administrator.CALL\Documents\Certificate request` folder and the filename is `cert-request-mysite.txt`. Click on **Finish**.

9. Let's open the `cert-request-mysite.txt` file:

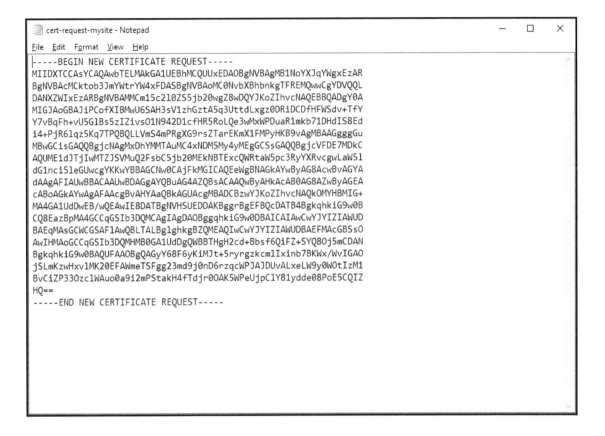

10. You can see we have the certificate request created in encrypted format. Now you can send the file to a certificate authority to buy an SSL certificate.

11. Now let's see how to import the certificate that we have purchased or generated.

12. Open IIS Manager and click on the **WIN2016IIS** IIS server. Go to the **Actions** pane and click on **Import Certificate**:

13. Now that you have the .pfx certificate, you can browse it and provide the password. You can also select the certificate store type: **Personal** or **Web Hosting**. Click on **OK**.

14. You can import the .cer type certificate; in the IIS server **Actions** pane, click on **Complete Certificate Request**, as shown here:

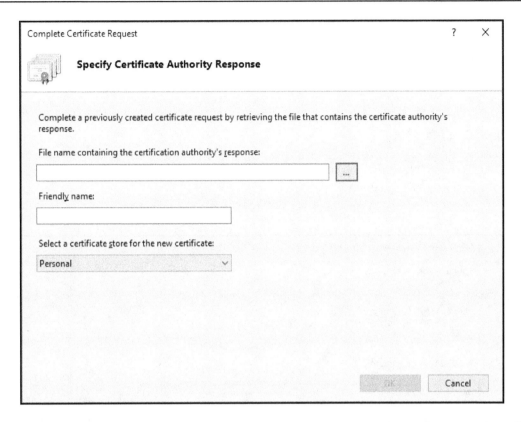

15. Go to the local path of the certificate where you've stored it and give it a friendly name for identification purposes. Select the type--**Personal** or **Web Hosting**--and click on **OK**.

How it works...

In this recipe, we opened IIS Manager on WIN2016IIS and created a certificate request to buy a third-party certificate. We also reviewed how we can import the third-party SSL certificate.

Creating an SSL certificate

In this recipe, we are going to open IIS Manager WIN2016IIS and create an SSL certificate on the local server WIN2016IIS.

Getting ready

To step through this recipe, you will need a running IIS 10.0 server and an administrator account, which will be used to make changes in IIS 10.0.

How to do it...

1. Go to **WIN2016IIS** and log in to the IIS 10.0 server. Open the Server Manager, and go to the **Tools** menu.
2. Open IIS Manager and click on **WIN2016IIS**, as shown here:

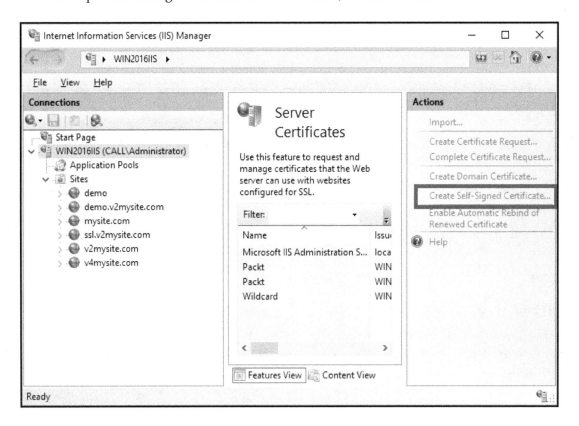

3. Go to the **Actions** pane and click on **Create Self-Signed Certificate**. We are using this only for testing purposes. This local server certificate is not valid for the internet. Now the **Create Self-Signed Certificate** window will open, as shown here:

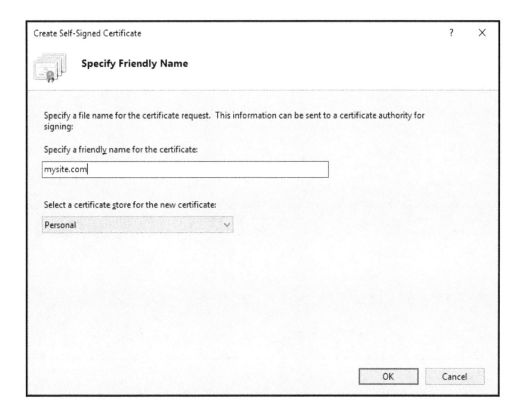

4. Here you can type a friendly name that you can use to easily identify the certificate. You can select the **Personal** or **Web Hosting** certificate store type; we'll select **Personal**. Click on **OK**. Now the certificate has been created, as shown here:

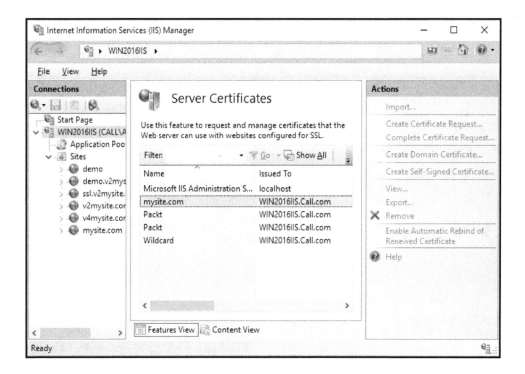

How it works...

In this recipe, we opened IIS Manager on WIN2016IIS. We also created an SSL self-signed certificate on WIN2016IIS with the Personal option.

Configuring websites with an SSL port and certificate

In this recipe, we are going to open IIS Manager on WIN2016IIS. We will also configure the SSL certificate on `mysite.com`.

Getting ready

To step through this recipe, you will need a running IIS 10.0 server and an administrator account, which will be used to make changes in IIS 10.0.

How to do it...

1. Go to WIN2016IIS and log in to the IIS 10.0 server. Open the server manager and go to the **Tools** menu.

2. Open IIS Manager and expand **WIN2016IIS**; you will get the **Application Pools** and **Sites**. Click on **Sites**, as shown here:

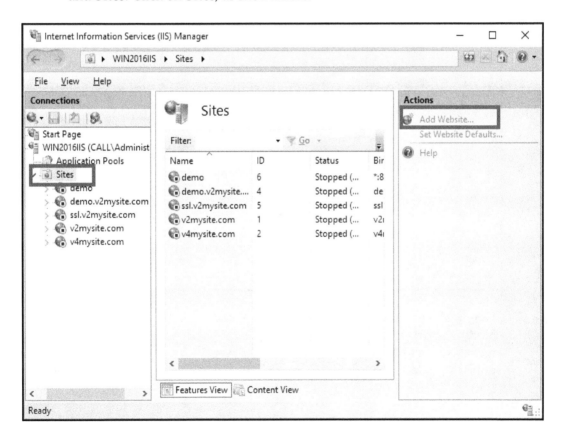

3. Go to the **Actions** pane and click on **Add Website.** You will get the **Add Website** window:

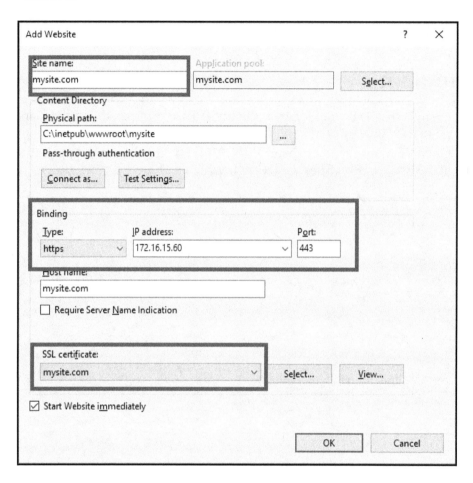

4. Here we'll enter the site name `mysite.com` and select the **Physical path**. In the binding information, we've selected `https` (SSL will not run on the `http` port; it must be `https`). Type the IP address of the website, and enter the HTTPS default port, `443`. Select the `mysite.com` certificate, which we created earlier. Click on **OK**.

5. Now you can see that the website has been created:

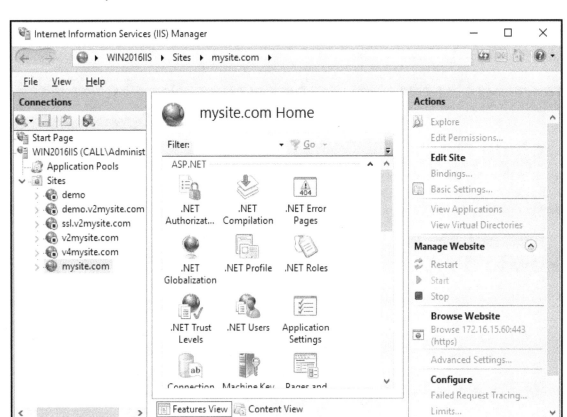

6. Go to the **Actions** pane, and in the the **Browse Website** section, there will be a link to **Browse 172.16.15.60:443 (https)**.

7. If you want to assign the certificate to an existing website, you can add a binding for the HTTPS protocol and select the certificate you've created or imported.

How it works...

In this recipe, we opened IIS Manager on WIN2016IIS, created the website `mysite.com`, added binding information for the HTTPS protocol, and configured the SSL certificate called `mysite.com`, which we'd created earlier.

Using PowerShell commands to create SSL certificates

In this recipe, we are going to open IIS Manager on WIN2016IIS. We will open PowerShell and create an SSL certificate called v3mysite.com. We will also verify that the certificate has been created through IIS Manager.

Getting ready

To step through this recipe, we are going to create an SSL certificate for v3mysite.com. We will use PowerShell to create a self-signed certificate. You will need a running IIS 10.0 server and an administrator account to make changes in IIS 10.0.

How to do it...

1. Log in to Windows Server 2016. The IP is `172.16.15.60` and the name of the server is **WIN2016IIS**.
2. Press *Windows + R*. You will get the Run window. Open PowerShell ISE with administrative rights, type `RunAs /user:Administrator PowerShell_ISE.exe` in the run command window, and press **OK**.
3. Now it will ask you for the administrator password of server **WIN2916IIS**. Type the administrator password and press **Enter**. The PowerShell window will open. Now you have to type `New-SelfSignedCertificate -DnsName v3mysite.com -CertStoreLocation cert:\LocalMachine\My`, as shown here:

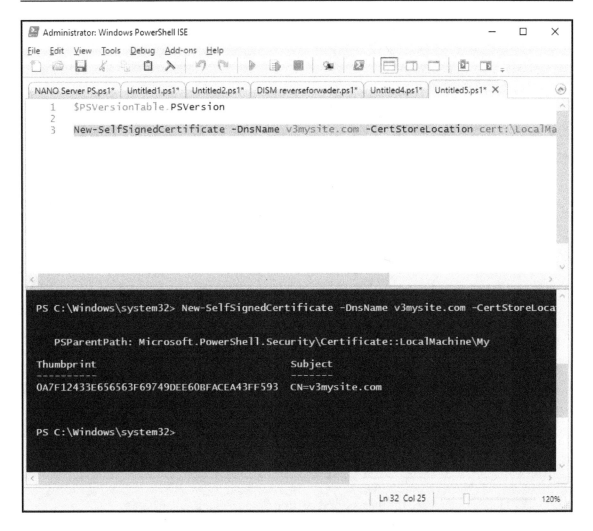

4. You can see in the PowerShell window that the certificate has been created. It is a self-signed certificate.

5. Let's open IIS Manager. Click on the **WIN2016IIS** server, and you'll see the **Server Certificates**.

6. Open the Server Certificates window from the **Features** pane, as shown here:

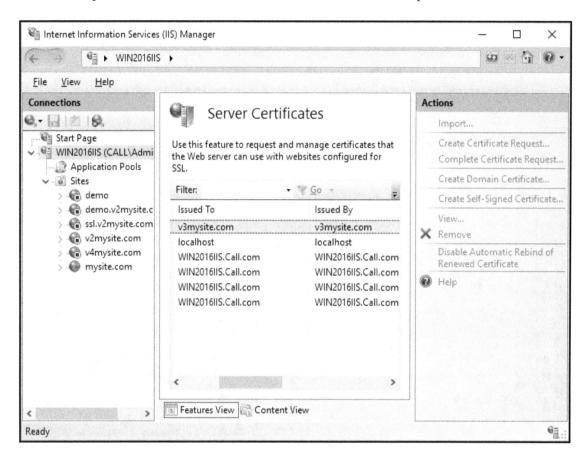

7. Here you can see the self-signed certificate v3mysite.com listed.

How it works...

In this recipe, we opened IIS Manager on WIN2016IIS. We opened PowerShell and created a SSLself-signed certificate called v3mysite.com. We verified that the self-signed certificate v3mysite.com has been created.

Testing SSL websites

In this recipe, we are going to open Internet Explorer on WIN2016IIS and open `mysite.com`. We will also verify the SSL certificate we created and configured on `mysite.com`.

Getting ready

To step through this recipe, you will need a running IIS 10.0 server, SSL-configured website `mysite.com`, and an administrator account to make changes in IIS 10.0.

How to do it...

1. Go to WIN2016IIS and log in to the IIS 10.0 server WIN2016IIS. Open the server manager and go to the **Tools** menu.
2. Open IIS Manager and expand **WIN2016IIS**. You will get the **Application Pools** and **Sites**. Expand **Sites**. You will the website **mysite.com** listed.
3. Right-click on **mysite.com** and click on **Explorer.** You will get the **mysite.com** website's physical directory, as shown here:

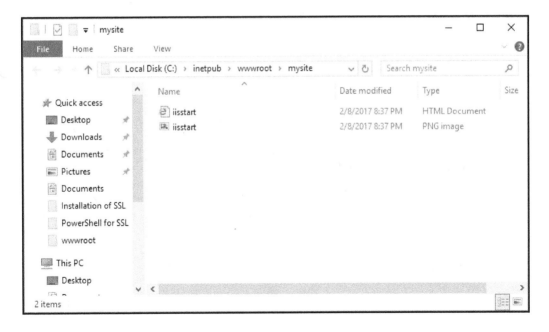

4. We've pasted the `iisstart.htm` and `iisstart.png` files inside the `mysite` physical directory. Now you have to make a host entry for `mysite.com` so that we can access it by name.

5. Go to the **WIN2016IIS** server's `C:\Windows\System32\drivers\etc` location. You will see the `hosts` file. Open it in Notepad, and add an entry for `172.16.15.60` and website name `mysite.com`, as shown here:

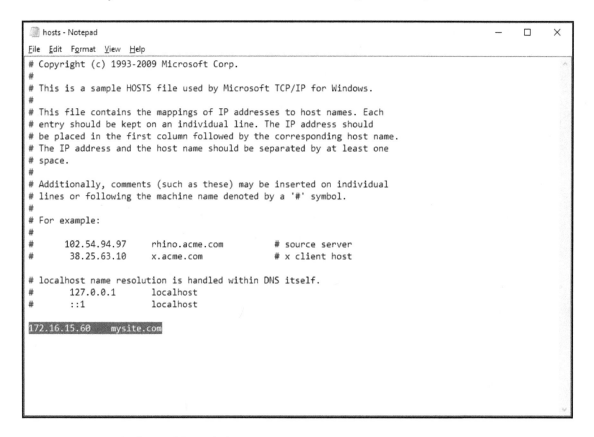

6. Save the hosts file and close it.

7. Open Internet Explorer and type `https://mysite.com`, and you will get a certificate error warning ignore the warning, it is coming because we have our self-signed certificate only on local Server, warning message will not be displayed If we have purchased a certificate installed, you shown in figure.

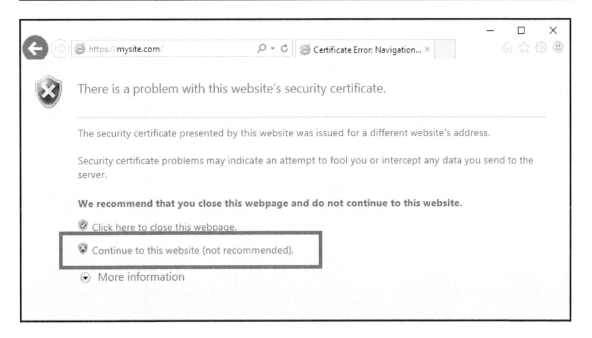

8. Click on **Continue to this website**, and you will get redirected to the
    mysite.com home page, as shown here:

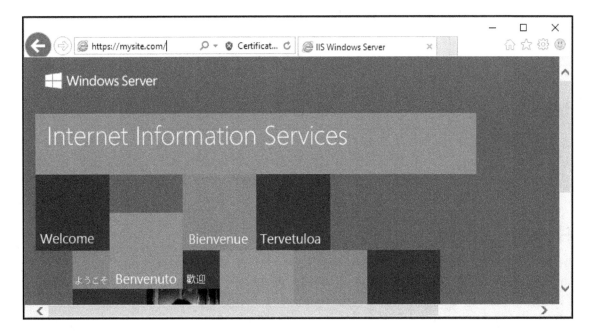

9. You can see here that we're accessing the website with the `https` protocol and a certificate (it's marked in red here as it is a local server certificate and not valid for the outside world--just for demonstration). Click on the certificate, and you will get the certificate properties:

10. You can see here that we have the certificate details **Issued to, Issued by, Valid from**, and valid **to**. Click on **OK**.

How it works...

In this recipe, we opened Internet Explorer on server WIN2016IIS and copied the `iisstart.htm` and `iisstart.png` files to the `mysite.com` physical directory. We created a hosts file entry and opened `https://mysite.com`. We also verified the SSL certificate we created and configured on `mysite.com`.

11
Extending IIS 10.0 to FTP

In this chapter, we will cover the following recipes:

- Understanding FTP
- Installing FTP on IIS 10.0
- Creating, securing, and configuring an FTP site
- Creating an FTP user and managing user permissions
- Testing our FTP server

Introduction

The **File Transfer Protocol (FTP)** is used to transfer files between two computers over a network and the internet.

FTP is a standard network protocol used for the transfer of computer files from a server to a client using the client–server model on a computer network. FTP's default network port numbers are 20 and 21.

FTPS, also known as FTPES, FTP-SSL, S-FTP, and FTP Secure, is an extension to the commonly used FTP that adds support for the **Transport Layer Security (TLS)** and **Secure Sockets Layer (SSL)** cryptographic protocols.

Understanding FTP

In this recipe, we will open the FileZilla FTP client software, which has already been installed on a Windows 10 PC. We will also open an FTP site hosted on a remote server. We will see how to upload and download files, folders, media files, and program files.

FileZilla is a third-party application available free online to download. Two types of FileZilla programs are available: FileZilla Clienta and FileZilla Server.

FileZilla is designed for FTP server connectivity for file download and upload.

In this book, the examples are covered with the FileZilla Client application, available at `https://filezilla-project.org/`.

Getting ready

To step through this recipe, you will need a running FTP site. You should also be have administrative privileges on the FTP site, FileZilla FTP client software (or any FTP client software), and an internet connection.

How to do it...

1. We have already installed the **FileZilla** FTP client software on our Windows 10 PC. Find the **FileZilla** client shortcut on the desktop and open it:

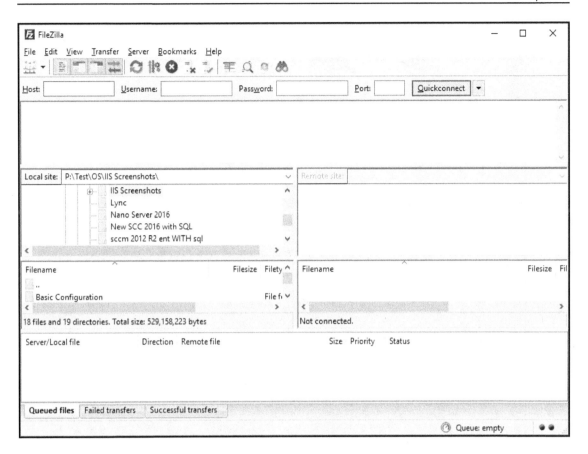

2. You can see that at the top, we have the **Quickconnect** option. You just need to input the FTP server name or IP in the **Host** field and the FTP username and password. If you have a custom port for your FTP server, you can set it here in the **Port** option. Let's connect to a remote FTP server.

3. Go to the **File** menu on the client and click on **Site Manager**:

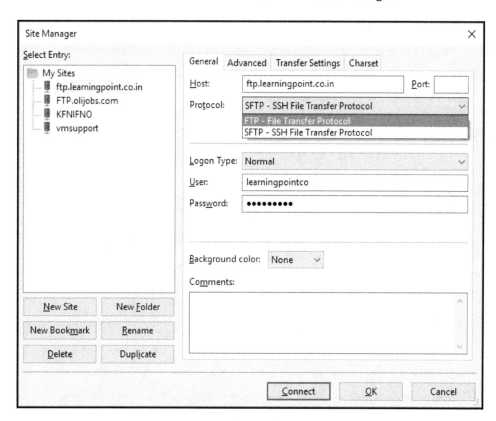

4. We already have several sites added, as you can see. We will select **ftp.learningpoint.co.in** and **Protocol FTP** or SFTP. Then, click on the **Connect** button. You will be connected to the remote FTP site, as shown here:

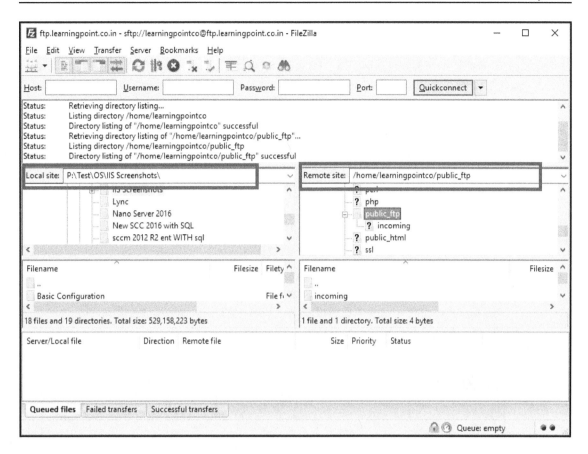

5. You can see that we have a **Local site**, which is on your Windows 10 PC, and a **Remote site**, which is the FTP site **learningpoint.co.in**. You can download **learningpoint.co.in** from the remote FTP site to your local site (your Windows 10 PC or server), and you can also upload files. If you have administrative rights, you can modify and delete files on the FTP server directly.

How it works...

In this recipe, we opened the FileZilla FTP client. We then remotely connected to the FTP site **learningpoint.co.in**, which is hosted on a public host server remotely, and we saw how to upload and download files, folders, media files, and program files.

Installing FTP on IIS 10.0

In this recipe, we are going to install an FTP server on Windows Server 2016. We will open IIS Manager to check whether the FTP server has been installed or not.

Getting ready

To step through this recipe, you will need a running Windows Server 2016 instance with IIS 10.0 installed. You should also have administrative privileges.

How to do it...

1. Log in to Windows Server 2016 with an administrator account.
2. Click on the **Start** menu or search for **Server Manager** and open it.
3. You have to click on the **Add roles and features** link, or you can find the same option in the **Manage** menu at the top:

4. Once you open the **Add Roles and Features** window, click on **Next** until you get to the Server Roles window.

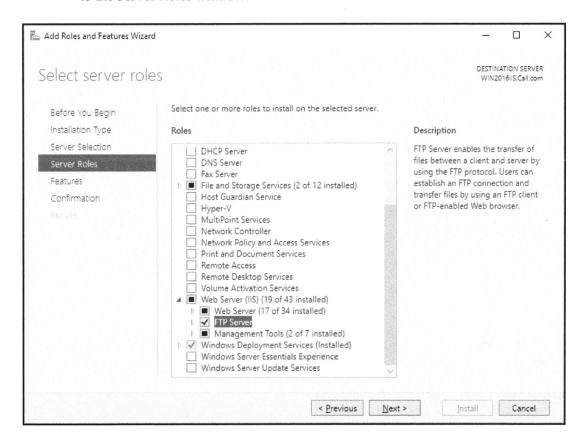

5. Select the **FTP Server** checkbox, click on **Next**, and then click on the **Install** button. You will get the **FTP server** installed on your **WIN2016IIS** Windows Server 2016 server:

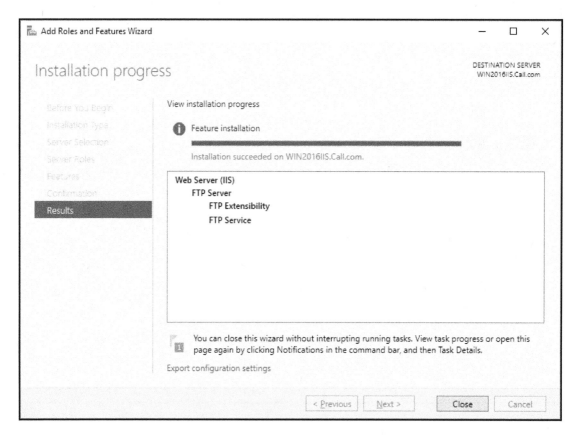

6. Click on the **Close** button. Now we have to check on the IIS server whether FTP features have been installed or not.

7. Open IIS Manager on Windows Server 2016. Click on the **WIN2016IIS** server. You will see the features view. We have successfully installed the FTP component, as shown here:

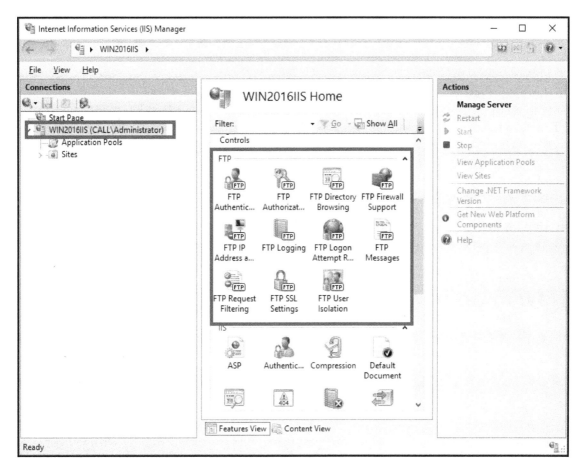

8. You will see the FTP features view highlighted.

How it works...

In this recipe, we installed FTP server on Windows Server 2016 and also opened IIS Manager to check whether it had been installed or not.

Creating, securing, and configuring an FTP site

In this recipe, we will create an FTP site and create an FTP site binding. We will discuss how to set up SFTP (Secure FTP). We will also see how we can add an SSL certificate to our FTP site to make it secure and create a basic FTP site with anonymous access. We will overview the properties of the FTP site.

Getting ready

To step through this recipe, you will need a running Windows Server 2016 instance with IIS 10.0 and FTP server installed. You should also have administrative privileges.

How to do it...

1. Log in to Windows Server 2016 with an administrator account.
2. Open Server Manager.
3. You have to click on **Tools** and go to IIS Manager. Open IIS Manager, and right-click on **WIN2016IIS**, as shown here:

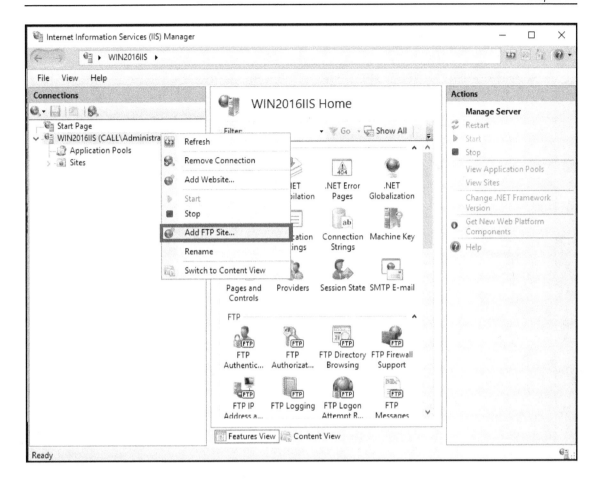

4. Click on **Add FTP site**, and you will get the FTP **Site Information** window, as shown here:

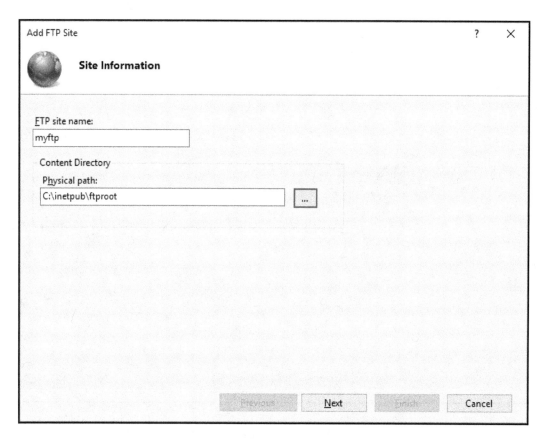

5. We've added an FTP site called `myftp`. Select the local default `ftproot` folder, `C:\inetpub\ftproot`. You can also create your own folder anywhere on the server. Click on **Next**, and you will get the **Binding and SSL Settings** window, as shown here:

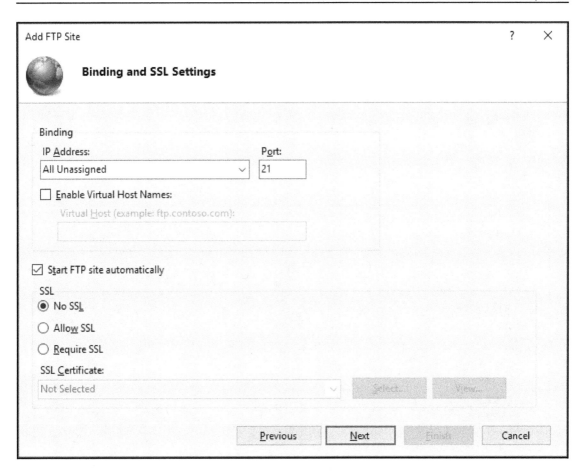

6. Here, you can provide a dedicated IP address for the FTP site. We are keeping it at the default **All Unassigned** and default port 21 (you can also create a custom port number for the FTP site if you need, but you need to configure a firewall rule for the custom port).

7. Here, we can secure the website. You have the options **No SSL, Allow SSL**, and **Require SSL**. Let's select the default option **Require SSL**:

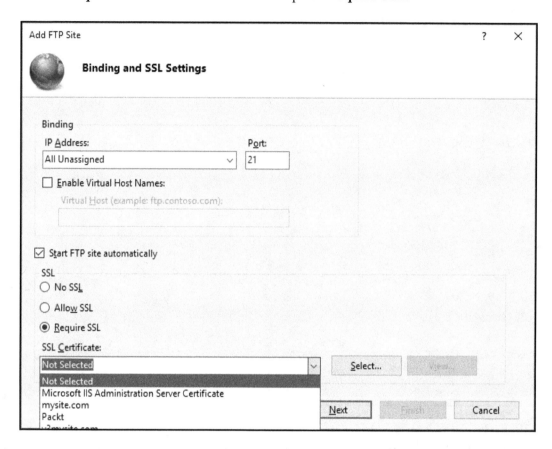

8. Now you can see that we get all our previously created SSL certificates listed. If you need a secure FTP site, you can select any one of the SSL certificates and use the following steps to create an SSL FTP site. We will go ahead with the **No SSL** option. After selecting the **No SSL** option, click on **Next**. You will get the **Authentication and Authorization Information**, as shown here:

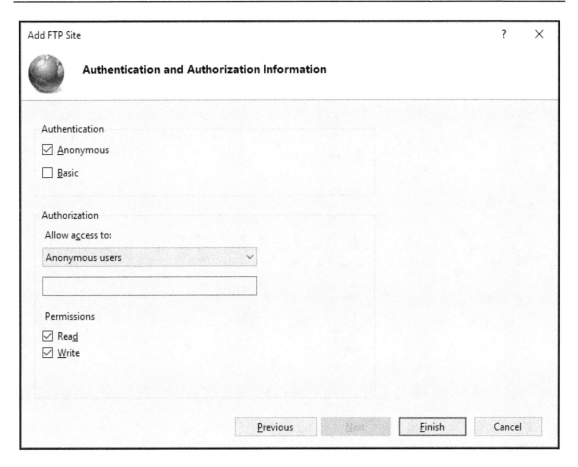

9. Let's select **Anonymous** authentication and **Anonymous user** authorization and provide permissions to **Read** and **Write.** Now an anonymous user can download and upload files on FTP. Click on **Finish**.

> When you create an FTP server with anonymous access, it means your FTP site is unsecured, and anyone can get access to it.
>
> I recommend you never create any FTP site with anonymous access; unauthorized users can harm your FTP server. FTP servers, whether configured over secure or normal protocols, must be restricted at least to allow only authorized user access.

10. Let's go to IIS Manager. Expand the **Sites** folder, and you will see the **myftp** site created:

11. Go to the **Actions** pane of the **myftp** site and click on **Bindings**. You will get the bindings window, as shown here:

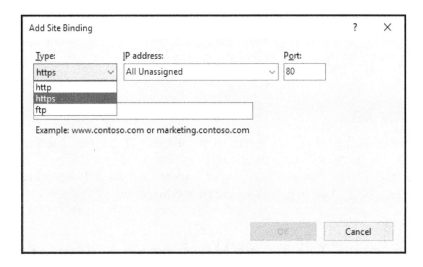

12. Click on **Type:** dropdown in the **Add Site Binding** window, and you will see that we have options to select **http**, **https**, and **ftp**. You can set the site binding to **ftp** if you have an existing site.

13. The basic properties are the same as the website properties, which we discussed in earlier chapters. Click on the **Advanced Settings...** option, and you will get the **Advanced Settings...** window, as shown here:

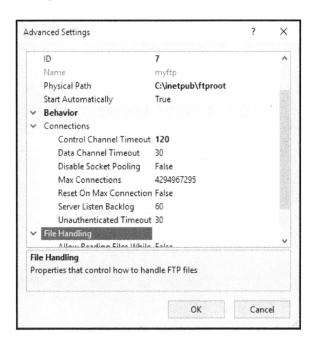

14. You need to set the connection properties here. You can create more specific connections if you want to, but we'll keep it default. Click on **OK** to close the **Advanced Settings...** window of the **myftp** site.

How it works...

In this recipe, we created the FTP site **myftp**. We made an FTP site binding and discussed custom bindings. We discussed how to set up SFTP (Secure FTP) and how an SSL certificate can be added to an FTP site to make it secure. We created a basic FTP site called **myftp** with anonymous access. We had an overview of the properties of the FTP site.

Creating an FTP user and managing user permissions

In this recipe, we will create a Windows Server 2016 user for FTP access and give that FTP user FTP folder permissions. We will also configure FTP authentication and FTP authorization rules. We will allow the Windows user to get access to the FTP site.

Getting ready

To step through this recipe, you will need a running Windows Server 2016 instance with IIS 10.0 and FTP Server installed. You should also have administrative privileges.

How to do it...

1. Log in to Windows Server 2016 with an administrator account.
2. Open Server Manager.
3. Click on **Tools** and open **Computer Management**.
4. In the **Computer Management** window of **WIN2016IIS**, expand **System tools.** Expand **Local Users and Groups**, as shown here:

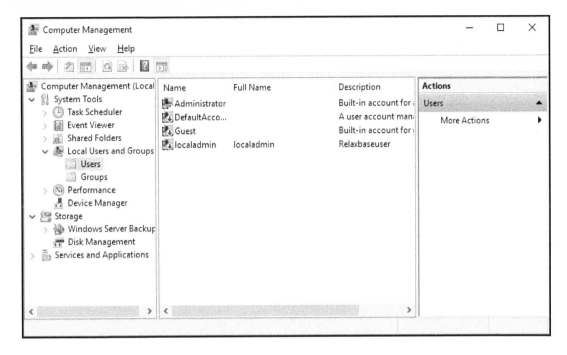

5. Right-click on the **Users** folder and select **New User.** The **New User** creation window will pop up:

6. Fill in the details of the user: **User name**, **Full name**, **Description**, user **Password**, and **Confirm password**. You can select any or all checkboxes if you need to set those options. Click on **Create**, and you will have the `ftpadmin` user created, as shown here:

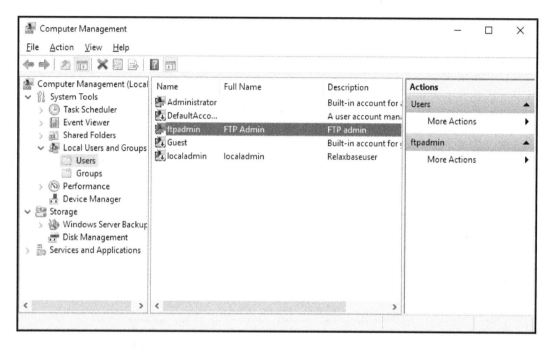

7. Now let's go to set user permissions on the `FTPROOT` folder. This is best practice to manage NTFS permissions on a folder.

8. Go to `C:\inetpub`, and find the folder named `ftproot`. Right-click on `ftproot`, and open its properties. In the properties window, go to the **Security** tab and click on the **Edit** button. The security window will open. Click on the **Add** button. Find the user window in **WIN2016IIS** (local computer) and select the **ftpadmin** user. Press **OK**, and the user will be listed in the security window, as shown here:

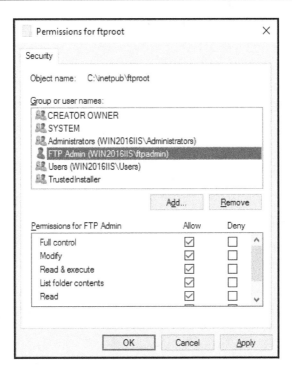

Here you can also restrict or provide the certain privileges by checking the box according to the user requirements. Permissions for FTP Admin which are below 1. Full Control 2. Modify 3. Read & execute 4. List folder contents 5. Read 6. Write

9. Now you can set the permissions. We'll allow all the permissions. Click on **Apply** and **OK**. Now we are done with the `ftproot` folder permissions. Let's move ahead to allow the user on our FTP site to access the FTP folder.

10. Open IIS Manager, expand **WIN2016IIS**, and expand the **Sites** folder. Click on **myftp**, as shown here:

11. Go to the ftpsite **Features View**, open FTP authentication, disable **Anonymous Authentication**, and enable **Basic Authentication**, as shown here:

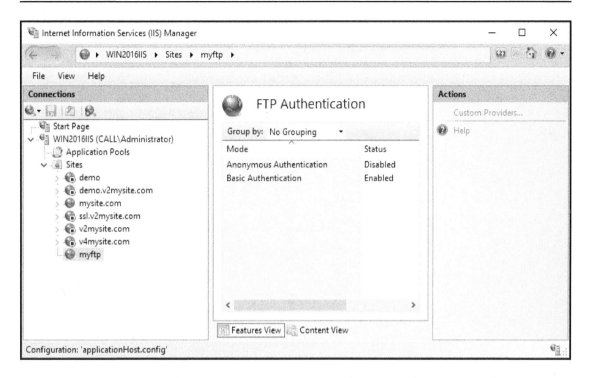

12. Next, go to the ftpsite **Features View**, open the FTP authorization rules, and add a new rule:

13. Select **All Users** and provide **Read** and **Write** permissions. Click on **OK**. Check the **FTP Authorization Rule**. If there are any other rules available, you can delete them. We will use the rule we created.

14. Next, go to the ftpsite **Features View** and open IIS Manager Permission. Here, you can allow the user to access the FTP site. Click on **Allow User...** from the **Actions** pane. You will get the **Allow User...** window, as shown here:

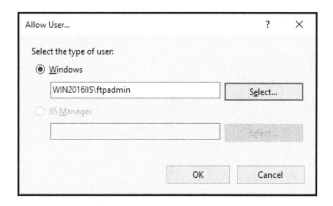

15. We selected the ftpadmin user from the **WIN2016IIS** server. Click on the **OK** button.

How it works...

In this recipe, we created a user on WIN2016IIS for FTP access and granted the FTP user full permissions to the ftproot folder. We configured FTP authentication and FTP authorization rules for all users. We allowed the Windows user to access the FTP site from IIS Manager Permission.

Testing our FTP server

In this recipe, we are going to test the FTP site called ftpsite using FileZilla. We will create the FTP site in FileZilla and connect to ftpsite on WIN2016IIS. We will upload a sample file and cross-check it in the ftproot folder.

Getting ready

To step through this recipe, you will need a running Windows Server 2016 instance with IIS 10.0 and FTP server installed. You need FileZilla or any other FTP client software installed on the PC or server. You should also have administrative privileges.

How to do it...

1. We have already installed the FileZilla FTP client software on our Windows 10 PC. If you do not have it already installed, look at the the tip in the first recipe to find the FileZilla download URL. Download and install it on your PC.
2. Open FileZilla, go to the **File** menu, and open the **Site Manager.** Create a new site, as shown here:

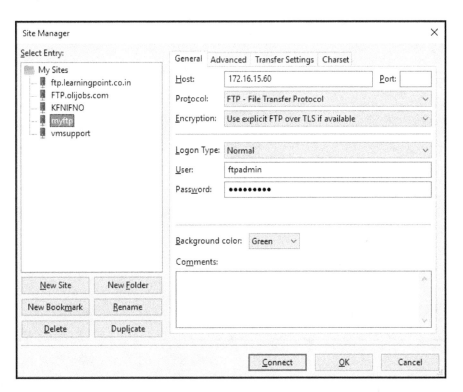

3. We set the IIS Server WIN2016IIS IP to `172.16.15.60`, the username to `ftpadmin`, and the password we set for the WIN2016IIS server. Click on the **Connect** button. You will be connected to **ftpsite**:

The IP is `172.16.15.60` in this case, but in your case, it may be different. Find out your FTP server's IP address to configure the FileZilla FTP client tool to get access. The IP can be obtained in various ways, but one of them is to open Command Prompt and run `ipconfig`. You will get all of your IPs listed; pick the IPv4 one.

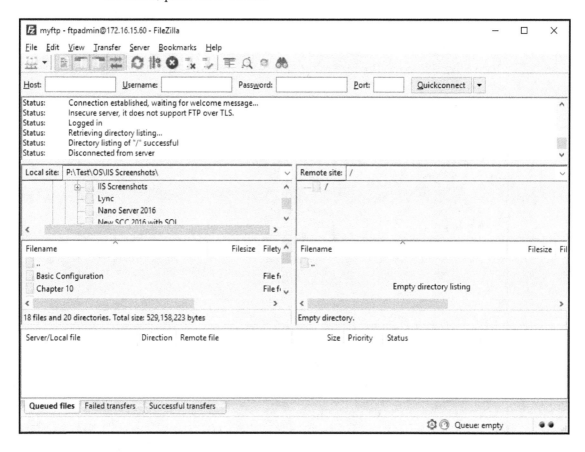

4. You can see that the **Remote Site** folder doesn't have anything in it. Let's upload the `chapter 7.rar` file. Select `chapter 7.rar` from your local site, and right-click and select the upload. You will see the file uploaded to the remote site:

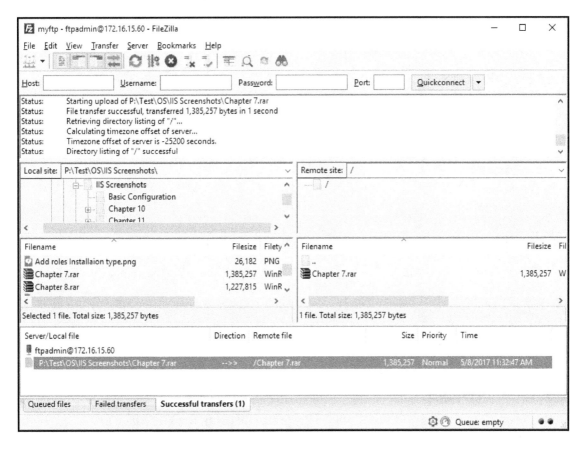

5. You can see in the figure that the **Remote Site** has the `chapter 7.rar` file, which we uploaded. Let's check out the `ftproot` folder.

6. Go to `C:\inetpub\ftproot` on the **WIN2016IIS** server:

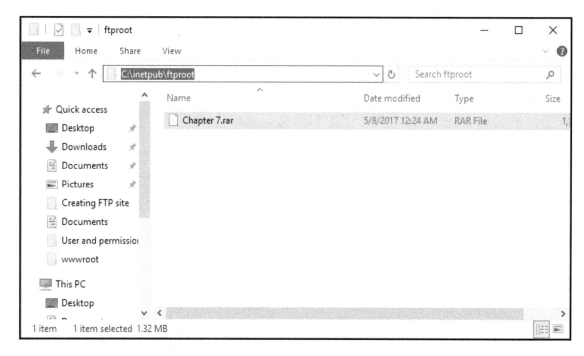

7. You can see in the figure that we have the file in the `ftproot` directory.

How it works...

In this recipe, we created and tested the FTP site **ftpsite** using the FileZilla FTP client software. We created and connected to the FTP site using FileZilla. We also uploaded `chapter 7.rar` and checked whether it was present in the `ftproot` folder.

12
Securing Your Websites on IIS 10.0

In this chapter, we will cover the following recipes:

- Understanding available security on IIS 10.0
- Configuring security on IIS 10.0
- URL authorization and authentication
- IP address and domain restrictions
- Testing security on IIS 10.0

Introduction

Web server security (IIS server), website security, and application security can be used to configure an IIS server to protect itself and the website.

The following are the security options available in IIS server:

- Machine key
- Authentication
- Authorization rule
- IP address and domain restrictions

- ISAPI and CGI restrictions
- Server certificate
- Request filtering
- IIS Manager permissions and IIS Manager users
- NTFS permissions

We can install and configure security components on an IIS server for our website or web application that needs secure hosting.

In this chapter, we will start with some of the security information of IIS 10.0. You can try more security options if you wish to. Here, we will cover a few important parts.

Understanding available security on IIS 10.0

In this recipe, we will install security components available in Windows Server 2016 and browse the available installed security features in IIS Manager. We will also understand NTFS permissions.

Getting ready

We require an up-and-running IIS 10.0 instance. You should have administrative privileges. There are no other prerequisites.

How to do it...

1. Log in to Windows Server 2016 from an account with administrative privileges.
2. Click on the **Start** menu or type `Server Manager` in the search window. You will see the **Server Manager** window.

3. Click the **Add roles and features** link, or you can find the same option in the **Manage** menu, as shown here:

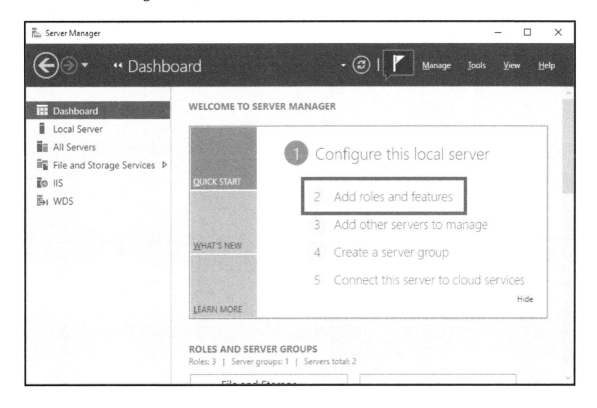

4. In the **Add Roles and Features** wizard, click on **Next** until you reach the **Server Roles** wizard. Expand **Web Server**, as shown here:

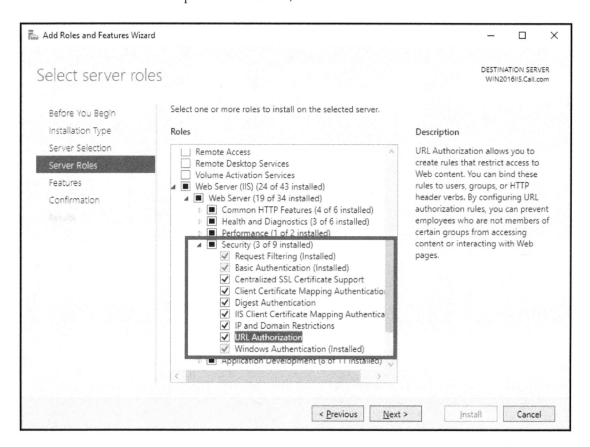

5. As seen in the figure, we expand **Web Server** and then we expand **Security**; here, we find some of security options already installed (the checked and grayed-out boxes). Check the rest of the available security features listed here, click on **Next**, skip the Features wizard, click on **Next**, and you will get the confirmation window, as shown in the following screenshot:

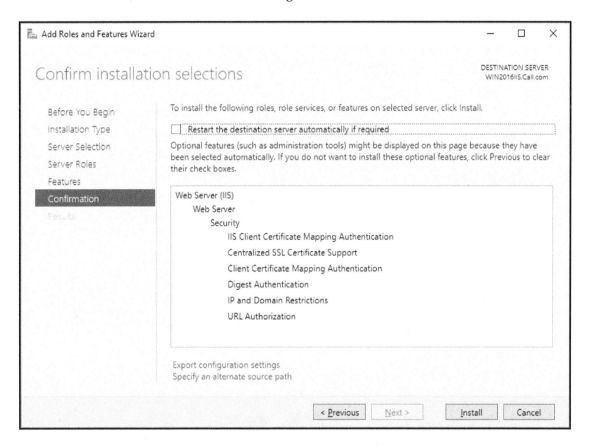

6. You can see that we have selected the security features that we are going to install. Click on the **Install** button. You can see in the next screenshot that they are installed successfully:

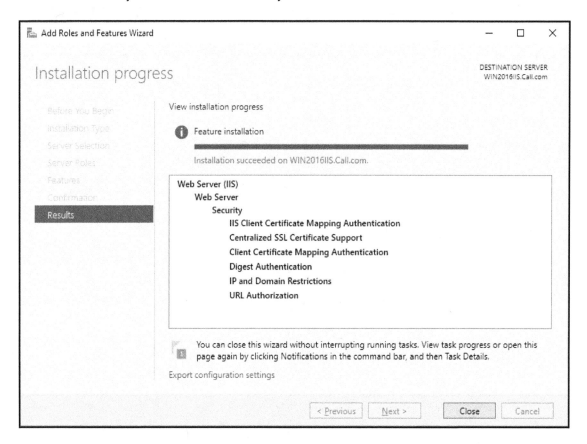

7. Click on **Close**. Now we have to open the IIS Manager. Click on the Start menu or type Server Manager in the search window on Windows 2016 Server. You will see the Server Manager window. Open the Server Manager, On the Server Manager click on **Tools** menu and select and open the IIS Manager, as shown in the following screenshot.

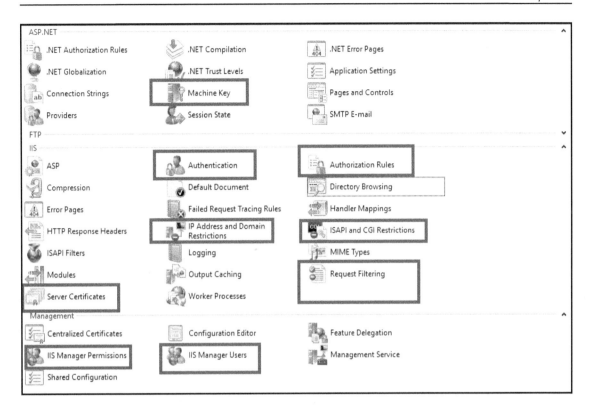

8. You can see here that we have several security features available in IIS Server: **Machine Key**, **Authentication**, **Authorization Rules**, **IP Address** and **Domain Restrictions**, **ISAPI** and **CGI Restrictions**, **Server Certificates**, **Request Filtering**, **IIS Manager Permissions**, **IIS Manager Users**, and so on. We can set them up according to the level of security we require for our website or web application. Let's check out NTFS permissions.

9. Go to IIS Manager, expand the IIS server, expand the **Sites** folder, and click on any existing site:

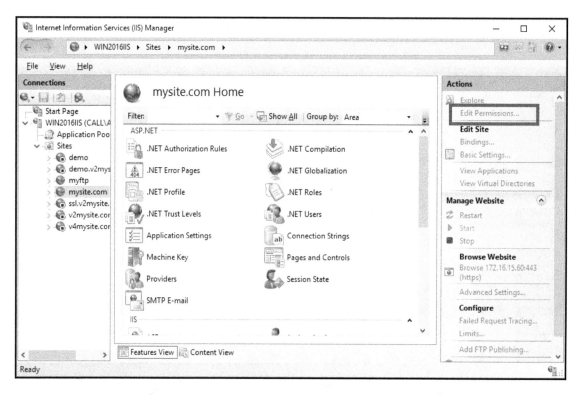

10. Go to the **Actions** pane, as highlighted in the previous screenshot, and click on **Edit Permissions....** This is the physical directory of the selected website, **mysite.com**. The `mysite` physical directory property will open, as shown here:

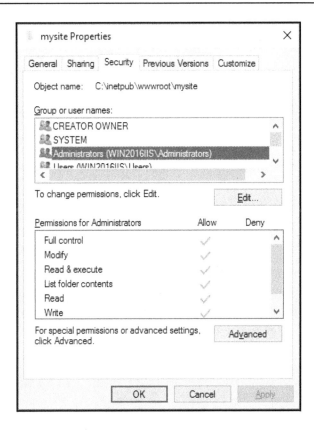

11. Click on the **Security** tab in the `mysite` property window. In the **Security** tab, you can add users and modify folder-level permissions. Not everyone can access and make changes to the `mysite` folder; only specific users who have permissions can. You can set this up according to how you've planned NTFS permissions.

How it works...

In this recipe, we installed available security components on Windows Server 2016 and browsed the available installed security features in IIS manager. We understand NTFS permissions on the `mysite` physical folder of the `mysite.com` website.

Configuring security on IIS 10.0

In this recipe, we will configure IIS Manager permissions and IIS Manager users. We will also configure the machine key.

Getting ready

We require an up-and-running IIS 10.0 instance. Security components should be installed. You should have administrative privileges.

How to do it...

1. Log in to Windows Server 2016 with an account with administrative privileges.
2. Open Server Manager from the Start menu or use the search window to find it.
3. Go to Tools | IIS Manager. Click on IIS server **WIN2016IIS**, go to **Features** View, and open **IIS Manager Users**, as shown here:

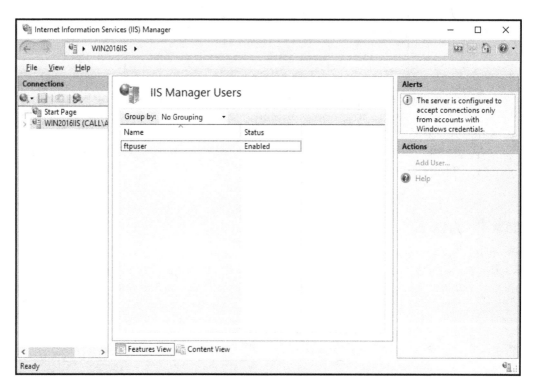

4. You can add the new IIS user from **IIS Manager Users** (these are different from Windows users). Let's move to **IIS Manager Permissions**. Expand the IIS server **WIN2016IIS**, expand the **Sites** folder, click on **mysite.com**, go to **Features View**, and open **IIS Manager Permissions**:

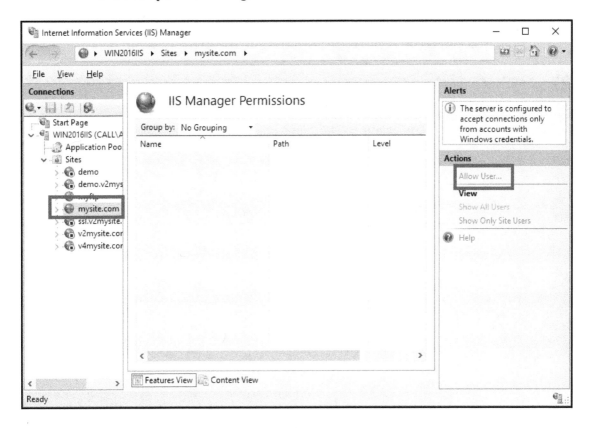

5. Go to the **Actions** pane, and click on **Allow User...**. IIS Manager permissions are used to allow users or user groups on the local computer to manage a website. Let's select **mysite.com**. Once you click on **Allow User** from the **Actions** pane, you will get the **Allow User...** window:

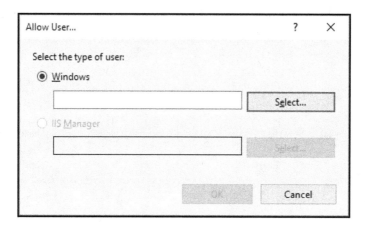

6. Click on the **Select...** option. You will get the **Select User or Group** window, as shown in the following screenshot:

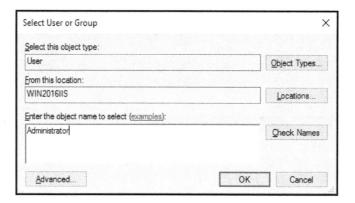

7. Here, we will search for and select Windows Server users. I want to select the administrator user, so I type `Administrator` and click on the **OK** button. You can see that the administrator user has been selected:

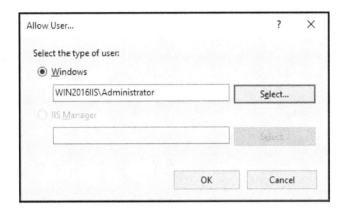

8. We have selected **WIN2016IIS\Administrator** (`<local server name>\<username>`). Click on **OK.** You can see in the **IIS Manager Permissions** pane that the administrator user has permission for `mysite.com`:

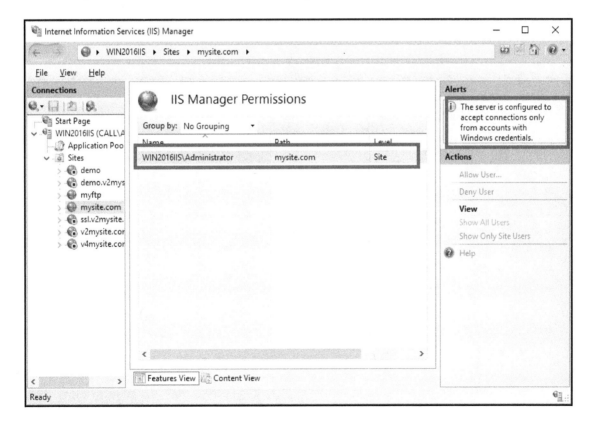

9. This action specifies that only allowed users can access your website. Let's move to the machine key.

10. Go to the **WIN2016IIS** IIS server and click on **WIN2016IIS**. Go to **Features View** and select **Machine Key**, as shown here:

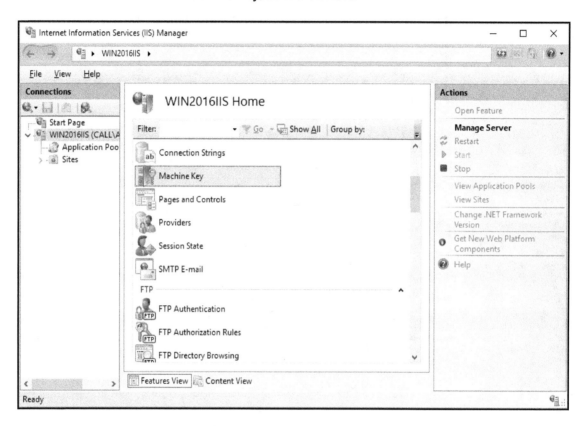

11. Go to the **Actions** pane, click on **Open Features**, and click on **Encryption Method.** You will see that we have several options we can select. We will keep it at the default of **Auto**:

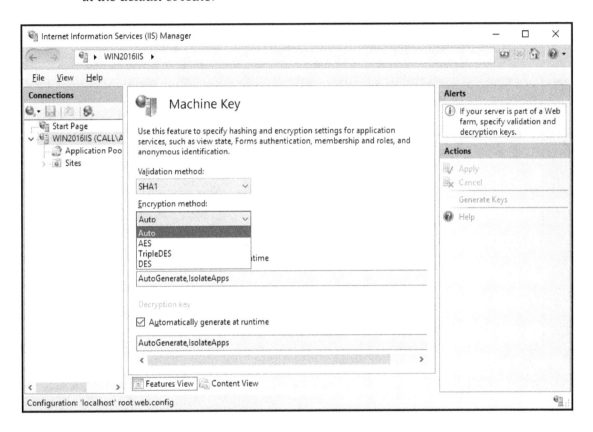

12. The **Machine Key** is what we use to apply the configuration settings on the IIS server. Machine key configuration settings will have an effect on the IIS server level. Now, click on the **Validation method** drop-down menu. You have a list of validation methods available. We will select the default one, as shown here:

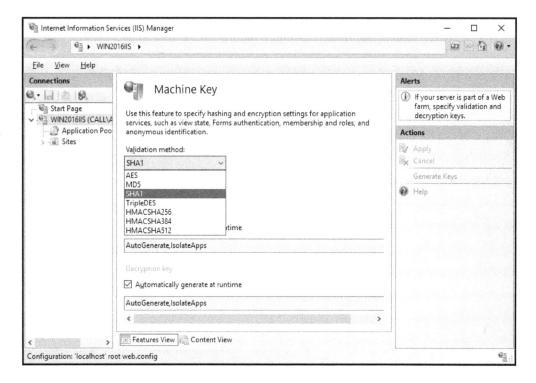

You can use the type of method and encryption you require.

How it works...

In this recipe, we configured and checked the IIS Manager permission, and we added the Windows user for IIS Manager permissions. We checked the IIS Manager user and also configured the machine key.

URL authorization and authentication

In this recipe, we will configure the URL authorization rule and enable and disable the authentication type of the website.

Getting ready

We require an up-and-running IIS 10.0 instance. Security components should be installed. You should have administrative privileges.

How to do it...

1. Log in to Windows Server 2016 with an account with administrative privileges.
2. Open Server Manager from the Start menu or use the search window to find it.
3. Click on the Tools menu from **Server Manager**; you will find IIS Manager. Open it and click on the **WIN2016IIS** IIS server. Go to **Features view** and select Authorization Rules:

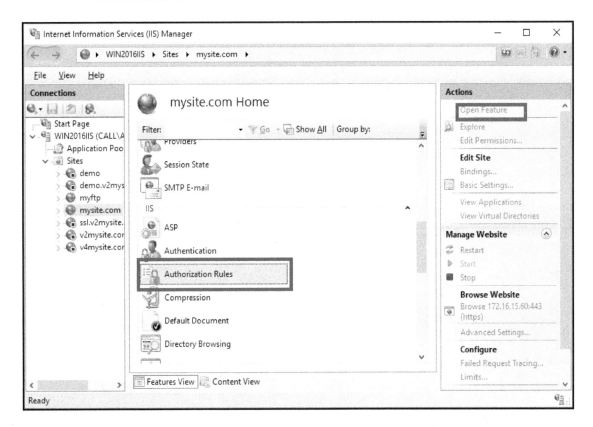

4. Go to the **Actions** pane of **Authorization Rules**. You have two options: **Add Allow Rule...** and **Add Deny Rule...**, as shown in the following screenshot. Click on **Add Allow Rule...**:

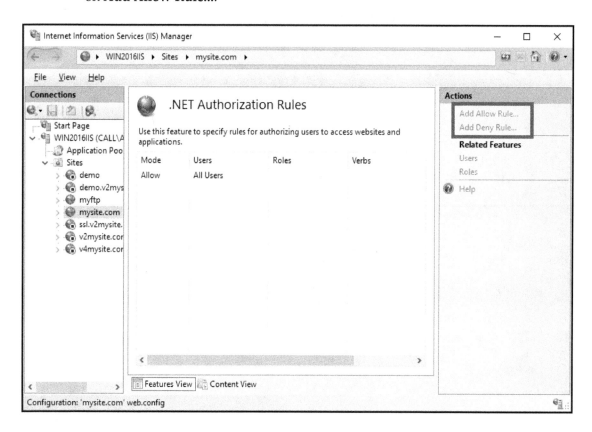

5. The following **Add Allow Authorization Rule** window pops up:

6. Here, we can select one out of **All users**, **All Anonymous users**, and **Specified roles or user groups.** Next, you can select any specified users you require. We can choose to allow them over here. You can use specific verbs in it, such as **GET** and **POST**. Let's see how we can add a deny authorization rule.

7. Go to the **Actions** pane of authorization rule and click on **Deny rule**, as shown here:

8. Here, in **Add Deny Authorization Rule**, we can select **All users**, **All Anonymous users**, or **Specified roles or user groups**. Next, you can select any specified users. Depending on our requirement, we can choose over here to deny them access to the website; you can use the specific verbs such as **GET** and **POST**. Let's see how we can disable an authorization rule.

9. Let's move to the authentication type; go to the **Features View** of `mysite.com`, as shown here:

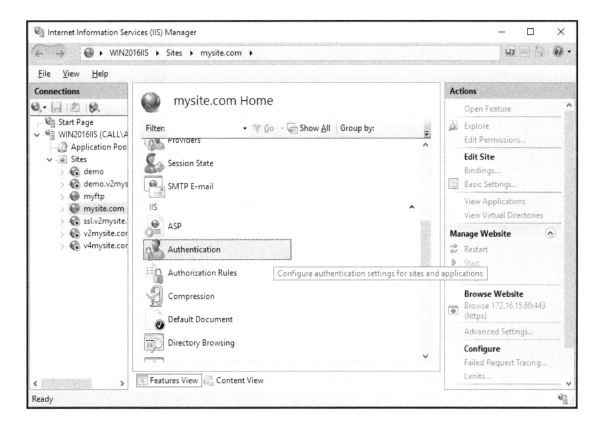

10. Open the **Authentication** option. You will see the listed **Authentication** type method available:

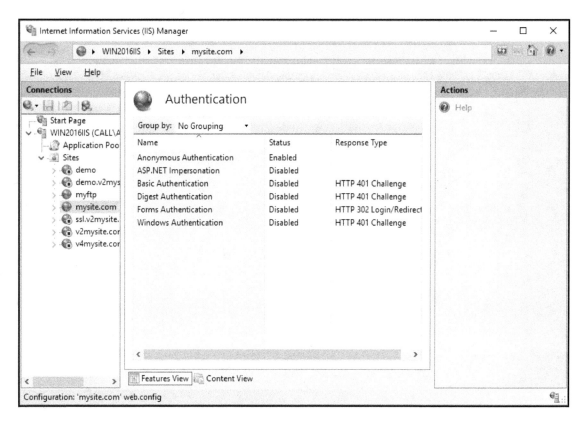

11. In the **Authentication Features View** pane, we can enable and disable the type of authentication. We have **Anonymous Authentication**, **ASP.NET Impersonation**, **Basic Authentication**, **Digest Authentication**, **Forms Authentication**, and **Windows Authentication**.

How it works...

In this recipe, we configured URL authorization allow and deny rules. We also enabled and disabled the authentication type of a website.

IP address and domain restrictions

In this recipe, we will log in to the IIS server first and then open the IP address and domain restrictions feature. We will add an allow rule and deny rule for specific IP addresses. We will discuss and review dynamic IP restriction.

Getting ready

We require an up-and-running IIS 10.0 instance. Security components should be installed. You should have administrative privileges.

How to do it...

1. Log in to Windows Server 2016 with an account with administrative privileges.
2. Open Server Manager from the Start menu or use the search window to find it.
3. Click on the **Tools** menu from **Server Manager**; you will find IIS Manager. Open it and click on the **WIN2016IIS** IIS server. Expand the **Sites** folder and click on `mysite.com`. Go to the **Features View** of `mysite.com` and select **IP Address and Domain Restrictions**:

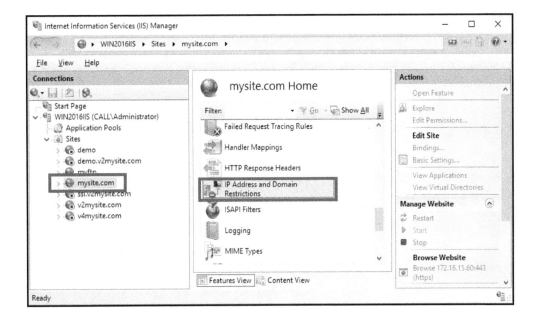

4. You will get the **IP Address and Domain Restrictions** configuration window, as shown in the following screenshot:

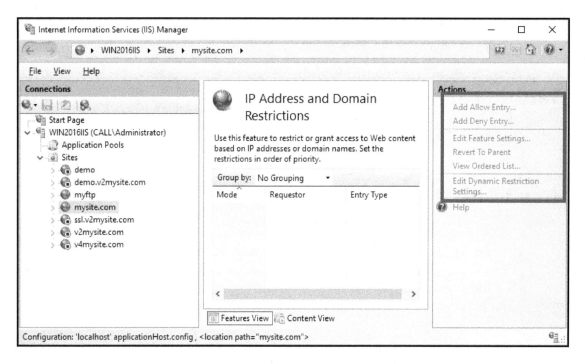

5. Go to the **Actions** pane, click on **Add Allow Entry,** and you will get the allow IP and domain window, as shown here:

6. **Add Allow Restriction Rule** will help us to allow specific IP addresses or domain names (`xyz.com`), or an IP address range with a subnet mask or prefix (domain name). Add the IP `172.16.15.60` and click on **OK**. You've now created the allow restriction rule. Let's move on to create a deny rule.

7. Go to the **IP Address and Domain Restrictions** Actions pane, click on **Add Deny Entry...**, and you will get the **Add Deny Restriction Rule** window:

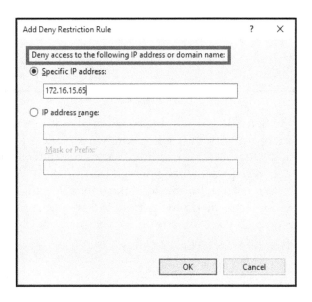

8. Here, we are creating a deny rule for the IP `172.16.15.65`. We can add a deny rule for a specific IP, domain, or range of IP addresses. We've added a single IP for now: `172.16.15.65`. Click on the **OK** button. We've now created the deny rule.

9. We need to configure the dynamic IP address restriction setting. Go to the **IP Address and Domain Restrictions Actions** pane. Click on **Dynamic IP Restriction Settings**. You will get a new window:

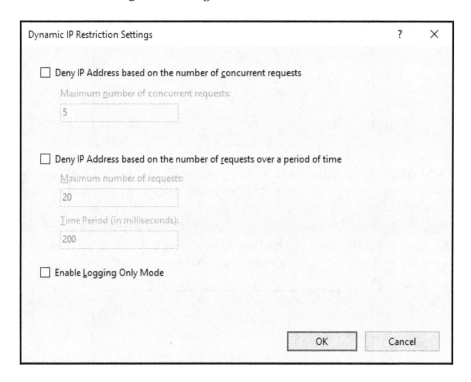

10. Here, we set the deny IP address rule based on the number of concurrent requests; for example, with the first option, we can allow a single IP address to access the website with a maximum of four simultaneous sessions. More than four website access requests will be denied (terminated). With the second option, we can require that each IP be able to make only a specific number of website access requests for a specified time period. We are not configuring this part here, but when you publish your website on the internet, you can do this to protect against certain cyber attacks.

How it works...

In this recipe, we looked at IP address and domain restriction features. We then added an allow rule the IP address `172.16.15.60` and a deny rule for the `172.16.15.65` address. We discussed and had an overview of dynamic IP restriction.

Testing security on IIS 10.0

In this recipe, we will log in to Windows Server 2016 WIN2016IIS and check the IP address access and deny rules we've set. We will access the website `https://172.16.15.60` (`mysite.com`) from the `172.16.15.60` server and access the website `https://172.16.15.60` (`mysite.com`) from the `172.16.15.65` server.

Getting ready

We require an up-and-running IIS 10.0 instance. Security components should be installed. You should have administrative privileges.

How to do it...

1. Log in to Windows Server 2016 with an account with administrative privileges.
2. Open Server Manager from the Start menu or use the search window to find it.

3. Click on the **Tools** menu from Server Manager; you will find IIS Manager. Open it and click on the **WIN2016IIS** IIS server. Expand the **Sites** folder and click on **mysite.com**. Go to the **Features View** of **mysite.com**, select **IP Address and Domain Restrictions**, and open the **IP Address and Domain Restrictions** settings, as shown here:

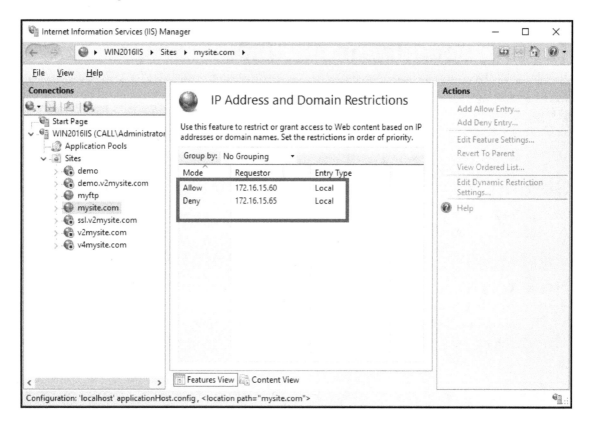

4. You can see in the figure that we have already created an Allow rule for IP address 172.16.15.60 and Deny rule for IP address 172.16.15.65. Let's test the IP 172.16.15.60.

5. We need to check the **WIN2016IIS** server IP address. Open Command Prompt and type `ipconfig`, as shown here:

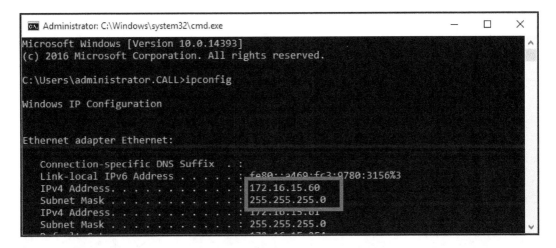

6. You can see in the result that we have `172.16.15.60`, the IP address of server WIN2016IIS. Now, let's open the `https://172.16.15.60` URL in Internet Explorer, as shown here:

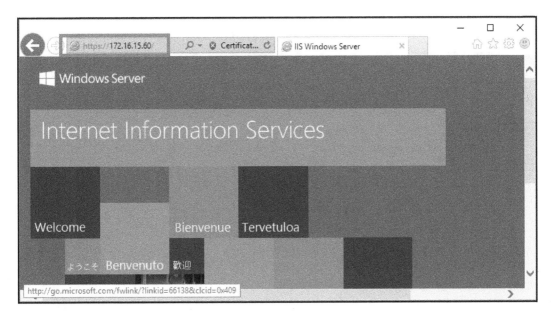

7. You see now how we can easily access the URL `https://172.16.15.60` (`https://mysite.com`) on server `172.16.15.60`. We added an Allow rule for the server IP `172.16.15.60` so that we can access it. Now we have to test the URL `https://172.16.15.60` on the server IP `172.16.15.65`.

8. Log in to server `172.16.15.65`, open Command Prompt, and type the command `ipconfig` to check the server IP address, as shown here:

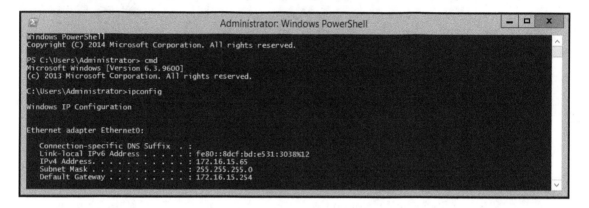

9. Now let's open the URL `https://172.16.15.60` (`https://mysite.com`) on server `172.16.15.65`. You will get a Deny message, as shown in the following screenshot:

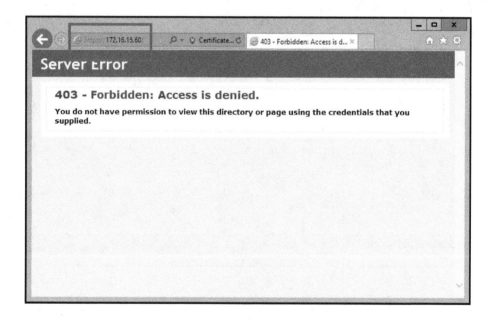

How it works...

In this recipe, we logged in to Windows Server 2016 WIN2016IIS and checked the IP address restriction rules and access and deny rules on the server. We accessed the website `https://172.16.15.60` (**mysite.com**) from server `172.16.15.60` and website `https://172.16.15.60` (**mysite.com**) from server `172.16.15.65`.

13
Managing and Troubleshooting IIS 10.0

In this chapter, we will cover the following recipes:

- Managing IIS 10.0
- Installing Health, Diagnostics, and Performance features
- Configuring Health and Diagnostics
- Configuring Failed Request Tracing Rules
- Configuring static content compression

Introduction

Health and Diagnostics provides an infrastructure to monitor, manage, and troubleshoot the health of a web server, sites, and applications.

The advantage is the detailed trace events that track a request throughout the complete request-and-response process. To enable the collection of these trace events, IIS Server can be configured to automatically capture full trace logs, in XML format, for any particular request based on elapsed time or error response codes.

Health and diagnostics includes the following features:

- Failed request tracing rules
- Logging
- Worker processes

 IIS Health and Diagnostics modules consume extra CPU resources and are often disabled in production IIS environments.

IIS exposes numerous configuration parameters that affect IIS performance. The following are things you need to do if you are looking for more performance; otherwise, keep the default settings:

- Disable IIS logging
- Disable IIS ASP debugging
- Tune the value of the ASP Threads Per Processor Limit property
- Enable IIS HTTP compression
- Configure ASP.NET 4 max ConcurrentRequests
- Disable WCF services tracing

Managing IIS 10.0

In this recipe, we will log in to IIS Server and open IIS Manager. We will open the features view of IIS Server to view the Health and Diagnostics features. We will also check the available Health and Diagnostics options by opening the `mysite.com` website's **Features View**.

Getting ready

In this recipe, we require an up-and-running IIS 10.0 instance. The health and diagnostics component should be installed. You should have administrative privileges.

How to do it...

1. Log in to Windows Server 2016 with an administrator account.
2. Open **Server Manager**.
3. Click on **Tools** and you will find IIS Manager. Open IIS Manager and click on the IIS server **WIN2016IIS**. Go to the **Features View**, as shown here:

4. You can see in the figure that we've selected **Worker Processes. Worker Processes** are only available in the IIS Server **Features View** and not in the website's **Features View. Worker Processes** enable you to view the application process' utilization of server resources.

5. Next, we have to expand the **Sites** folder and click on `mysite.com`, as shown here:

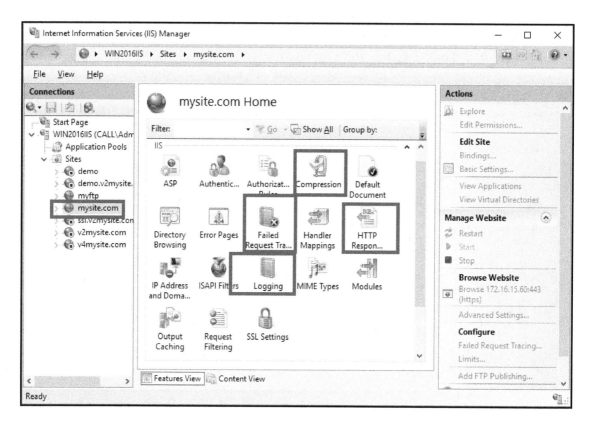

6. As you can see, we're selecting **Compression, HTTP Responder, Failed Request Tracer,** and **Logging**. These are features of the health and performance of IIS Server. In the next recipe, we will go on to install the health, diagnostics, and performance features.

How it works...

In this recipe, we logged in to IIS Server and opened IIS Manager. We went through the features view of IIS Server to view the Health and Diagnostics features and the `mysite.com` features view to check the available Health and Diagnostics options.

Installing Health, Diagnostics, and Performance features

In this recipe, we will log in to Windows Server 2016, on which we have already installed IIS 10.0. We will open Server Manager and install the Health and Diagnostics features of IIS 10.0 Server. We will then install the performance features of IIS 10.0 Server.

Getting ready

For this recipe, we require an up-and-running IIS 10.0 instance on Windows Server 2016. You should have administrative privileges.

How to do it...

1. Log in to Windows Server 2016 with an administrator account.
2. Open Server Manager.

3. Click on the **Add roles and features** link; you can find the same option in the **Manage** menu, as shown here:

4. In the **Add roles and features** window, click on **Next** until you reach the **Server Roles** wizard. Expand **Web Server**, as shown here:

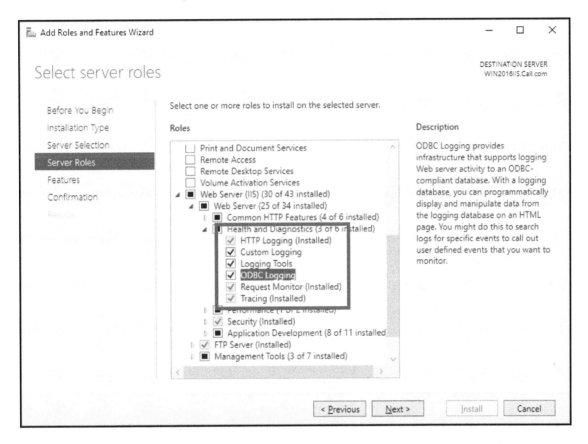

5. Select **Custom Logging, Logging Tools, ODBC Logging**; the preinstalled options are **Request Monitor, Tracing**, and **HTTP logging.**

6. Expand the **Performance** features option from **Server Roles** to install them on IIS, you can see the details in this figure:

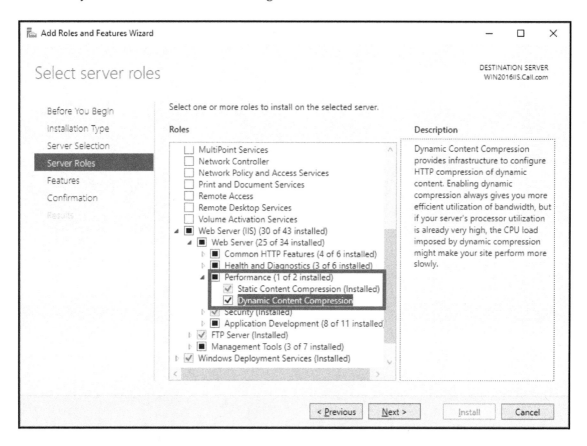

7. We have already installed **Static Content Compression**. Now select **Dynamic Content Compression**.

8. Click on **Next**, skip the features wizard, and click on **Next** again. You will get the **Confirmation** window, as shown here:

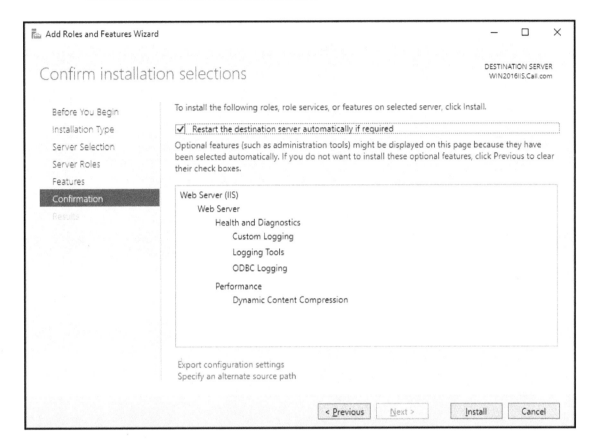

9. You can see that we have selected the **Health and Diagnostics** and **Performance** features, which we are going to install. I also selected the restart checkbox at the top. Next, you have to click on **Install**. You can see in the next figure that it's installed successfully:

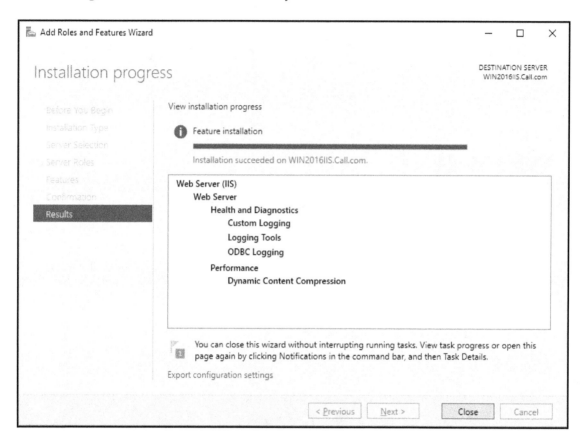

10. We've now finished the installation. In the next recipe, we will set up the configuration.

How it works...

In this recipe, we logged in to Windows Server 2016, on which we have already installed IIS 10.0. We opened Server Manager and installed the **Health and Diagnostics** features of IIS 10.0 Server. We also installed the Performance features of IIS 10.0 Server.

Configuring Health and Diagnostics

In this recipe, we will log in to IIS Server and open IIS Manager. We will go through the Features View of IIS Server to configure the worker process features. We will configure the Logging features and discuss the HTTP Response Header features.

Getting ready

For this recipe, we require an up-and-running IIS 10.0 instance. The Health and Diagnostics component should be installed. You should have administrative privileges.

How to do it...

1. Log in to Windows Server 2016 with an administrator account.
2. Open Server Manager.

3. Click on the **Tools** menu in Server Manager, and you will find IIS Manager. Open IIS Manager and click on the IIS server called **WIN2016IIS**. Go to the **Features View**, and select **Worker Processes**, as shown here:

4. Go to **Actions**, and click on **Open Feature.** This will open the **Worker Processes**, as shown here:

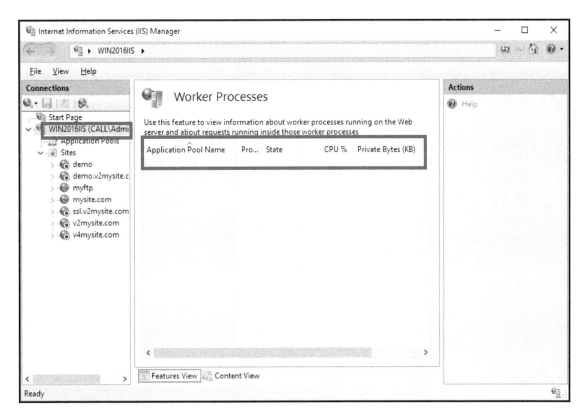

5. You'll see in the figure that we don't have any application pool in the worker processes because we are not using any application pool right now. If your web server hosts a website application, here you will find the application pool's server-utilization details. You can manage the application pool load in IIS Server.

6. Let's go to **Logging**. Expand **WIN2016IIS**, expand **Sites**, click on `mysite.com`, go to **Features View**, and click on **Logging**, as shown here:

7. Open the **Logging** option. **Logging** can be configured at the site level or IIS server level. We will configure it at site level. If you want to trace all website logs on IIS Server, you can configure it as a server, as shown here:

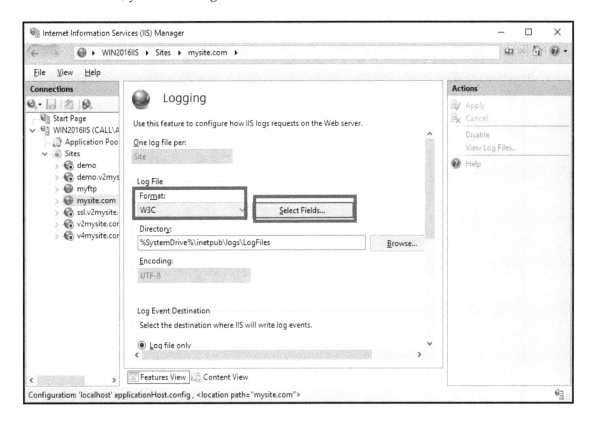

8. You can see **Log File** | **Format** in the figure, which we've selected to default to W3C . Now you have to click on the **Select Fields...** button. You will get the **W3C Logging Fields**, as shown here:

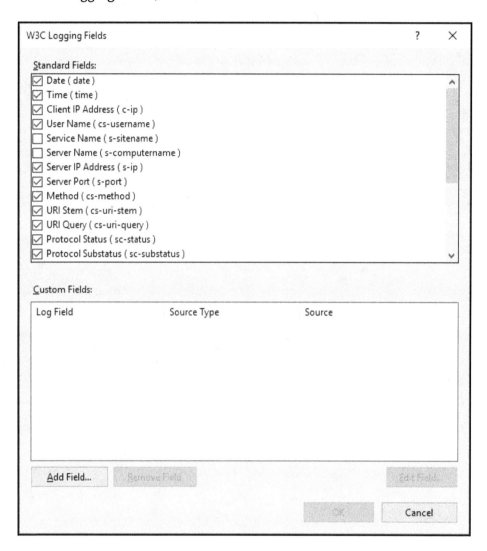

9. Here in this **W3C Logging Fields** window, you can select checkboxes as per your requirements to generate the log file. Click on the **Cancel** button. We'll use the default.

10. Click on `mysite.com`, go to the **Features View**, and click on **HTTP Response Header**, as shown here:

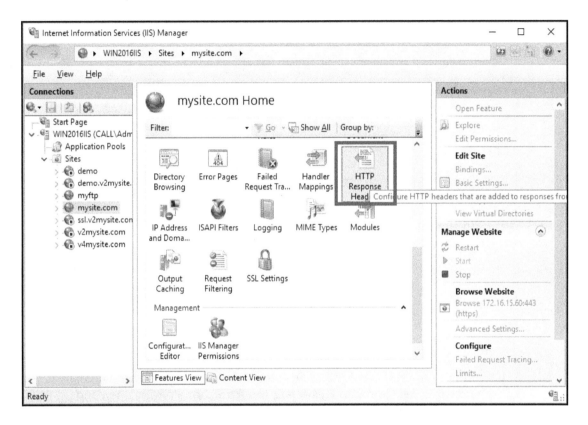

11. Open the **HTTP Response Header**; you can see the header information listed here:

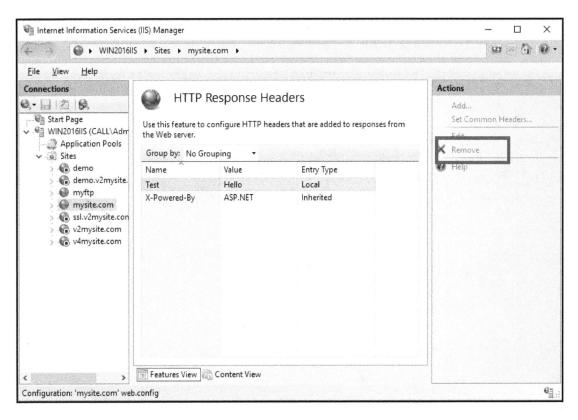

12. If you have more HTTP response headers for your site, you can manage them from here and **Set Common Headers...**, use **Add...** for a new header, and use **Remove** to remove a header.

How it works...

In this recipe, we logged in to IIS Server and opened IIS Manager. We opened the features view of IIS Server to configure the worker-process features. We also configured logging features and discussed the HTTP Response Header features.

Configuring Failed Request Tracing Rules

In this recipe, we will log in to IIS Server and open IIS Manager. We will open the **Features View** of `mysite.com` to add **Failed Request Tracing Rules**. We will check out how to edit them. We will also check out the Failed Request Tracing Rules log file directory and enable the rules.

Getting ready

In this recipe, we require an up-and-running IIS 10.0 instance. The Failed Request Tracing Rules component should be installed. You should have administrative privileges.

How to do it...

1. Log in to Windows Server 2016 with an administrator account.
2. Open Server Manager.

3. Click on **Tools** and you will find IIS Manager. Open IIS Manager, and expand the IIS server **WIN2016IIS**. Expand the Sites folder, click on `mysite.com`, go to the **Features View** of **mysite.com**, and select **Failed Request Tracing Rules**, as shown here:

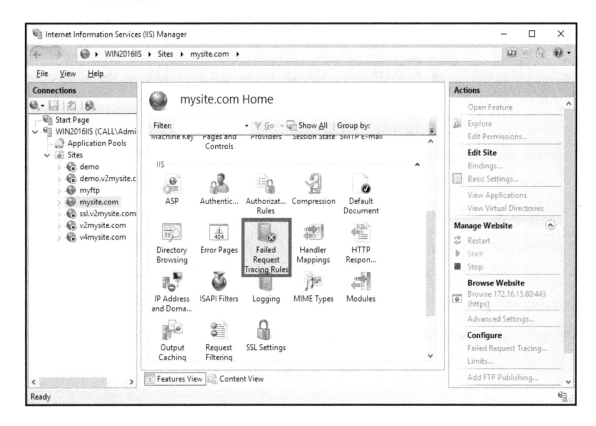

4. Open the **Failed Request Tracing Rules** option, as shown here:

5. You can see that we've selected the **Actions** pane. We have a list of options available. We are going to add **Failed Request Tracing Rules**. Click on the **Add** option in the **Actions** pane:

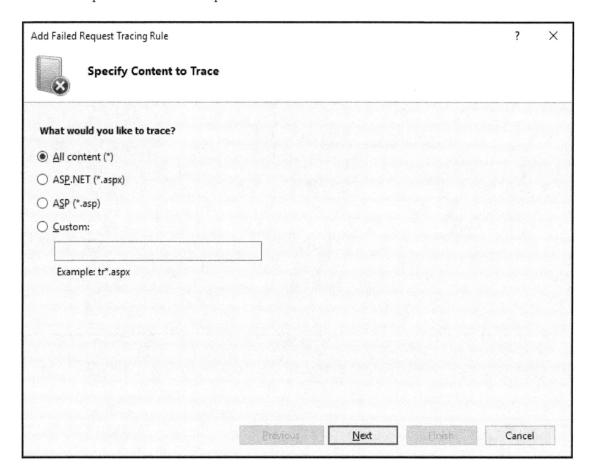

6. Select the **All content (*)** radio button. You have some more choices over there; **ASP.NET** or **ASP** and custom. Click on **Next**:

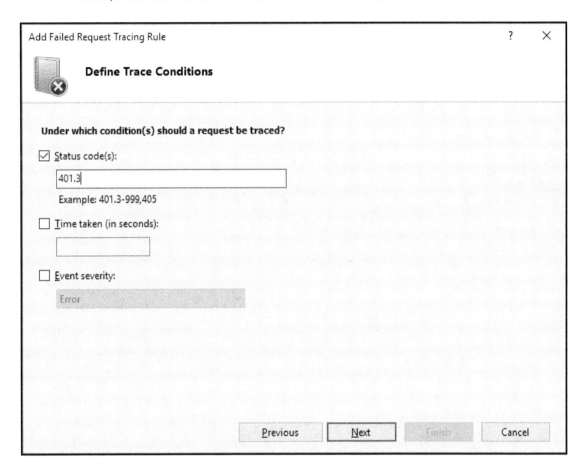

7. Now we have defined the trace conditions, and we can select any **Failed Request Tracing** code. Let's add `401.3` and click on **Next**:

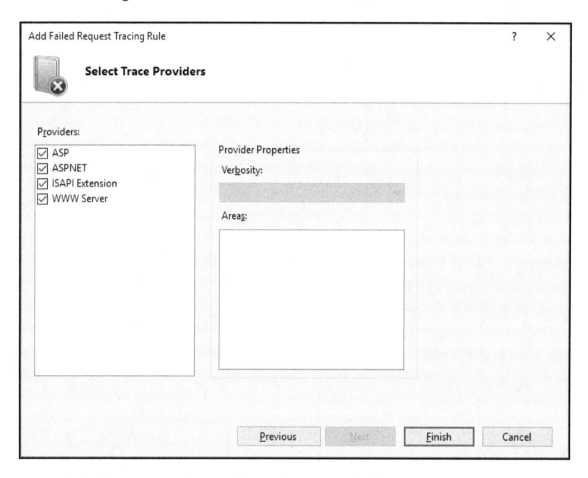

8. In the trace providers window, select any or all of them. Here we're selecting all. Click on **Finish**, and you will have the rule created, as shown here:

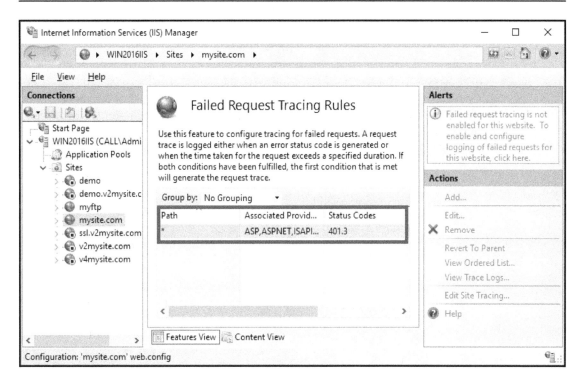

9. Once you've created a **Failed Request Tracing Rules**, you can edit it. Just follow the edit options from the **Actions** pane of **Failed Request Tracing Rules**.

10. Let's enable the **Failed Request Tracing Rules** we just created for `mysite.com`. Click on the **Edit Site Tracing...** option from the **Actions** pane, and you will get the Enable **Failed Request Tracing Rules** window for `mysite.com`, as shown here:

11. Click on **Enable** at the top. You can see in the screenshot that we have the **Directory** path of the Failed Request Tracing log and maximum number of trace files as 50. Click on **OK**. Now your **Failed Request Tracing Rule** is enabled for **mysite.com**.

12. Let's check the log file directory. Go to the **Actions** pane of **Failed Request Tracing Rules** and click on **View Trace Logs....** You will get the log file directory of **Failed Request Tracing Rules**, as shown in this figure:

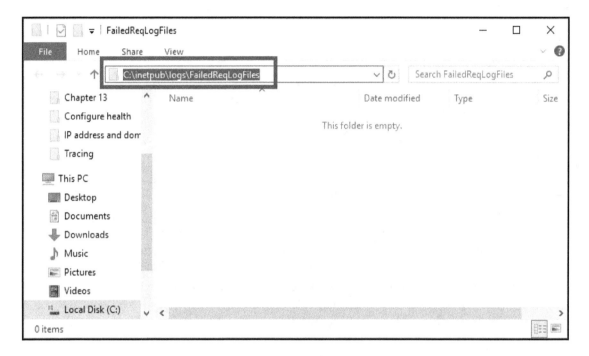

13. Currently, we don't have any log files, but if our website has failed operations, the log file will be generated automatically.

How it works...

In this recipe, we logged in to IIS Server and opened IIS Manager. We went through the **Features View** of mysite.com to add **Failed Request Tracing Rules**. We saw how to edit the **Failed Request Tracing Rules** and checked the **Failed Request Tracing Rules** log file directory. We then enabled the Failed Request Tracing Rules.

Configuring static content compression

In this recipe, we will log in to IIS Server. In IIS Manager, we will open the **Features View** of IIS Server WIN2016IIS to configure content compression. We will open the features view of mysite.com to enable or disable and dynamic content compression.

Getting ready

In this recipe, we require an up-and-running IIS 10.0 instance. The Compression component should be installed. You should have administrative privileges.

How to do it...

1. Log in to Windows Server 2016 with an administrator account.
2. Open Server Manager.

3. Click on the **Tools** menu from Server Manager, and you will find IIS Manager. Open IIS Manager and click on **WIN2016IIS**. Go to **Features View** and select **Compression**, as shown here:

4. Now open the **Compression** file, and you will get the configuration options for **Compression**, as shown here:

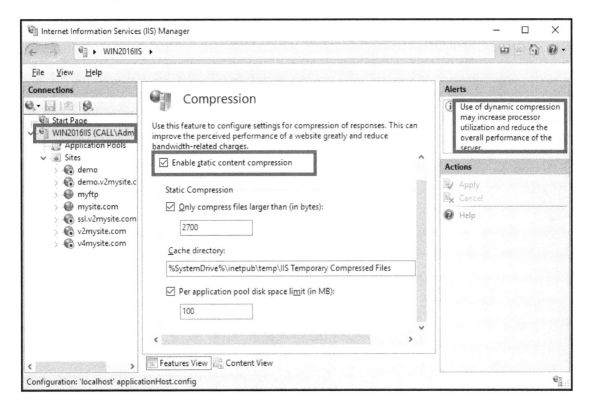

5. As you can see in the figure, we have some default settings. These settings are applicable on IIS Server. After setting them, you have to enable the website you want to apply compression on. You'll see that we have enabled static content compression, which will compress files larger than 2700 (in bytes). The Cache directory location is where temporary files can be compressed or decompressed. The Per application pool disk space limit is 100 MB.

6. You can see in the figure that I have highlighted the Alerts section. If you use dynamic compression, it will use more server resources, which might slow down the server.

7. Let's see how to enable and disable compression on the website.

8. Expand the IIS server **WIN2016IIS**, expand the Sites folder, click on **mysite.com**, go to the **Features View** of **mysite.com**, and select **Compression**, as shown here:

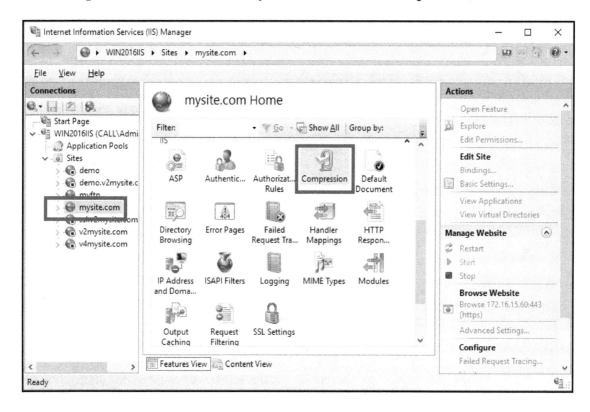

9. Open the **Compression** option, and you will get the enable and disable window, as shown here:

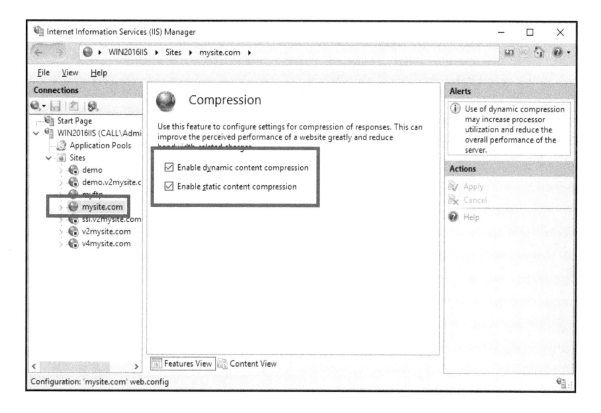

10. We have the Enable checkbox ticked so that compression is enabled. If we uncheck the **dynamic content compression** or static content compression checkboxes, they will be disabled when you click on the **Apply** button in the **CompressionActions** pane.

   IIS routine to maintain at next level of the IIS Server performance of your web application considerably.

   1. Application Pool Suspension through advance property.
   2. Make your page asynchronous if application support.
   3. Don't write in wwwroot.
   4. Remove unused view engines and language.
   5. Pipeline mode.
   6. Remove unused modules.
   7. runAllManagedModulesForAllRequests.
   8. Kernel mode Cache.
   9. Remove methods from Glabal.asax.
   10. Don't use SqlDataSource.
   11. Use HTTP Keep Alive.
   12. Remove ETag Generally, people ignored these tips but they have enormous performance enhancement potential and can be applied quickly on IIS Server to boost in a health prospect.

How it works...

In this recipe, we logged in to IIS Server and opened IIS Manager. We opened the features view of IIS Server WIN2016IIS to configure content compression. We opened the Features View of `mysite.com` to enable and disable static and dynamic content compression.

Index

.

.NET web page
  hosting 68, 71, 72
  uploading 127, 129, 149, 151
  uploading, to wildcard hosts 172, 175
.NET website
  different versions, hosting 73, 75

2

2and3.5AppPool 122, 132

A

advanced IIS 10.0 website
  creating, on Nano Server 223, 230
application pools
  about 45
  benefits 46
  configuration 61, 64, 66
  creating 57, 60
  in IIS 10.0 46, 49
architecture
  components and modules 13
  components, reviewing 11
ASP.NET Core
  about 247
  configuring, on Nano Server 251, 259
  creating, on Nano Server 248, 251
  reference link 259

D

default web site 45
DefaultAppPool 122
demo.v2mysite.com
  uploaded web pages, testing 175, 177, 180
domain restrictions 347, 349, 350, 351
DuoEnabled 142

F

Failed Request Tracing Rules
  configuring 375, 383
features
  FTP 8
  FTPS 8
  HTTP/2 8
  IIS 10.0 on Nano Server 8
  multi-web hosting 9
  PowerShell 5 cmdlets 8
  virtual directories 9
  wildcard host headers 8
File Transfer Protocol (FTP)
  about 297, 298, 301
  installing 302, 305
  server, testing 320, 324
  site, configuring 306, 314
  site, creating 306, 314
  site, securing 306, 314
  user permissions, managing 314, 320
  user, creating 314, 320
FileZilla
  about 298
  URL 298

H

Health and Diagnostics features
  configuring 367
  installing 361
HTML page
  testing 130, 132
HTML web page
  hosting 39, 41, 43
HTTP request
  in worker process 16
  overview 14

HTTP.sys 14
HTTP/2
  about 133, 134
  configuring, on IIS 10.0 143
  installing, on IIS 10.0 136, 139, 140, 142, 145, 148
  working with 134, 136
HttpPlatformHandler x64
  URL 252
Hyper Text Transfer Protocol (HTTP) 79
Hyper Text Transfer Protocol Secure (HTTPS) 276

I

IIS 10.0 installation
  on Windows Server 2016 17, 20, 24
IIS 10.0
  about 7
  application pool, configuration 61, 64, 66
  application pools 46, 49
  application pools, creating 57, 60
  architecture 10
  basic configuration 34, 36, 38
  features 8
  installing, on Nano Server 185, 195
  managing 358
  managing, on Nano Server 195, 199
  prerequisites 9
  security components, installing 326, 327, 328, 329, 330, 332
  security, configuring 334, 335, 336, 338, 339, 340
  security, testing 351, 352, 353, 354
  virtual directory 115
  virtual directory, configuring 117
  virtual directory, constructing 112, 114
  website, configuring on Nano Server 203, 208
  website, creating on Nano Server 199, 203
IIS administration
  IIS administration 216
  reference link 198
  with PowerShell cmdlets 216, 223
IIS server
  connecting, with IIS Manager 25, 28, 31
internet 80
Internet Information Services (IIS) 7

intranet 79
IP address 347, 349, 350, 351

L

lower framework version
  installation 49, 52, 54, 56

M

Microsoft
  URL 274
multiple websites
  hosting 80, 82, 84, 85, 86

N

Nano Server
  about 181
  advanced IIS 10.0 website, creating 223, 230
  ASP.NET Core, configuring 251, 259
  ASP.NET Core, creating 248, 251
  IIS 10.0 website, configuring 203, 208
  IIS 10.0 website, creating 199, 203
  IIS 10.0 websites, uploading 236, 240
  IIS 10.0, installing 185, 195
  IIS 10.0, managing 195, 199
  overview 182, 185
  v5mysite.com, configuring 231, 235
  virtual directory, creating 259, 262
nanosite.com 206

P

performance features
  installing 361
PowerShell cmdlets
  IIS administration 223
PowerShell DSC 216
PowerShell ISE 216
PowerShell
  commands, using to create SSL certificates 290, 292
  reference link 216
prerequisites
  hardware requirements 10
  operating system media 10
  OS requirements 9

push 134

S

Secure Sockets Layer (SSL)
    about 273, 297
    installing 276, 283
security
    configuring, on IIS 10.0 334, 335, 336, 338,
        339, 340
    installing, on IIS 10.0 326, 327, 328, 329, 330,
        332
    testing, on IIS 10.0 351, 352, 353, 354
SSL certificate
    creating 283, 286
    creating, PowerShell commands used 290, 292
    websites, configuring 286, 289
SSL port
    websites, configuring 286, 289
SSL websites
    about 274, 276
    testing 293, 296
static content compression
    configuring 383, 388
static website page
    testing 43, 44

T

Transport Layer Security (TLS) 297

U

uploaded web pages
    testing 211, 214
URL
    authentication 340, 342, 343, 344, 345, 346
    authorization 340, 342, 343, 344, 345, 346

V

v4mysite.com
    uploaded web pages, testing 152, 155
    URL 153
v5mysite.com
    configuring, on Nano Server 231, 235
    uploaded web pages, testing 241, 246

virtual directory
    about 111, 112, 115
    configuring 117, 121, 263, 267
    configuring, with different application pools 123,
        125
    constructing 112, 115
    creating, on Nano Server 259, 262
    reference 130
    web pages, testing 268, 272
    web pages, uploading 268, 272

W

web pages
    testing, in virtual directory 268, 272
    uploading 209, 211
    uploading, in virtual directory 268, 272
website access port
    configuring 94, 96, 97, 98
website folder
    configuring 92, 94
    creating 87, 88, 90
website IP
    configuring 99, 100, 102, 104
websites
    configuring 90
    configuring, with SSL certificate 286, 289
    configuring, with SSL port 286, 289
    deploying 104, 106, 110
    testing 107
    versions, testing 75, 78
Wide Area Network (WAN) 80
wildcard hosts
    .NET web pages, uploading 172, 175
    about 157, 158, 161
    configuring 167, 171
    creating 161, 167
    reference 167
WIN2016IIS 194, 353
Windows Activation Service (WAS) 14
Windows Server 2016
    IIS 10.0 installation 17, 20, 23
World Wide Web Publishing Service (WWW
    Service) 14

www.ingramcontent.com/pod-product-compliance
Lightning Source LLC
LaVergne TN
LVHW081329050326
832903LV00024B/1091

* 9 7 8 1 7 8 7 1 2 6 6 7 1 *